CW01269740

WEAVING

Structure and Substance

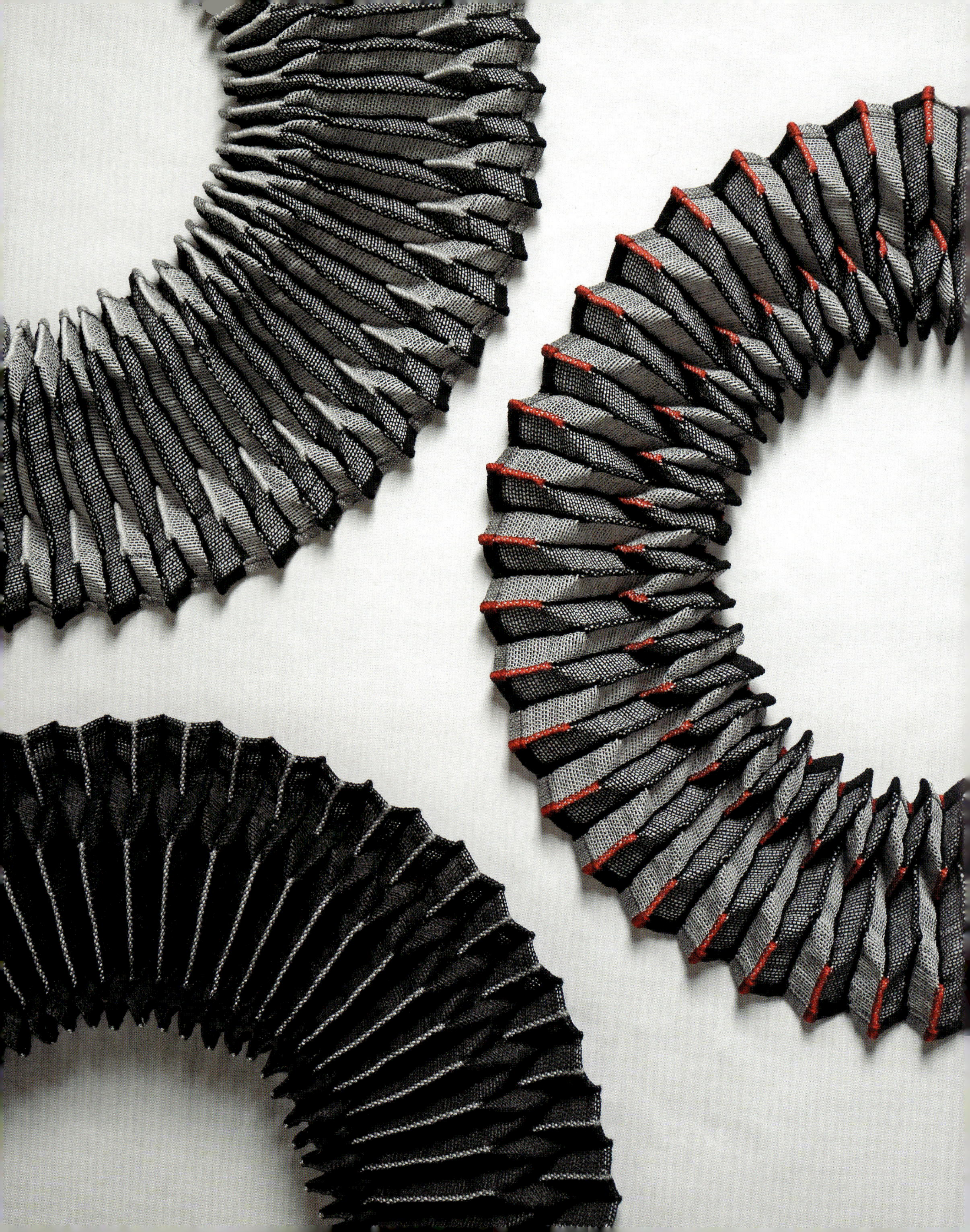

WEAVING

Structure and Substance

ANN RICHARDS

✳ THE CROWOOD PRESS

First published in 2021 by
The Crowood Press Ltd
Ramsbury, Marlborough
Wiltshire SN8 2HR

enquiries@crowood.com
www.crowood.com

© Ann Richards 2021

All rights reserved. No part of this publication may be reproduced or transmitted in any form or by any means, electronic or mechanical, including photocopy, recording, or any information storage and retrieval system, without permission in writing from the publishers.

British Library Cataloguing-in-Publication Data
A catalogue record for this book is available from the British Library.

ISBN 978 1 78500 929 7

Cover design: Peggy & Co. Design
Frontispiece: Self-folding origami neckpieces. Silk, steel and paper.

Graphic design and typeset by Peggy & Co. Design
Printed and bound in India by Parksons Graphics Pvt. Ltd., Mumbai.

Contents

	Acknowledgements	6
	Introduction: The Interplay of Material and Structure	7

Part 1 Nature as Designer — 11
1. Endless Forms Most Beautiful — 12

Part 2 Resources for Design — 21
2. Material Resources: Fibres and Yarns — 22
3. Structural Resources: Simple Gifts — 36
4. Structural Resources: Beyond Plain Weave — 60

Part 3 Designing for Fabric Qualities — 91
5. Fold Here — 92
6. Light Work — 109
7. Both Sides Now — 119
8. Off the Grid — 134

Part 4 Designing Through Making — 151
9. From Sample to Full-Scale Fabric — 152
10. Reflective Practice and the Butterfly Effect — 160

Bibliography	169
Online Resources	172
Suppliers	173
Index	174

Acknowledgements

I have to begin on a sad note because five people who have given me a great deal of help and encouragement have died since the publication of my first book. Margaret Bide accepted me as a student at West Surrey College of Art and Design, so changing the direction of my life, and she later worked hard to ensure a continuing supply of high-twist woollen merino yarn – it is used for many samples in this book. Deryn O'Connor and Amelia Uden, who were my stimulating tutors at college, later became good friends and were always supportive and encouraging. Amelia generously gave me a sample of her design in Russian cords, which I have included in this book. Susi Dunsmore worked for many years with the weavers of Nepal, promoting their textiles, particularly those made of 'allo', and holding wonderful 'Nettle Days' that will be greatly missed by many of us. A final loss is the Japanese designer Junichi Arai, co-founder of Nuno, an important influence on my work, especially in the use of high-twist yarns. I shall continue to miss all these people who were inspirational, encouraging and full of an infectious enthusiasm for textiles.

I would like to thank the many designers and artists whose work is included here: Paulette Adam, Lotte Dalgaard, Alison Ellen, Mariana Eriksson, Berthe Forchhammer, Stacey Harvey-Brown, Denise Kovnat, Gilian Little, Noriko Matsumoto, Andreas Möller, Wendy Morris, Anna Nørgaard, Tim Parry-Williams, Geraldine St Aubyn Hubbard, Reiko Sudo, Ann Sutton, Rezia Wahid, Margrit Waldron, Angus Williams and Deirdre Wood. A special thank you to Wendy Morris for not only allowing me to use examples of her work but also reading the text and making valuable suggestions. I am also grateful to those designers who I am unable to acknowledge individually because they are unknown to me – I have collected many fabrics over the years, and some of these were not attributed to a named designer. They range from simple tea towels to elegant scarves, but all are pieces that I picked up because I knew them to be useful and believed them to be beautiful.

Many thanks to Greta Bertram of the Crafts Study Centre for her help in obtaining photographs of work in the collection and to Martin Conlan and Gina Corrigan for photographs of textiles by the Miao people. I would also like to thank two archaeologists. Noortje Kramer introduced me to the remarkable *Rippenköper* textiles and commissioned me to attempt to replicate their effect, a fascinating process that has also fed into my own work. Johanna Banck-Burgess was responsible for the analysis of the original textile fragment that I worked from and generously allowed me to include her photograph.

The photographs have been taken by the designers and artists themselves, and by: Ole Akhøj, Johanna Banck-Burgess, Alan Costall, Sanne Krogh, Håkan Lovallius, Joe Low, Loucia Manopoulou, Colin Mills, James Newell, Takao Oya, Karl Ravn, and David Westwood. Textiles and photographs not otherwise attributed are by the author.

While writing this book I have had ongoing encouragement from my friends and collaborators in the exhibition *Soft Engineering: Textiles Taking Shape*: Alison Ellen, Julie Hedges and Deirdre Wood. I hope we will be working together again soon.

And a final thanks to Alan for support and advice, especially with photography.

INTRODUCTION

The Interplay of Material and Structure

> Although structure is all-important, the physical characteristic of an object is naturally also influenced by the material used in its making. The resulting interaction between material and structure is an absorbing study; for sometimes the material is dominant – compare a silk sari with a wooden fencing panel, both interlaced in plain weave – and sometimes the structure is dominant – compare a felted piano hammer with a knitted Shetland shawl, both made from wool fibre.
>
> Peter Collingwood, *Textile and Weaving Structures*

Of the many features characteristic of woven textiles, the aspects that probably attract the most immediate attention are colour and pattern. But underpinning these obvious features, textiles necessarily possess textural qualities and deeper tactile properties – they have substance. Such aspects often receive less attention than they deserve, even though all weavers know that they are essential to the success of woven fabrics. So, although colour and pattern will feature in this book, there will be particular emphasis on the ways that tactile properties emerge from the interaction of material and structure.

Weave structure is crucial to the design of woven textiles but, being simply a plan of interlacement, it does not in itself specify what a fabric will be like. It remains an abstraction until embodied in a fabric, since fibre, yarn structure, sett, scale and finishing techniques can create so many different results. Peter Collingwood draws attention to this issue when he invites us to 'compare a silk sari with a wooden fencing panel, both interlaced in plain weave.'

Recently, the ease of computer drafting has encouraged some designers to become absorbed in complex manipulations of structure, using programs that generate new weaves. It has even been suggested that, from the multitude of structures that result, the 'successful' weaves could be woven as a physical record of these particular 'weave species'. But this begs the question of how any interlacements are to be judged as successes when none have been tested as real objects.

Rather than seeing weave drafts on paper (or screen) as inherently 'successful', it is probably more reasonable to think of them as looking promising or having potential for particular purposes, with ultimate success or failure depending on their interplay with the material. For example, plain weave is potentially the firmest structure but nevertheless not all plain weave fabrics are firm, as this quality will vary with the texture and stiffness of the fibre, the character of the yarn and the sett. Collingwood's comparison of the silk sari and the wooden fence deliberately captures extremes of possibility in terms of fineness, stiffness and lustre of material.

More complex weaves can be thought of as having promise for particular uses on account of their characteristic styles of interlacing or length and placement of floats. But since long floats tend to allow substantial changes, through yarns sliding over one another, pulling on other threads or shrinking, the structures as weave drafts may bear little resemblance to the finished fabric. Once again, their success will depend on their interplay with the material.

When initiating a design, a common approach is to draw on the long tradition of woven textiles by exploring the possibilities of a well-known structure, a material or a

A pleated dress twisted into a skein for storage. This flexible tube of self-pleated fabric makes a simple garment that moulds itself to the body, but other weave structures can create fabrics that transform themselves into shaped pieces for more complex 'loom-to-body' garments.

particular combination of the two. But an equally valid starting point can be some outside source of ideas or perhaps a desired fabric quality. In practice, it is often necessary to move between these different strategies as the fabric takes shape in a process of reflective design. Anni Albers gives the example of a fabric intended for the walls of a museum, where there is a focus on the desired functional characteristics of the fabric, but with constant references back to the constraints of material and structure. At the end of this problem-solving process of moving between practical requirements and the possibilities of material and structure, she concludes: 'Here, now, we have a fabric that largely answers the outlined requirements. It formed itself, actually...'

This book is arranged in four parts, looking at weave design from different viewpoints. It begins with the idea of nature as designer, because interesting parallels have been drawn both by designers and biologists between evolution and design. The following section deals with resources and the ways that materials and weave structure can serve as starting points for design, while the third part considers design from an alternative viewpoint of aiming for desired qualities of cloth, considering various possible solutions. Moving between these different approaches will often be the best way to resolve a design, so there is a good deal of cross-referencing between chapters – a book is necessarily sequential but designing is more like a network. At every stage a responsive attitude is helpful, allowing unexpected results or chance occurrences to become starting points for new designs, so the final part of the book considers the practicalities of designing through making, emphasizing the need to be a reflective practitioner.

One important aspect of textiles is the tremendous range of functions that they can fulfil, from the mundanely practical to the highly decorative and beautiful. As a student, and later a tutor, at the Surrey Institute of Art and Design (now the University for the Creative Arts, Farnham), I was struck by how this range was reflected in the college's textile collection. There were stunningly beautiful and valuable pieces in richly coloured silks but also very down-to-earth, everyday textiles, such as towels, and even a baby's nappy – a member of staff noticed that the nappies she was using for her baby were interchanging double cloths, so donated one to the collection! In this spirit my selection of textile examples spans a wide range and celebrates not only the obviously striking or unusual but also humble everyday pieces of cloth. For a weaver, these too have their beauty.

This detail of a skirt shows how a piece of fabric woven in a combination of double cloth and 1/3 twill can shape itself during wet finishing. The complete skirt is shown in Chapter 8.

10

PART 1

Nature as Designer

> Whilst this planet has gone cycling on according to the fixed law of gravity, from so simple a beginning endless forms most beautiful and most wonderful have been, and are being evolved.
>
> Charles Darwin, *The Origin of Species*

Interesting parallels have been drawn, both by designers and biologists, between evolution and design, with each side seeing lessons for their own practice and taking ideas from the other. For example, fabric shear has been informative to biologists investigating worm biology while, working in the other direction, natural forms provide a familiar source of ideas for designers in all media. In textiles such inspiration most often concerns pattern and colour, but textile designers can usefully draw lessons from practitioners in other fields, such as architecture, where greater attention is paid to the deeper structures and growth processes of nature, since these can be highly instructive in shaping the form and functioning of textiles. This approach can be most clearly seen in the various high-tech fabrics that have been developed through biomimetic research, but it can equally well be applied to the structure and substance of textiles designed for more everyday purposes. Some of the lessons from natural forms that are discussed in this part of the book will be picked up later in a series of chapters concerned with designing for specific fabric qualities.

The water lily *Victoria regia* (now *Victoria amazonia*). This is something of a design icon as the ribbing on the underside of the leaf is reputed to have inspired the roof structure of Joseph Paxton's Crystal Palace, though this is probably a myth. The leaf does however provide a good example of nature's ability to produce an effective structure with great economy of material, offering a useful lesson to designers in all fields. (Photo: Alan Costall)

CHAPTER 1

Endless Forms Most Beautiful

> Design in nature is hedged in by limitations of the severest kind... On the other hand, complexity in itself does not appear to be expensive in nature, and her prototype testing is conducted on such a lavish scale that every refinement can be tried.
>
> Michael French, *Invention and Evolution*

Over the last century and a half interesting parallels have been drawn, both by designers and biologists, between evolution and design, and this has definitely been a two-way street, with each side seeing lessons for their own practice and taking ideas from the other. In the introduction to their book *Mechanical Design in Organisms*, the zoologist S. A. Wainwright and his colleagues explain their use of the term 'design':

> The idea that biological materials and structures have function implies that they are 'designed'; hence the book's title. We run into deep philosophical waters here, and we can do little but give a commonsense idea of what we mean. In our view structures can be said to be designed because they are adapted for particular functions... The designing is performed, of course, by natural selection.

Writing elsewhere, Wainwright has suggested that the science of biomechanics would benefit from developing a concept of 'workmanship', while E. J. Gordon, in his book *Structures*, describes how the fabric shear produced by cutting garments on the bias of a woven fabric has proved inspirational to biologists investigating worm biology. As an aside, he mentions that he has himself used the bias cut as a source of ideas for the construction of rockets, an interesting example where the 'soft' engineering of textiles has been inspirational to the 'hard' engineers!

Robin Wootton, researching the folding of insect wings, makes extensive use of paper models to investigate the mechanisms involved and remarks on the many connections to be found with other disciplines:

> When we began research on insect wing folding, we quickly discovered that the mechanisms we were identifying also occur in many other kinds of folding structures; and we found that we were talking with engineers, origami masters, mathematicians and the designers of pop-up books... in nature, similar mechanisms can be identified in the expanding leaves of hornbeams and in the respiratory air-sacs of hawkmoths.
>
> Robin Wootton, *How do insects fold and unfold their wings?*

Structures such as the hornbeam leaf and the hawkmoth air-sac provide examples of a kind of 'natural origami' that has been widely discussed by engineers concerned with deployable structures – compact forms that can be unfolded and refolded with ease. Robin Wootton describes a number of these interesting objects, ranging from folding maps to expanding solar panels for satellites in space, before finally concluding 'But the beetles and earwigs got there first.'

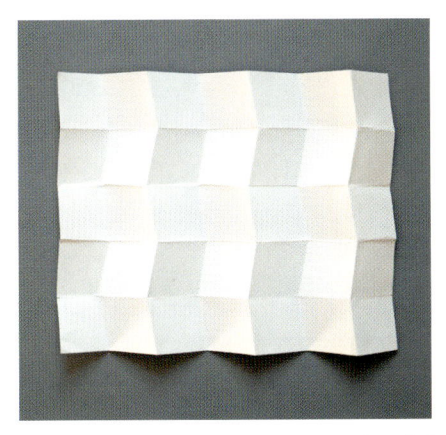

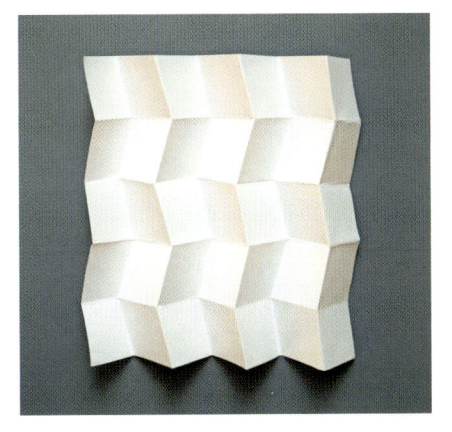

The Miura-ori structure shown open and partially closed. The structure can be folded completely flat in a single movement by pushing on opposing corners of the sheet.

The reference to expanding solar panels concerns the fold called Miura-ori, named after the Japanese engineer Koryo Miura. Though his ultimate aim was to design deployable structures for use in space, Miura used the problems of folding and unfolding maps as a way to explore basic principles of packing flat sheets into small packages. The V-shaped fold that he worked with was already known in origami but Miura investigated the effect of using different angles on the ease of folding and unfolding and on the size of the folded package. He found that with a large angle there are limits to how small the folded package can be made, but with an angle of only 1 degree there are difficulties in folding and unfolding. He concluded that for easy folding into a very small package angles of 2-6 degrees are optimum, creating a sheet that can be unfolded in a single movement simply by pulling on two diagonally opposed corners. Most instructions currently available for constructing the Miura fold suggest an angle of 6 degrees (see Online Resources).

The designer Biruta Kresling noticed that a similar problem of packing a large sheet into a small space occurs with the hornbeam leaf, because the bud is both shorter and narrower than the leaf that will emerge. As the leaves have a pleated structure she wondered whether the V-folds that Miura had investigated could model the process of opening and expanding that occurs when the leaf emerges from the bud. This proved to be the case and she produced the fold known as Ha-ori ('leaf fold'), which nicely models both the lengthening and broadening of the opening leaf (Peter Forbes gives good instructions for constructing this fold). Leaves on various other plants, such as the raspberry, show similar unfolding and such examples of 'natural origami', together with the origami tradition itself, are very instructive when it comes to designing self-folding textiles with origami-like effects. Paper folding is a good way to experiment with the possibilities when planning a design and exploring the impact of different V-fold angles on the overall form of the piece (more detail is given in Chapter 5).

Raspberry leaves, showing the compact folded leaf and some fully open leaves.

Ha-ori (leaf fold) shown closed and open.

CHAPTER 1: Endless Forms Most Beautiful 13

INSPIRATION FROM NATURE

Such cases of 'natural origami' provide good examples of nature's ability to get there first, giving some explanation of why natural forms and processes provide inspiration for designers in all media. Architects seem particularly conspicuous in this respect, partly because of the scale on which they work. For example, it is frequently suggested that Joseph Paxton was inspired by the leaf of the water lily *Victoria regia* in designing the roof of the Crystal Palace, though it seems unlikely that there was a direct connection.

The water lily *Victoria regia*, showing the longitudinal and cross-ribbed underside of the leaf.

A section of the dragonfly wing. (After Hertel)

This cross section shows the pleated structure of the leading edge of the wing. (After Hertel)

Paxton certainly does appear to have been impressed with the 'engineering' of the ribbed structure of the leaf, having posed his eight-year old daughter on one to demonstrate its strength, but the ribbing is only modestly three-dimensional, while the most notable feature of the roof of the Crystal Palace was the deeply folded ridge-and-furrow system, which had already been invented by John Loudon. Heinrich Hertel notes that this ridged structure closely resembles the pleated structure of an insect wing, though he refers also to the popular story about Paxton and the water lily.

> The roof structure of Sir Joseph Paxton's gigantic steel and glass exhibition hall, the London Crystal Palace, bears an amazing similarity to the lattice-work and articulation of the dragonfly's wing... Paxton said he conceived this extremely fine-membered structure in his youth, as a gardener, by studying the leaf skeleton of the tropical water lily *Victoria regia*.
> Heinrich Hertel, *Structure, Form, Movement*

A deeply folded structure provides extra stiffness as compared with a less three-dimensional ribbed surface such as the lily leaf and the roof of the Crystal Palace certainly did resemble an insect wing. There is no evidence that the dragonfly was a direct source of inspiration for the ridge-and-furrow system, but it seems a particularly accurate analogy because the folds in the dragonfly wing are not deployable pleats – the wings are rigid structures that cannot be folded up and the function of the pleating is to provide stiffness.

I have myself used the dragonfly wing as a source of ideas for pleated scarves to deal with some similar issues to those of glasshouses – a desire to combine translucency with strength and stiffness. My requirements were not exactly the same, given that I wanted deployable pleating, but stiffness was still an issue as my delicate pleats were tending to buckle and collapse. Fortunately the structure of the dragonfly wing combines longitudinal ribs with many finer cross-bars that act as 'struts' to support the pleating, a strategy I gratefully adopted.

Detail of a pleated fabric. Warp: Linen. Weft: Crepe silk and hard silk, with picks of linen at intervals serving as 'struts' to stiffen the pleating.

Many insects of the grasshopper family are able to conceal themselves by folding away their delicate pleated flying wings under protective fore wings that imitate leaves. (Photo: Alan Costall)

The ribs and cross-bars in the dragonfly wing are particularly conspicuous, but similar structures can be seen in the many insects that are able to fold their wings when not in flight, though such ribbing is often more delicate in wings that are protected when not in use. In insects such as grasshoppers and beetles the pleated rear wings that are used for flying can be folded away under hard fore wings – in the example shown here it is clear that when it comes to the process of imitating nature, this is another case of nature getting there first!

The design of many modern buildings can clearly be seen as making references to natural forms, and this theme was beautifully explored in the exhibition *Zoomorphic* at the Victoria and Albert Museum, together with an accompanying publication by Hugh Aldersey-Williams. One of the most prominent architects working in this way was Frei Otto who based designs on various structures such as crab shells, the skulls of birds, spider webs and bubbles. It is clear in many of these designs that architects have learnt from nature in achieving strong structures with great economy of materials, as thin shells or sheets of fabric are supported and stiffened through strategically placed ribs, struts or tension cables. It is easy for weave designers to feel that such concerns are not so pressing in textiles as they are in architecture, but similar structural issues of strength, stiffness and so on do still arise on this smaller scale, particularly with fabrics that have a strong three-dimensional character, so natural forms offer lessons in terms of substance and performance as well as in the appearance of the cloth.

BIOMIMETIC TEXTILES

Good examples of learning from nature can be seen in the many biomimetic investigations that have led to designs for high-performance textiles. Veronika Kapsali describes many of these innovative textiles in her book on biomimetics, including a fabric for sportswear that imitates the transpiration of plant leaves, Stomatex, and the swimsuit fabric FastSkin based on the structure of sharkskin.

Studies at the Centre for Biomimetics at Reading University on the opening and closing of pine cones in dry and damp conditions inspired the design of an adaptive fabric that responds to moisture. Colin Dawson, who carried out this work, discovered that the scales of the pine cone are composed of two different types of wood cell, and that although these both absorb water they have very different swelling properties. These different responses cause the scales to open out or close up according to the atmospheric conditions. Dawson applied this to textiles by bonding a synthetic woven fabric to a non-porous membrane and cutting U-shaped perforations that formed flaps that would open or close in response to changes in the moisture in the air.

Like the cells in wood, the various textile fibres have different properties and do not all swell to the same extent when wetted out. Natural fibres swell considerably when they absorb water and this is the basis for textured effects that are created by the creping reaction (which will be explained in Chapter 2). In contrast most synthetics swell relatively little, so many further designs on the principle of the pine cone might be possible with various combinations of natural and synthetic fibres in backed or double cloths.

Veronika Kapsali followed up Dawson's work on the pine cone to produce a self-regulating fibre INOTEX. This takes an unusual approach because, unlike the fibres in traditional crepe yarns that swell and make the yarn thicker, INOTEX fibres are engineered to become thinner as they absorb moisture, making a textile that is more permeable and so more comfortable to wear over a range of different conditions.

Another interesting development is Morphotex, a yarn that imitates the structural colours seen in nature, for example in the feathers of some birds and perhaps most strikingly in the wings of the brilliant blue Morpho butterfly. Such colours do not rely on pigments but are produced by interference effects when light is reflected from microscopic layered structures in scales, feathers or shells. The Morphotex yarn produced so far, though attractively iridescent, is nowhere near as intensely coloured as the butterflies it imitates and this exemplifies one of the great difficulties in biomimicry. In many cases, not only has nature got there first but, as a result of the lavish prototype testing of natural selection, does it much better. While Morphotex yarn uses sixty-one alternating layers of polyester and nylon to produce a pale, iridescent effect, the Morpho butterfly needs only ten layers of chitin with air spaces in between to create its extraordinary brilliant colour. However, this particular biomimetic design aims to use structural colours as a substitute for more environmentally damaging dyes, which seems a worthwhile strategy to pursue. Peter Forbes points out that the problem in the case of Morphotex is insufficient contrast between nylon and polyester, so 'If two cheap high-contrast fibre materials could be found, some dazzling textiles would result' (see Bibliography).

Birds' feathers often combine both pigments and structural colours as in this jay feather where brown pigments lie alongside the brilliant blue produced by the fine structure of the feather.

ECONOMY IN NATURE

As described above, the water lily leaf and dragonfly wing, together with the crab shells and birds' skulls that so inspired Frei Otto, are all efficient structures in which strength and stiffness are achieved with minimal material. Julian Vincent, formerly head of the Centre for Biomimetics at Reading University, sums up this characteristic of many natural structures with the phrase 'In nature materials are expensive and shape is cheap' and emphasizes the increasing need for human designers to work in a similar way to avoid a wasteful use of limited resources:

> Most of our resources, especially materials, are treated by economics as if the supply were infinite, when demonstrably it is not for those that are non-renewable. In his engineering, use of materials and energy, man lets design take second place, whereas nature treats materials as expensive and designs with apparent care and attention to detail. This results in durable materials and cheap structures that are easy to recycle under ambient conditions.
>
> Julian Vincent, 'Survival of the Cheapest' (see Online Resources)

In textiles, attempts to economize on materials often focus on substituting inferior materials, particularly where it is assumed that they will not be too noticeable. For example the term 'backed cloth', often used for fabrics with a supplementary warp or weft, derives from the industrial system of using inferior materials for yarns that will not be seen on the back of the cloth. Stacey Harvey-Brown describes the widespread use of this practice in the industrial production of matelassé fabrics, but comments that as a handweaver she would prefer not to use inferior materials in this way. The solution, as Julian Vincent suggests, is to accept that materials *are* expensive and to design with the care and attention necessary to use them to best advantage.

NATURAL FORMS AND TEXTILE QUALITIES

Although the visual qualities of natural objects suggest many ideas for colour and pattern in textiles, the development of high-tech biomimetic fabrics shows the value of considering the deeper structures and growth processes of nature as a source of ideas. This approach can equally well be applied to the structure and substance of textiles designed for more everyday purposes. It will often be found that even a single object may have multiple ideas to suggest and this feeds particularly well into textile design since fabrics inevitably have multiple qualities. It is worth examining natural objects closely and on many scales – inexpensive but effective digital microscopes are now readily available and can reveal beautiful details.

In this courgette flower a series of deep folds are responsible for bending adjacent thin flat areas to create an overall effect of pleating. This is a principle that can also work in textiles since pleating can be achieved even when only alternate stripes are actually structural folds, provided that the adjacent flat cloth is soft and flexible. An example using a combination of Han damask and plain weave will be shown in Chapter 5.

The sculptural seed pods of *Nicandra physalodes* show a beautiful combination of strong curved ridges interspersed with thinner concave surfaces, creating striking three-dimensional forms.

Both outer and inner surfaces of this bivalve shell have attractive qualities, with rippled ridges on the outside and subtle colour gradations and delicately toothed pink edging on the inside. The outer surface rewards close inspection, revealing tiny cross-ribs running across the main ridges. This efficient way of achieving strength with a minimal use of materials echoes the structure of the water lily leaf.

Later in this book I have chosen four fabric qualities as starting points for design: ribbed/pleated textures, translucency, textiles that are different on the two sides and those that escape the grid of the woven structure. Many other qualities could equally well have been selected, and even the four that have been chosen are obviously not mutually exclusive. Ribbed or pleated fabrics lend themselves particularly well to creating double-sided effects and translucent gauze fabrics may also spontaneously develop wavy effects or pleats, and so on. A few examples of natural objects that might offer both structural and visual ideas for the fabric qualities to be discussed later in the book will give a sense of these multiple possibilities.

For ridged and pleated textures the origami-like structures of leaves and insect wings have already been mentioned, but many other strongly textured forms can provide ideas. Flowers often have quite thin, delicate petals and these may be given adequate stiffness through regularly spaced ribs or folds. Seed pods are often also deeply ridged to provide stiffness with great economy of material, an arrangement that can also work well in textiles.

The diversity of structure in shells is a great resource and lovely examples of ridged textures are shown in Hans Meinhardt's remarkable book *The Algorithmic Beauty of Sea Shells*, which also offers plenty of inspiration for pattern and colour. Not only do many objects such as leaves and shells have interesting textures but frequently they are also different on the two sides, so can offer ideas for fabrics that are both highly textured and double sided. As well as living things, other aspects of the natural world such as stones, rocks and various geological formations can be a wonderful source of ideas. Stacey Harvey-Brown draws on the forms of sand ripples, volcanoes and mountains in her highly textured fabrics.

Examples of transparency and translucency abound in the natural world and can be very instructive, both visually and in terms of cloth quality since the substance of translucent surfaces can vary greatly, ranging from the crisp quality of honesty seed heads to the soft creped texture of poppies. Beautiful lacelike effects can be seen in leaf skeletons, and the different weights of the supporting ribs, from main stems down to the smallest vessels, provide appropriate strength where necessary while also making the visual effect of the surface more varied and interesting. The way that local dense areas serve only to emphasize the transparency of the whole is a lesson that can usefully be applied to textiles.

CHAPTER 1: Endless Forms Most Beautiful **17**

Leaves have large variations in scale from major to minor ribbing and this is particularly well revealed in leaf skeletons.

Physalis seed pods produce exceptionally beautiful skeletons and these can be particularly interesting when only partly skeletonized.

This detail of a guinea fowl feather shows the delicate structure of the barbs and barbules and the attractive variation in pigmentation.

Feathers also provide beautiful examples of translucency, with their delicately interlocking barbules, particularly where there are contrasts of pigmentation. Another interesting aspect of transparency in nature is that often another surface can be seen behind the transparent one, so the experience is one of looking *through* rather than simply at the surface, something that can be exploited in textiles by using double or multiple layer cloths.

Some of the natural objects that have already been mentioned in relation to textured or transparent textiles can also suggest ideas for double-sided fabrics, but there are many other possible sources of ideas. As well as the many beautiful leaves that have strikingly different sides, other plant structures such as pieces of bark can show attractive contrasts between the inner and outer surfaces. And when it comes to textiles that aim to escape the formal grid of warp and weft, the list of examples that could provide inspiration must be endless – what in nature is perfectly straight and rectangular? Perhaps this is precisely why weavers so often want to break out of their grid.

OTHER LESSONS FROM NATURE: FIBONACCI TO FRACTALS

Philip Ball's book *Patterns in Nature* includes many dramatic images, while his trilogy *Shapes*, *Flow* and *Branches* provides more detailed scientific explanations of the forces involved. He deals extensively with the mathematics behind natural patterns, ranging from the Fibonacci series, which can be seen in many plants, to fractal forms that show self-similarity over many scales. Such natural patterns can be a source of ideas for designers in many fields.

Philip Ball opens *Shape*, the first of his trilogy, with a discussion about whether it should be possible to use shape, pattern and form as a signature of life: 'That doesn't seem an unreasonable thing to do, does it? Surely, after all, we can distinguish a crystal from a living creature, an insect from a rock?' He goes on to explain that on many occasions making this apparently obvious distinction is not at all easy. He quotes extensively from D'Arcy Thompson, a biologist whose book *On Growth and Form* strongly emphasizes the underlying forces behind the development of form, giving numerous examples where inorganic and organic forms closely resemble one another because similar forces have been involved in their creation. Just as the ripples on the shore, the outline of the hills or the shape of clouds are subject to physical forces so also are all living things: 'Cell and tissue, shell and bone, leaf and flower, are so many portions of matter, and it is obedience to the laws of physics that their particles have been moved, moulded and conformed.'

Thompson goes on to suggest that objects themselves reveal the forces involved in their formation, so any object, organic or inorganic, can be thought of as a 'diagram of forces.' Designers and makers in all fields are being offered a useful hint here because thinking about how natural forms have developed, what forces have shaped them, can sometimes allow us to exploit underlying principles of growth and form in our designs as well as being inspired by the beauty of nature.

WEAVING AS INSPIRATION AND METAPHOR

The beginning of this chapter described how the relationship between design and the study of nature is a two-way street. As designers and makers we must gratefully acknowledge our debt to nature itself and also to the scientific ideas that help us make sense of it, but we may also take some satisfaction from the way that scientists in their turn have drawn upon the human activities of designing and making as sources of both practical ideas and vivid metaphors. Weaving seems to bear this out, perhaps more than any other branch of design. The close interplay of different elements in weaving is so well known to everyone and so perfectly captures something important about the interconnectedness of the natural world that it appears irresistible as an image. When D'Arcy Thompson discusses the relation between evolution by natural selection and the mechanical constraints of physics that govern all living things, he concludes that these ideas are woven together 'like warp and woof'. And when the physicist Richard Feynman suggests that understanding things in detail can lead to a broader understanding of the universe, it is weaving that provides him with the perfect metaphor: 'Nature uses only the longest threads to weave her patterns, so each small piece of her fabric reveals the organization of the entire tapestry.'

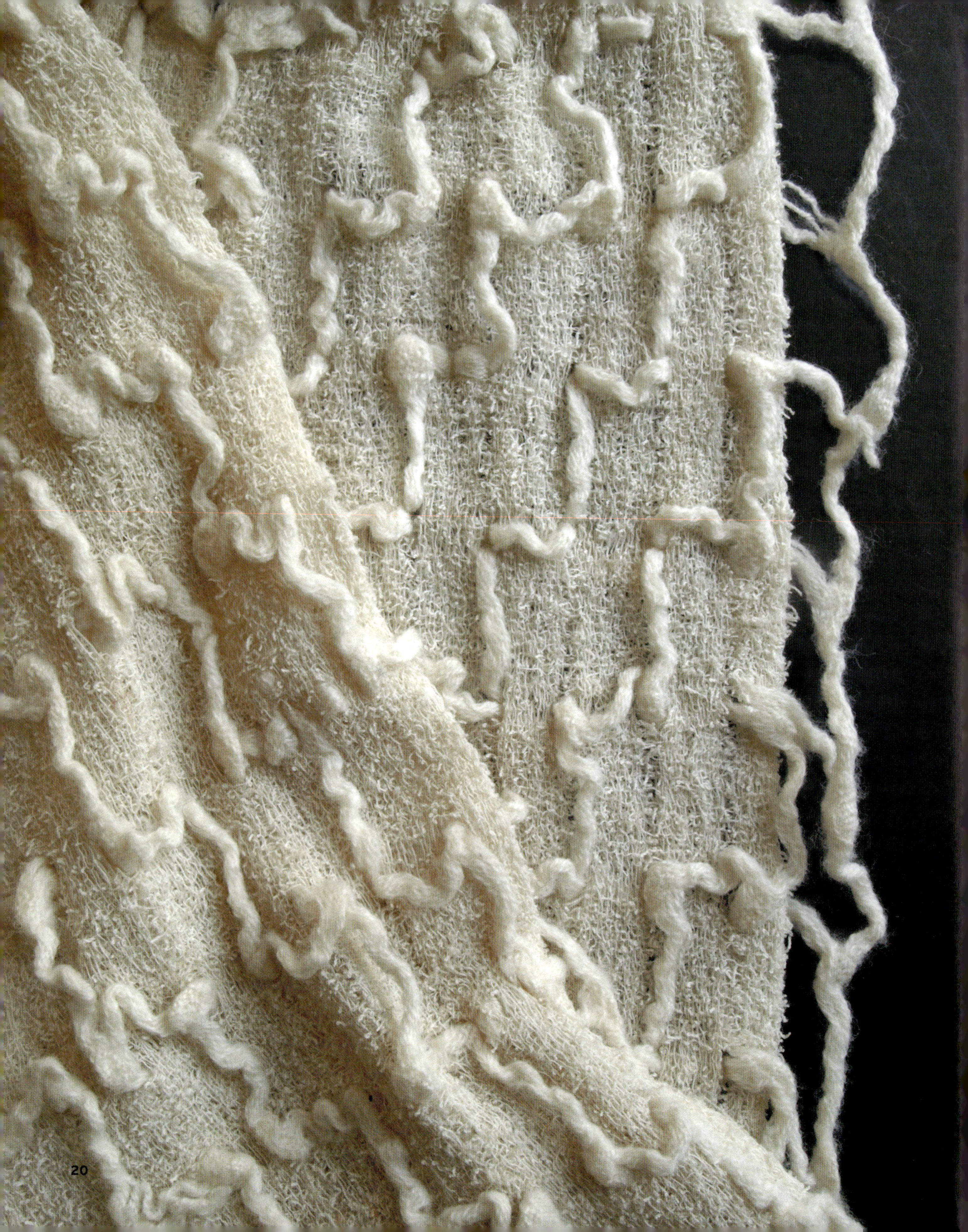

PART 2

Resources for Design

> The material itself is full of suggestions for its use if we approach it unaggressively, receptively.
>
> Anni Albers, *On Designing*

The range of fibres that can be used for textiles is too wide for an attempt at a complete overview here, but some commonly used fibres with very different qualities will be described. The interplay of these materials with weave structure is complex and provides a useful starting point for design but when working with traditional weaves, it is often worthwhile to 'play around' with them in an experimental way as well as using them in their 'classic' forms. With different materials or on different scales some of them may become interestingly unrecognizable! An awareness of the characteristics of various materials and structures and how they interplay will give a sense of their potential for design, so these 'resource' chapters will take a selection of traditional weaves and show how versatile they can be depending on material, scale and sett. Many techniques stretch back over hundreds of years, even millennia, so in these cases there will also be some account of their history.

The interplay of material and structure creates a striking effect in this scarf by Gilian Little. Two sets of wool yarn of different weights and with very different felting properties are arranged so that each weaves only with itself. The easily fulled yarn floats above and below the fine high-twist yarns that form the main part of the scarf. The structure is similar in principle to a deflected double weave but the high-twist wool is itself woven as a double layer. During wet finishing the floating yarns felt together while the high-twist wool shrinks and crinkles but resists felting. (Ann Sutton Collection)

CHAPTER 2

Material Resources: Fibres and Yarns

> Structures are made of materials... but in fact there is no clear-cut dividing line between a material and a structure. Steel is undoubtedly a material and the Forth bridge is undoubtedly a structure, but reinforced concrete and wood and human flesh – all of which have a rather complicated constitution – may be considered as either materials or structures.
>
> J. E. Gordon, *Structures*

WHAT IS A MATERIAL AND WHAT IS A STRUCTURE?

It is quite common to talk about materials and structures as though they were distinct categories but, as Professor J. E. Gordon explains, the dividing line is not always sharp. When talking of materials, most weavers tend to conflate the properties of the fibre and the yarn – for example, the inherent strength and stiffness of linen fibres are properties that are also evident in the yarns constructed from these fibres. In a general way this works fairly well but it is still worth taking time to consider the basic properties of fibres and the ways these may be impacted by different preparation and spinning methods and also finally modified by any finishing processes applied to the woven cloth. There will be no attempt here to be comprehensive because the range of fibres that are usable for textiles is vast. A brief survey of some commonly used fibres that vary greatly in their physical properties will give a sense of the range of possibilities.

MATERIALS AND THEIR PROPERTIES

It helps to start by considering some general properties of materials so that the specific behaviours of textile fibres can be seen in a broader context. Professor Gordon has a lively and amusing way of capturing the fundamentals about materials and structures and he particularly emphasizes strength and flexibility:

> A biscuit is stiff and weak, steel is stiff and strong, nylon is flexible and strong, raspberry jelly is flexible and weak. The two properties together describe a solid about as well as you can reasonably expect two figures to do.

But he then goes on to discuss a third important property, that of *toughness*, the ability of a material to absorb energy without breaking. This is particularly relevant to weavers as our materials are greatly in need of this energy-absorbing capacity as we stretch them under high tension and abrade them with the heddles and reed. So, if we include toughness, the four main natural textile fibres can be characterized in this way:

- Flax is strong and stiff but has poor toughness.
- Wool is weak and flexible but moderately tough.
- Cotton is moderately strong and flexible but not very tough.
- Silk is also moderately strong and flexible but it is extremely tough.

Immediately some of our familiar experiences in handling these fibres begin to make sense. It is clear that flax is strong because it is hard to break a linen yarn by pulling on it, yet it is a notoriously 'difficult' yarn. Its lack of flexibility means that it is unforgiving of tension variations and its lack of toughness makes it subject to breakage through the abrasion of the heddles and reed. In contrast, although wool is not strong, its flexibility makes it easy to work with and its moderate toughness resists abrasion fairly well, although the range of qualities of wool is so immense that there is much variation. It is interesting to compare cotton and silk, both flexible fibres that are easy to handle. Silk is often regarded as an immensely strong fibre, but cotton is almost as strong (or equally strong according to some authorities). It is the greater toughness of silk as well as its beauty that accounts for its pre-eminence as a textile fibre.

HOW YARN STRUCTURES MODIFY FIBRE PROPERTIES

The intrinsic properties of the various fibres will inevitably be modified by techniques of fibre preparation and spinning. Yarns fall into two groups, continuous filament yarns such as silk, and staple yarns composed of shorter fibres. Filament yarns are strong even without being twisted, though in the case of silk it is usual to give a light twist to give extra strength and cohesion, but staple yarns need to be twisted to bind the short overlapping fibres together – the process of draft spinning. There are some exceptions in the case of bast fibres that are long enough to be formed into yarn through splicing or knotting lengths of fibre, but these techniques are now used on a relatively small scale and mass production of bast fibre yarns is done through draft spinning.

For staple yarns a major issue is the extent to which the fibres are made to lie in parallel alignment; long-stapled fibres are treated by combing to line them up to produce smooth, compact yarns, while shorter fibres are carded to create a more random arrangement of fibres for softly textured, loftier yarns. This distinction can be seen in the contrast between worsted and woollen yarns, combed and carded cottons and smooth line linen spun from long fibres as compared with the rougher texture of tow, spun from shorter fibres.

BASIC PROPERTIES OF YARNS

Although the various methods of fibre preparation have an important impact on the final properties of yarns, there are two aspects of construction that apply to all yarns, regardless of fibre and method of preparation: their thickness and the amount and direction of twist applied to them.

Yarn Counts

Yarn thickness is indicated by various count systems, based on the relation between weight and length of yarn, using a fixed weight system (length/unit weight) or a fixed length system (weight/unit length) (see box). In spite of an attempt to impose a standard system (Tex), yarns are still sold under various count systems so it is important when buying yarn to check which count system has been used. It is not safe to assume a yarn count is metric just because it has not been produced in an English-speaking country – a cotton yarn from Japan may be using a traditional cotton count rather than the metric system! To avoid confusion it can be helpful to choose one system, such as metres/kg, and draw up a standard chart of all your yarns, converting any other counts so that you are always working from the same system when doing calculations (see box for conversion factors). To check the count of yarns you are unsure of, weigh a small sample of known length – Handweavers Studio has some suitable digital balances.

The yarn count is needed for calculating the quantity of material required for a particular piece of work, but it can also be used to estimate the yarn diameter, information that is useful for cloth setting and twist calculations (details of such calculations will be given in Chapter 3). Using a yarn diameter calculation, such as Ashenhurst (see box), provides a quick and effective alternative to the traditional process of 'wrapping' (winding the yarn round a ruler to see how many threads occupy a centimetre or inch). Although much beloved by handweavers, the wrapping technique is both time consuming and unreliable, with estimates varying from one individual to another especially when working with fine yarns. Also, importantly, estimates of yarn diameter made by calculation and by wrapping are simply *not the same*. Wrapping will always flatten the yarn a little – on average, a wrapped estimate of diameters/cm (or inch) will be about two thirds of the figure given by the Ashenhurst formula. This needs to be kept in mind when using yarn diameters for calculations of sett or twist angle.

FIXED WEIGHT YARN COUNT SYSTEMS

Traditional systems
These base the count on the number of unit lengths (skeins, hanks and so on) to a fixed *weight*. The yarn becomes finer with increasing count. There are several systems based on yards/lb.

YARN TYPE	UNIT	LENGTH/LB
Woollen spun – Galashiels	cut	200 yd
Woollen spun – Yorkshire	skein	256 yd
Worsted (wc)	hank	560 yd
Linen (lea or Nel)	lea	300 yd
Cotton (cc or Ne)	hank	840 yd
Spun silk	hank	840 yd

For example, a cotton yarn with a count of 8. The cotton unit is 840 yd, therefore:

$$\text{Cotton } 8 = 8 \times 840 = 6{,}720 \text{ yd/lb}$$

For a plied yarn the count is written with the ply number, followed by the count of the singles.

$$\text{For example, cotton } 2/8 = \frac{8 \times 840}{2} = 3{,}360 \text{ yd/lb}$$

Metric system
The metric count is based on km/kg and is normally indicated by Nm (occasionally m.c.). For plied yarns, in the metric system, the count of the component yarns is given first, followed by the ply number.

$$\text{For example, spun silk } 30/2 \text{ Nm} = \frac{30{,}000}{2} = 15{,}000 \text{ m/kg}$$

FIXED LENGTH YARN COUNT SYSTEMS

These use a fixed length and a variable weight. The yarn therefore becomes thicker with increasing count.

Tex system
This has been proposed as a universal system, to replace all other count systems. The Tex count is the weight in grams of 1,000 m (g/km).

For example, 1,000 m of a 15 Tex yarn weighs 15 g

When a yarn is plied the resultant count is the sum of the component yarns and the direction of the ply may also be given.

For example, 20/2 S indicates a yarn composed of two threads of 10 Tex, plied together with an S twist.

Denier system
This is a traditional system originally developed for filament silk, but is sometimes also used for man-made extruded fibres.

Denier = weight in grams of 9,000m

For example. 9,000m of a 40 denier yarn will weigh 40 g

YARN COUNT CONVERSIONS

Fixed weight counts can be converted to Tex:

$$\text{Tex} = \frac{496{,}000}{\text{Yards/lb}} \qquad \text{Tex} = \frac{1{,}000}{\text{km/kg}}$$

Tex counts can be converted to fixed weight counts:

$$\text{Yards/lb} = \frac{496{,}000}{\text{Tex}} \qquad \text{km/kg} = \frac{1{,}000}{\text{Tex}}$$

Denier can be converted to fixed weight counts:

$$\text{Yards/lb} = \frac{4{,}464{,}500}{\text{denier}} \qquad \text{km/kg} = \frac{9{,}000}{\text{denier}}$$

Denier can be converted to Tex:

$$\text{Tex} = \frac{\text{denier}}{9}$$

ASHENHURST FORMULA FOR YARN DIAMETERS

Yarn diameters/inch = $\sqrt{\text{yards/lb}}$

Multiply by: 0.85 for woollen yarns
0.90 for worsted yarns
0.92 for cotton, silk and linen

METRIC ASHENHURST FORMULA

Yarn diameters per cm = $\sqrt{\text{m/kg}}$

Multiply by: 0.236 for woollen yarns
0.25 for worsted yarns
0.255 for cotton, silk and linen

YARN TWIST AND ITS IMPACT ON YARN PROPERTIES

Although continuous filaments such as silk are strong even without twist, they may be lightly twisted for increased cohesion and can also have further twist applied to achieve particular yarn qualities. The shorter fibres of cotton, wool and linen require twist to form usable yarns, but may also have extra twist added beyond the minimum needed for strength. Not only the amount but also the direction of twist can vary and though both will ultimately have an impact on the quality of the cloth, variations in the amount of twist *directly* affect the physical properties of the yarn itself, while variations in the direction of twist only make an impact within a finished fabric.

The amount of twist can vary greatly, with lightly twisted yarns being usable only as weft, while with increasing twist a yarn will gain sufficient strength to be suitable for warp. However, increasing twist will only strengthen a yarn up to a certain point, beyond which it will become weakened due to stress. Also, even the level of twist that gives maximum strength often produces a rather hard yarn so lower twists are often used to satisfy other requirements, such as a soft handle. Levels of twist are usually quoted as turns/m (tpm) or turns/inch (tpi), but yarns vary in thickness, and fine yarns need more twist than thick ones to have the same properties, so the angle of twist is a more fundamental measure. For more information about the relationship between tpm (tpi) and twist angle see my book *Weaving Textiles That Shape Themselves*.

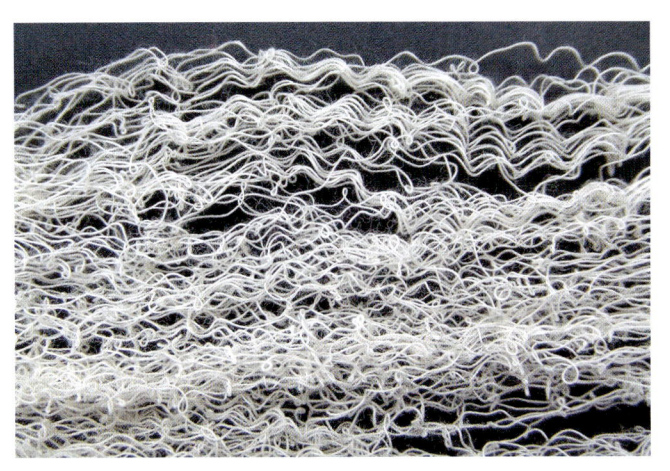

Samples of high-twist wool yarn, shown before and after being soaked in water.

Yarns can be twisted by different amounts, giving varied angles of twist, and also in different directions, indicated by the letters S and Z.

The Creping Reaction

A yarn composed of a single strand will often ply back on itself or even become snarled up, particularly if it is very highly twisted. This is because the stress imposed on the yarn by twisting makes it unbalanced – it has surplus energy that can be released through such plying or snarling movements. This stress reaction forms the basis for the construction of plied yarns, in which single threads are folded together in the opposite direction to their original twist, so producing a balanced, stable yarn. However the extreme instability that occurs at very high levels of twist can be put to good use in creating textured effects and such high-twist yarns are often referred to as crepe yarns.

Rather than plying back on themselves these highly energetic yarns can also escape stress by curling and crinkling, and when this happens within the weave structure it will disturb the surface of the fabric. Some slight movements may be obvious as soon as a fabric comes off the loom, but usually texture develops only when the fabric is soaked in water. Natural fibres swell when wetted and this increases the stress on the yarn, so triggering the creping reaction. Silk, wool and cotton are the main fibres used for crepe yarns, as they are fairly soft and tend to form a fine crinkled texture, but other natural fibres will also give the reaction, though modified by other properties such as stiffness. Unlike natural fibres most synthetics do not swell much on wetting so cannot give a creping reaction, but because reconstituted cellulose fibres do so, rayon is effective as a crepe yarn.

Direction of Twist

The direction of twist, S or Z, does not affect the physical properties of the yarn such as strength or stiffness but does make an impact on the woven cloth. The different directions of twist reflect the light differently so can be used to create 'shadow stripes' that show up in the cloth. If the yarns are also highly twisted then striking textural effects can be produced and these will be described in Chapter 3.

VEGETABLE FIBRES

Bast Fibres

Bast fibres lie in the stem of the plant between the outer epidermis and woody centre of the stem and give strength and support to the plant. The major textile plants are flax, hemp, ramie, and jute. While jute is mainly suitable for coarse fabrics such as sacking the others are all useful for both clothing and furnishings. All need extensive treatment to separate the fibres from the woody parts of the plant and prepare them for spinning. They have an important shared quality in their lack of flexibility and so all of them contrast strongly with softer and more flexible fibres such as cotton, silk and especially wool. This means that the bast fibres are all suited to similar *kinds* of use, but as there are variations in the fineness and stiffness of their fibres they are not completely interchangeable.

Flax

Flax has a long history as a textile fibre and exceptionally fine linen was produced in ancient Egypt. In modern times the main processing technique has been retting, which involves allowing plant stems to partly decompose either by soaking them in water or laying them out on the ground (dew retting). The fibres are then separated from the stems by breaking and scutching, ready for draft spinning. In contrast, the technique employed in ancient Egypt was to separate long fibres from the stem and to splice these end to end, which may give some explanation for the exceptionally fine quality of linen produced for the pharaohs.

The possibility that ancient Egyptian linen might be spliced was first raised many years ago but remained a matter for dispute until the combined efforts of archaeologists and textile technologists made the evidence overwhelming (*see* the Bibliography for details of the fascinating paper by Cooke et al. which settles this argument once and for all). Splices can actually be seen in examples of cloth from ancient Egypt; these are visible because of the different character of the thread in the spliced and non-spliced sections. When untwisted strands are thrown together to form a thicker yarn they merge to form a single thread, but the splices are not able to blend in and so short lengths of yarn are produced that appear to be plied. These splice points can also be seen in hanks of unwoven linen yarn from ancient Egypt, as for example in a hank on display in the Nebamun gallery at the British Museum.

A strick of flax that has been water retted, giving a light golden colour. It is easy to see how the expression 'flaxen hair' came into use. Alongside are skeins of handspun linen yarn, water retted on the left and dew retted, giving a brownish-grey colour, to the right.

Modern Techniques of Fibre Preparation for Linen

In recent times the water retting and dew retting techniques of loosening the fibres from the stems have been supplemented by methods of enzyme and chemical retting. Chemical treatments are obviously undesirable from an ecological point of view, but the traditional method of water retting can also be a serious source of pollution if carried out in rivers rather than in ponds or tanks. Dew retting, though slower, is definitely the 'greenest' technique. After retting, breaking and scutching the flax, fibres are treated by hackling, a combing technique that separates shorter fibres from the better quality long fibres. Flax is thus separated into two grades; the long fibres are subjected to a wet-spinning process, producing smooth, lustrous line linen, while the shorter fibres are spun dry, creating a more rough-textured tow yarn.

These differences can be further enhanced in cloth woven from line linen by processes that flatten the fibres to give a glossy surface – mangling or beetling (beating with mallets) either by hand or machine. Even in plain weave these techniques can produce a highly lustrous cloth, but float weaves such as huckaback for towels and damask for tablecloth are also widely used and are very effective in making the most of the lustre of the yarn. A detailed study of the history and traditional use of linen is given by Patricia Baines. Although a smooth, lustrous finish is a classic use of the material, high-twist linen yarns are able to give a creping reaction. In a close weave this can give a lively quality to the surface, while with more open setts the stiffness of the yarns causes them to curl into quite large spirals, giving a larger-scale texture than the fine crinkling produced by crepe yarns in softer materials such as silk, wool or cotton.

Hemp

This is another bast fibre broadly similar to flax (microscopically they can be difficult to tell apart) but the fibres are not quite so fine. Preparation is similar to that for linen, involving retting, breaking and scutching, followed by hackling to separate the fibres into line and tow. It was once used mainly for cordage, ropes and coarse fabrics, but is increasingly being used for clothing as part of a drive for an increased use of more sustainable fibres as it has low requirements for water and pesticides.

Ramie

This requires a different method of preparation from flax and hemp because of the large amount of gum associated with the fibres. There may be an initial retting process to loosen the fibres but they are then pulled from the stems in strips, which are dried and later degummed. The fibres can be extremely fine and are very strong and durable. Some authorities suggest that ramie may be three times as strong as hemp and four times as strong as linen, though others suggest there is little difference in strength between the three fibres. Such varied results are probably due to differences in both sources of fibre and processing methods.

Compared with other bast fibres, ramie is particularly stiff and inflexible making it very suitable for achieving stability in open, delicate-looking cloths. Though potentially a good sustainable fibre because, like hemp and flax, it has little requirement for irrigation, it does tend to deplete the soil and so requires fertilizer. There is also the impact of the degumming process to consider, as this may involve strong alkalis, though attempts are being made to introduce more eco-friendly processes.

After spinning, the weavers of Nepal wind allo yarn into these elegant balls. The woven fabric is used for a variety of articles, including towels, garments, cushion covers, tablecloths, mats and bags.

Samples of cloth made from pineapple (left) and banana (right). These rather stiff yarns can form a relatively open and translucent cloth with a crisp handle.

Table mats designed by Angus Williams and woven in Nepal using allo yarn.

Nettle

Though nettles are no longer a major source of textile fibre there is a long history of the use of *Urtica* species, particularly *Urtica dioica* (great nettle or common stinging nettle), especially in Scandinavia, and Margrethe Hald suggests that its use as a textile fibre may well predate that of either flax or wool. Gillian Edom gives a good account of the historical use of nettle fibre around the world, together with some notes on fibre preparation. Nettles can be retted like linen but also can be broken down and spun like cotton, a technique that has been described in detail by Birthe Ford.

Another important species is the Himalayan giant nettle (*Girardinia diversifolia*), commonly known as allo. This plant is processed by stripping away the outer bark and fibres from the stems and preparing them for spinning by boiling. The books by Susi Dunsmore give a detailed account of the processing and use of the nettle fibre in Nepal.

Structural or Hard Vegetable Fibres

These are fibres obtained from stems and leaves but they are composed of the fibrovascular fibres that transport water and food through the plant and tend to be larger and stiffer than the bast fibres. They include manila (abaca), sisal and New Zealand flax and generally yield fibres suitable for cordage, paper or relatively coarse cloth, but this group does also include some fibres such as pineapple and banana that can be used to make very fine fabrics. Although pineapple fibre can be retted like linen and spun, both pineapple and banana are sometimes processed by splitting the fibres and

Neckpiece woven with a silk/steel warp and a paper weft, which gives the piece enough stiffness to resist crushing.

knotting long lengths together to make a fine but stiff yarn that produces a delicate but very crisp cloth.

Pineapple has also recently been developed commercially as a non-woven fabric, Piñatex, by the firm Ananas Amam. This material uses the waste from the farming of pineapple for fruit and is sometimes known as pineapple leather due to its successful use for items such as bags and shoes.

Paper

The use of paper yarn in weaving has a long tradition in Japan in the form of shifu, and such textiles were known and admired in the West as long ago as the eighteenth century. However it was only in the 1890s that the industrial production of paper yarn began in Germany as a way to avoid relying on imports of more conventional textile materials. Since then paper yarns have greatly increased in popularity and have been used for a wide variety of items, including clothing, bags, mats and even furniture.

Paper yarns are generally smooth and stiff, though they are now available in a wide range of weights and qualities and some finer yarns may be reasonably flexible. Heavier yarns are excellent for items like mats, though if used as warp their stiffness and springiness can make them difficult to handle; although dampening can make them more flexible, this needs to be done carefully as it tends to weaken them. Some very fine qualities have recently become available, particularly from Japan and the finest of these, made from manila (abaca), are particularly strong, dye well and are suited to a wide range of applications. Even the finest yarns have some degree of stiffness and this makes paper useful where a fabric needs body, such as pieces intended as jewellery, and it also works well as a foil to more flexible materials for creating textured effects. *Paper Textiles* by Christina Leitner provides an excellent survey, covering a detailed history and a wide range of textiles techniques.

Seed Fibres

Cultivated cotton is the main seed fibre in use for woven textiles although a number of wild cottons are produced in small quantities. Cotton fibres show a strong correlation between length and fineness so a very wide range of qualities can be produced, as carded yarns using short, thick fibres have a very different character from those spun from long, fine fibres that are suitable for combing. Also, given that long fibres need less overlap in spinning, this correlation between fineness and length means that exceptionally fine yarns can be spun from the long-fibre cottons.

The other important distinction between yarn qualities depends on a finishing treatment – mercerization. This involves treating yarns with sodium hydroxide while under tension, giving a highly lustrous finish, although this well-known characteristic was not achieved with the original technique. In the mid nineteenth century when John Mercer developed the process now bearing his name, he applied sodium hydroxide without keeping the yarn under tension. The main results were that the cotton shrank and became stronger and that its affinity for dyes was increased, this last property being the one that Mercer himself regarded as the most important. It was not until 1890 that Horace Lowe discovered that imposing tension during the sodium hydroxide treatment could create the silk-like lustre now associated with mercerized cotton.

Cotton works well as a crepe yarn, normally unmercerized since high levels of twist are incompatible with maintaining a high lustre. As the cotton fibre is much less stiff than flax, the creping reaction tends to produce a finer texture, though different qualities of cotton give different effects, with short-fibre carded cotton forming smaller crinkles than longer-fibre combed yarns. Crepe-like effects can also be produced with normal cotton yarns by means of the original mercerization process, that is to say by treating the fabric with sodium hydroxide but without tension. The swelling of the fibres will then cause contraction of the cloth.

Cotton is the most widely used of the natural fibres, valued for its good laundering qualities, cheapness and durability. Its reputation has suffered recently because of its high demand for water and pesticides, which has led to the promotion of less environmentally damaging fibres such as hemp and also to experiments with a wide variety of plants that might be produced more sustainably as sources of regenerated fibres.

ANIMAL FIBRES

Wool

Wool fibres vary so much that only a few general points can be made here. Unlike cotton, the relationship between fibre fineness and length is an inverse one. Fine merino fibres may be only 5 cm long, while a coarse long-staple breed can produce fibres as long as 30 cm, so fineness of fibre, rather than length, is the main determinant of how fine a yarn can be spun. However crimp, another measure of quality, appears to be directly related to fineness, with the finer, shorter wools having a larger number of crimps/cm.

The main distinction in wool yarn construction is between worsted and woollen spinning. The aim in worsted spinning is to produce a smooth, firm yarn by combing the fibres to lie parallel with one another, while for woollen spinning they are carded, creating a more random arrangement that results in a softer, loftier yarn. Although worsted spinning is generally applied to long fibres and woollen spinning used for short fibres, some wools of intermediate length could be prepared and spun either way. For the very finest worsted yarns, moderately short fibres must be used because they are finer than the longwools.

Wool is famous for its ability to felt, but this varies greatly from one breed to another. Felting occurs mainly because the scales that cover the surfaces of the fibres become enmeshed when fibres, yarns or fabric are subjected to heat, agitation and soap. But although there is generally a good correlation between felting ability and the scaliness of the fibres from the various breeds, there are exceptions so clearly other factors such as strength, elasticity and crimp must also be involved.

Wool forms excellent crepe yarns and, as with cotton, different effects are produced depending on whether fibres have been prepared by carding or combing, with soft, woollen-spun yarns tending to form small crinkles while stiffer worsted yarns form relatively large spirals.

Mohair

Mohair is derived from the fleece of the Angora goat and the fibres are long, stiff and lustrous. Although the surface of the fibre has scales, these lie almost flat and hardly overlap so the fibre is very smooth and resists felting. Though mohair is both strong and beautiful its smoothness and springiness can present difficulties in handling. Clifford W. Ashley, writing in *The Ashley Book of Knots,* describes being asked to design a special mohair knot that would not untie in fast-running power looms: 'The yarn is both slick and springy, in the same way that piano wire is… and none of the customary WEAVER'S KNOTS will serve'. Two pages of knots follow that are devoted to mohair and other difficult slippery yarns. The handweaver is not likely to have quite the same problems, but it is useful to be aware of the very smooth character of these yarns.

Everything about the characteristics of this fibre might seem to work against it being a good creping yarn and certainly it will not produce the fine crinkled effects given by silk, wool or cotton, but its stiffness and springiness mean that it responds surprisingly strongly to very modest amounts of twist and examples will be shown later in this book.

Alpaca and Camel Hair

These fibres cannot be bleached so can only be dyed to colours darker than their natural shades but although this could be seen as a disadvantage, their natural colours are very attractive. In the case of the alpaca, fibres may occasionally be white but are mainly in a range of browns, greys and black, while camel hair has the characteristic shades of yellow to brown. The alpaca produces lustrous hairs that have little crimp and generally do not felt easily, and these

Bundles of horsehair showing attractive variations of natural colour.

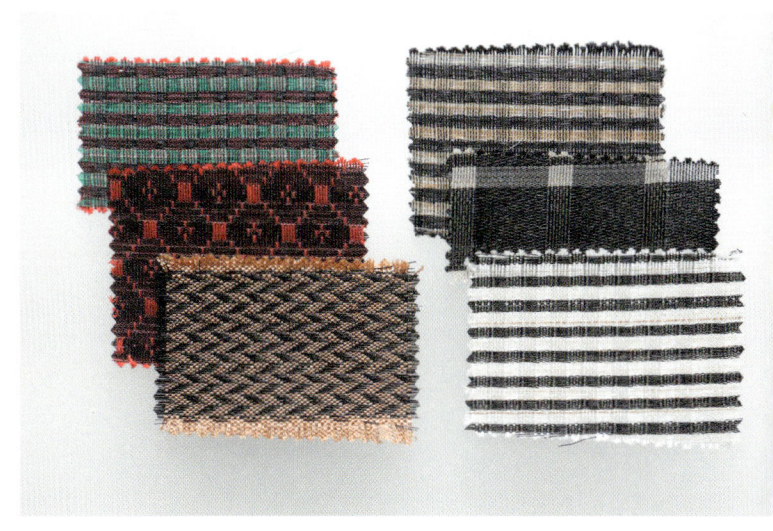

Samples of fabrics using horsehair as weft, woven by John Boyd Textiles. *See* Online Resources for more information about the company.

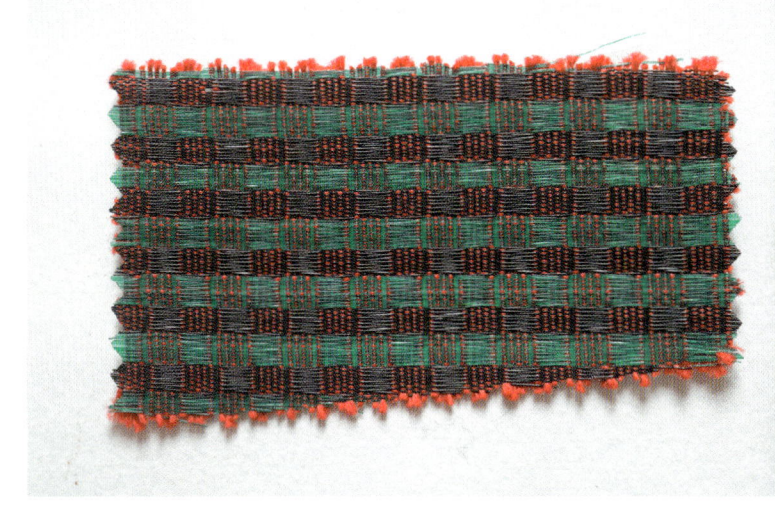

This close-up of a fabric swatch shows a horsehair weft dyed a brilliant green that is shown off well by the float weave that has been used, and the contrast with the red cotton warp.

smooth, straight fibres can give a good creping reaction at modest levels of twist. The camel has a mix of long coarse hairs, used for belting, ropes and so on, and soft short wool which has traditionally been used for overcoats because of its good insulating properties.

Horsehair

Hair from both the manes and tails of horses can be used to produce very hardwearing upholstery, with hair from the mane being generally the softer of the two. Although very popular in the eighteenth and nineteenth centuries, horsehair upholstery is no longer so widely used but there is still some demand because of its beauty and durability. John Boyd Textiles was established in 1837, in Castle Cary, and is now one of the few companies in the world still weaving this cloth, using the tail hair as weft, with warps of silk, cotton or linen. Horsehair naturally comes in a variety of attractive colours but also dyes well. The fibre is extremely smooth, stiff and springy – considerably more like piano wire than is the case with mohair!

CHAPTER 2: Material Resources: Fibres and Yarns **31**

This silk scarf shows how weave structure interacts with the properties of the material. The plain weave areas have an attractive sheen, but it is only where the float pattern is used that the full gloss of the silk weft is revealed. (Designer unknown. Lent by Irene Galant)

Silk

Silk produced by the mulberry silkworm, *Bombyx mori*, is the most widely used fibre, though there is a fairly substantial use of tussah silk, from the *Antheraea pernyi* moth, and a smaller local use of other wild silks. The continuous fibre reeled from the cocoons of the silkworm is the best quality, but there is a large production of other qualities from the waste that is generated as a by-product. The best quality waste uses quite long fibres and produces highly lustrous spun silk yarns, while shorter fibres are spun into rough-textured bourette and noil yarns. Tussah has greater elasticity than cultivated silk and is normally produced as spun silk yarns that have more 'tooth' than the glossier spun silks made from cultivated fibres. It cannot be bleached but its soft golden colour is very attractive and it also dyes well, though the intrinsic colour naturally influences the shades that are produced.

Silk reeled directly from the cocoon, known as hard or raw silk, is produced by combining filaments from between three and eight cocoons, giving yarn thicknesses ranging from 8/10 to 20/22 deniers. The silk filaments become held together by a coating of sericin (silk gum), which gives the yarn considerable strength and cohesion, though at the expense of the very high lustre normally associated with silk since this is only revealed once the gum has been removed. Hard silk is also much stiffer than degummed silk and this can be an advantage in achieving stability in very openly set fabrics. William Willetts has commented on the fact that early Chinese silks from the Han period appear to have used completely twistless warps, while silk weavers in the West always used twisted silk for their warps. He suggests that the Han weavers probably used raw silk, as this would be strong and cohesive enough for warps, and then degummed the woven fabric to reveal the high lustre of the twistless yarn.

Degummed silk with very little twist can of course be easily used as weft, and its lustre is best displayed in fabrics that include floats. However, although the high lustre of silk is one of its main attractions and lightly twisted yarns are generally desirable, higher levels of twist can be added for specific purposes, for example the firm twist applied to produce organzine yarn for organza, a crisp and open fabric. Silk also makes an excellent crepe yarn.

MAN-MADE FIBRES

The first known reference to the idea of creating artificial fibres was by Robert Hooke in his beautifully illustrated book *Micrographia*, published in 1664, but it was to be another 300 years before this was accomplished with the production of the first artificial silk, rayon. Since then a huge number of artificial fibres has been developed, with a vast range of properties, going far beyond the scope of this book. However two general issues are worth mentioning briefly, firstly that of learning to handle them, and secondly their environmental credentials.

On the first point, some man-made fibres clearly imitate natural ones and may to some extent have similar properties, so prior experience with natural fibres provides a starting point, while others have quite new and unfamiliar properties and need considerable experiment to really judge their strengths and weaknesses. On the second point, there is an increasing need to consider the sustainability of all textile fibres, so new materials need to be looked at carefully and bold claims of 'greenness' treated cautiously.

Man-made yarns fall into two groups; reconstituted fibres, derived from natural sources such as plant cellulose, and those that are true synthetics. The first group are more likely to be imitative of natural fibres though they may also be used to create yarns with quite different characteristics. As new materials with unusual properties became increasingly available during the twentieth century they were embraced with enthusiasm both by industry and by at least some craftsmen. Cellophane, for example, was used both by Anni Albers at the Bauhaus and by handweavers such as Ethel Mairet in her workshop 'Gospels' at Ditchling.

The true synthetics may also imitate or at least substitute for natural fibres, as when silk stockings were replaced by 'nylons', but they also have more scope for producing yarns with new properties such as being reflective, glowing in the dark or imitating the natural iridescence of butterfly wings. Synthetic elastomers can be used successfully as a substitute for crepe yarns in some situations but they do behave differently, shrinking along their length rather than acquiring the spiral structure of crepe yarns. Used as weft across a closely set warp the result is likely to be a flat fabric with elasticity rather than a textured surface, though with a more open sett a random texture that is a little like a coarse crepe may be produced. They also work well in designs that rely on long floats, where their strong shrinkage can push other yarns into a pronounced texture.

This 'Bubble' scarf by Lotte Dalgaard shows a good use of an elastomeric yarn, because strong shrinkage is required to push the adjacent wool yarns into a texture. Lotte gives instructions for weaving this fabric in *Vävmagasinet*. (Photo: Sanne Krogh)

On the environmental question, there is little point in condemning cotton as damaging if it is merely replaced by new fibres that may be no more sustainable when the whole production process is taken into account. Bamboo, for example, is rightly praised for its sustainable cultivation but processing the fibres requires damaging chemicals, so more work is needed to make it truly sustainable. Tencel can better justify its reputation because it is a closed-loop process that recycles the majority of the chemicals involved. Most regenerated fibres utilize cellulose and aim to substitute for cotton, but a yarn has also been developed based on protein extracted from soy beans, which is marketed under the name soysilk and is promoted as 'vegan silk'. Many different plants are now being considered as sources of regenerated fibres and their true sustainability will depend on building in closed-loop or other eco-friendly processing systems to ensure that not just cultivation but the entire production process avoids damaging the environment.

Metal yarns can vary greatly in their properties. Left: 'Heavy Metal', a handmade yarn formed from a viscose core wrapped with a flat strip of silver-plated copper. This construction results in a shiny yarn that makes an attractive weft but is not strong enough for warp. Centre: Silk/steel yarn, composed of a silk yarn tightly plied together with a fine steel wire. This yarn has only a faint sheen, but it is strong enough for warp and creates fabrics that are highly mouldable. Right: Bekinox (Alphatex), a 100 per cent steel yarn designed by Junichi Arai. This has a high gloss and creates a fabric that is drapable rather than mouldable.

METALS

Early examples of the use of metals in textiles usually involve decorations that are attached in various ways, such as the corded skirts decorated with metal tubes found in Bronze Age burials in Denmark, but entire items have also been constructed in wire using textile techniques, especially in Japan. Luxurious woven textiles were also produced with wefts of fine wire or yarns constructed by wrapping flat metal strips around a textile core. The use of wire for textile techniques became more widespread in the late twentieth century and was given much impetus by the work of Arline Fisch and her influential book *Textile Techniques in Metal*.

Wires are now available to weavers in a very wide range of gauges, but a new type of metal/textile combination has also been developed recently. These yarns have a very different character from metal-wrapped weft yarns because they are constructed by plying together a textile yarn and a very fine metal wire. The textile fibres can be silk, wool, cotton, linen or polyester while the wire may be steel, copper or brass. These yarns have an interesting intermediate character between textile and wire and are strong enough to be used as warp as well as weft. I have used them extensively for textile jewellery as they offer both a crisp texture and a 'memory' for imposed pleats and folds.

The Japanese designer Junichi Arai designed an extraordinary metal yarn with a completely different character from wire. Bekinox (Alphatex) is a 100 per cent steel yarn made out of fine metal fibres, is extremely heavy and, rather than being stiff like a wire, drapes like a textile yarn. Peter Collingwood used this remarkable yarn for a large and dramatic wall piece for the Kiryu Performing Arts Centre in Japan, and his account of working with it (described in Chapter 9) provides an excellent example of reflective practice, in getting to grips with a new and challenging material.

RESPONDING TO THE MATERIAL

Anni Albers is quoted in the introduction to this section because her concern with materials was central to her work, and her writings capture the importance of the *substance* of a cloth as well as its appearance. In her classic book *On Weaving*, she points out that the pre-preparation of many materials in everyday life, though convenient, has a downside: 'we merely toast the bread. No need to get our hands into the dough. No need – alas, also little chance – to handle materials, to test their consistency, their density, their lightness, their smoothness.' She believed that this lack of experience with unformed material caused a neglect of the sense of tactility, commenting that: 'there seems to be no common word for the tactile perception of such properties of material, related to inner structure, as pliability, sponginess, brittleness, porousness, etc.'

Another designer who strongly emphasized the importance of material as a source of inspiration was Marianne Straub:

> I always feel rather unhappy about the word 'design' because it sounds so superimposed… By design I mean the pattern that is made by the interlacing of the threads. And can there be anything lovelier than a material woven, one thread up and one thread down with the right yarns? There is nothing to compete with the character of the thread, and the shadows produced through the simple interlacing of the yarn gives such depth and vibration to the cloth.
>
> Quoted in: Mary Schoeser, *Marianne Straub*

This self-pleated neckpiece is constructed with copper/polyester yarn in both warp and weft. The stiffness of the copper/polyester gives body to the piece, which is assembled from a number of separately woven sections.

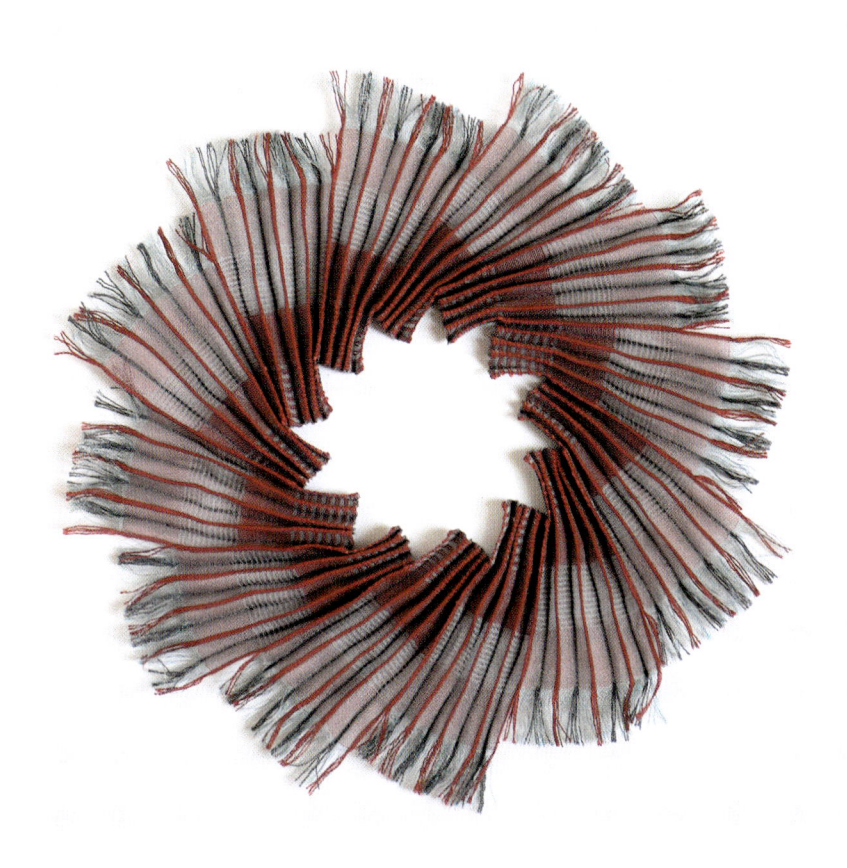

MATERIAL AND STRUCTURE

It is in the process of handling and using materials that ideas often emerge, as particular characteristics and properties become obvious. Sometimes it is only in handling the finished fabric itself that certain qualities are fully appreciated as the impact of different structures on the behaviour of a material becomes clear. Anni Albers has described this interplay of material and structure as 'the essence of weaving', and the next two chapters will look at this interplay, first with plain weave and then with a selection of more complex weaves. Many of these structures are most familiar to us in particular guises – they are 'towel weaves' or 'lace weaves' or 'rug weaves' – but variations of material or scale can make them look and feel quite different, so a sense of the great variety of possible cloth qualities will be particularly emphasized.

Chevron neckpieces. Warp: Silk/steel and spun silk. Weft: Crepe silk and linen. The radiating pleats are 'natural', emerging during wet finishing through the combination of material and structure, while the chevron folds are imposed, relying on the 'memory' of the silk/steel warp yarn.

CHAPTER 2: Material Resources: Fibres and Yarns 35

CHAPTER 3

Structural Resources: Simple Gifts

'Tis the gift to be simple, 'tis the gift to be free.

(Shaker dancing song by Elder Joseph Brackett)

Any weave structure can be used in numerous ways to give very different fabric qualities, and this important principle is exemplified by the simplest structure, plain weave. Although its simplicity might at first glance appear to be a limitation, in reality it offers immense freedom and need not be 'plain' at all. This was well understood by the Shakers who, while deeply committed to simplicity, made imaginative use of this most fundamental of structures, plying yarns and rags in different twist directions to pattern their rugs and producing very fine, richly coloured, iridescent silk scarves.

Although working with colour is perhaps the most obvious way to make the most of plain weave, the substance of the cloth is also subject to wide variation. Major factors that can be varied include fibre, yarn construction and thickness, sett and finishing technique, all of which can produce vastly different qualities of fabric, so it makes sense to discuss plain weave in some detail before moving on to other weave structures. Where there are variations in the naming or classification of fabrics or weaves, I am in most cases relying on the terms given by Irene Emery in *The Primary Structures of Fabrics*.

The inherent properties of individual textile fibres have already been discussed in Chapter 2, and given how varied they are, especially when modified by techniques of preparation, yarn construction and finishing technique, it is easy to see how even fabrics that are identical in terms of yarn thickness, sett and weave structure can still be vastly different in character. Once additional modifying effects are brought into play the range of possibilities is endless.

For the sake of clarity various influences will be considered in turn, beginning with yarn twist and followed by variations in sett and relative yarn thicknesses. But of course these factors are not operating in isolation from one another; a hard-twisted yarn in a close sett will behave quite differently from an identical yarn that is very openly set. With yarns of similar thickness in a very open sett, a stiff or rough-textured yarn might make a cohesive fabric while a softer or smoother yarn would probably give an unstable, sleazy effect. This is why sampling is so important – even with the simplest structure the interplay of factors can be complex and difficult to predict.

AMOUNT AND DIRECTION OF YARN TWIST

Yarns can be twisted by different amounts, giving various angles of twist that impact strongly upon fabric quality. High levels of yarn twist make very hardwearing fabrics, particularly if the sett is close, and this is likely to have been an important concern throughout history. Archaeologists studying Bronze Age and Iron Age textiles excavated from the salt mines in Hallstatt, Austria (1300-200 BC), record the yarn twists as being 'mostly hard to very hard' with twist angles of 40-50 degrees being common, and many of these fabrics are also very closely set. Ancient Egyptian textiles also frequently show fairly high levels of twist. For example, at Amarna (1353-1336 BC) the majority of the textiles that have been excavated have yarn twists between 25 and 45 degrees, as described by Kemp and Vogelsang-Eastwood in their detailed study *The Ancient Textile Industry at Amarna*.

Although high levels of twist have advantages for hardwearing fabrics, there are of course many other fabric qualities that may be desired. Hard-twisted yarns may give a somewhat harsh feel to a fabric and so lower twists may be required for softer fabrics, for example for scarves. With fibres that have a natural lustre, such as silk and linen, high-twist will tend to subdue the gloss, so lower levels of yarn twist are often used to exploit the lustrous qualities of the fibres. Although the lustre of silk is noticeable in a relatively open plain weave, it may be partly subdued in a closely set fabric, and so float weaves are often preferred to make best use of the natural character of the fibre. However, it can be particularly interesting to combine areas of plain weave with float weaves to vary the extent to which the natural lustre of silk is expressed, and some examples will be given in Chapter 4.

As well as being twisted by different amounts, yarns can be twisted in two different directions, S and Z, and historically one or the other seem to have been preferred at different times and by particular communities. This can be useful to archaeologists and historians as evidence for a particular provenance, and the possible reasons for such preferences have been a source of some speculation. For example, Elizabeth Barber suggests that different spinning techniques, combined with the fact that most people are right-handed, might be a possible explanation for different directions of twist. On this argument, the ancient Egyptians with their technique of rolling high-whorl spindles down the thigh will end up with an S-twist yarn, while communities that use low-whorl spindles tend to flick these to the right with a thumb and fingers and so will naturally produce a Z-twist yarn.

This is an interesting theory, though it does perhaps beg the question of how the different spinning techniques evolved, if not to achieve these different spin directions. A possible answer in some cases may lie in different methods of yarn construction; linen yarns in ancient Egypt were constructed by splicing lengths of fibre together, so the 'spinning' process was simply one of adding twist to an existing yarn. This may perhaps be relatively easy to do with a high-whorl spindle, while the teasing out of wool fibres in draft spinning may be more easily controlled with a low-whorl spindle.

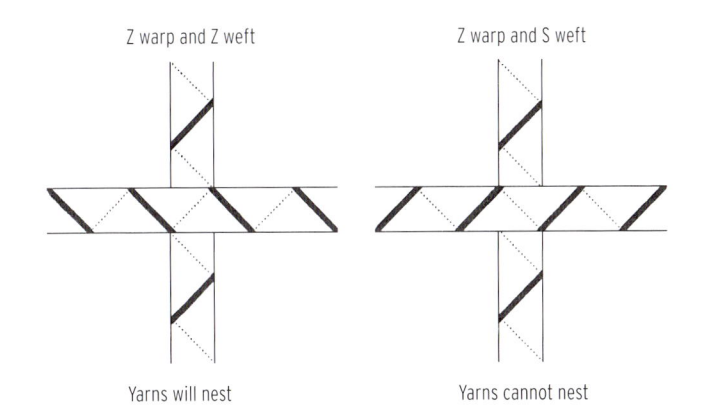

Z warp and Z weft — Yarns will nest

Z warp and S weft — Yarns cannot nest

Direction of yarn twist and fabric quality. Fabrics may either be woven with the same direction of twist in warp and weft or with opposite twists. If the same twist is used, the yarns nest or bed into one another, because when a Z pick lies over a Z end the fibres on the *underside* of the weft pick will be in line with those on the *surface* of the warp end. The direction of yarn twist is shown here as a solid line for the surface of the yarn and as a dotted line for the underside. With opposite twists the fibres on the underside of the weft pick will run counter to those on the surface of the warp end so that nesting is prevented. The yarns tend to push away from one another, giving a fuller handle to the fabric.

CHAPTER 3: Structural Resources: Simple Gifts

This Bronze Age belt from Borum Eshøj in Denmark has alternating stripes of S, Z and S spun yarn. Although it is in plain weave, the alternation of yarn twist direction together with its warp-faced sett creates the illusion of reversing twill stripes that run in the *opposite* direction to the twist in the yarn. The weaver has emphasized the effect by using paler wool for the central stripe. (Photo: Alan Costall)

Although textiles can be woven entirely with one direction of yarn throughout, combining *different* directions of twist within a textile can produce interesting effects, both visual and tactile, and such techniques seem to have a considerable history. For example, using different directions of twist in warp and weft creates a fabric with a fuller feel, because these yarns become pushed apart rather than nesting into one another, and this effect (even if not the mechanism) seems to have been understood quite early on. A large proportion of the textiles excavated from Bronze Age burials in Denmark use such combinations of S and Z twist, as do many of the Hallstatt textiles, especially those dating from the Iron Age. Using different twist directions in this way also avoids the tendency for a 'crowsfoot' or 'tracking' pattern to appear, which may happen when warp and weft yarns are of the same twist. This texture is not unattractive and some handweavers regard it as a gift, since it can create the illusion of a diamond twill in a plain weave fabric, but it may not always be desired. In woollen fabrics, using different twist directions in warp and weft has the further advantage of producing a cloth that will full more easily.

As well as influencing the handle of the cloth, S and Z yarns reflect light differently so they can be used to produce 'shadow' stripes and checks. The earliest example that I am aware of is the famous Borum Eshøj belt, dating from Bronze Age Denmark (1400–1200 BC). In this case, as the fabric is strongly warp-faced, the alternation of S and Z twist creates the illusion of reversing twill stripes. This beautiful belt is on display at the National Museum in Copenhagen, and it is well described in detail by Elizabeth Barber in *Prehistoric Textiles*.

Crepon fabric, where only one direction of twist is used in the weft.

Crepe fabric, where S and Z yarns are used for weft in a 2S, 2Z arrangement. (Designer unknown. Gift from Sheila Reimann)

Textured Effects with High-Twist Yarns in Open Weaves

Although highly twisted yarns that are closely set can produce a firm, hardwearing fabric, very different effects result from a more open sett. High levels of twist impart energy to a yarn (as described in Chapter 2) but this is only released when the yarn is wetted out, causing it to curl and crinkle. When this reaction takes place within a loosely woven fabric, various distortions are produced, depending on the amount and direction of twist. The simplest case is where a normal-twist yarn is crossed by high-twist yarn of a single direction of twist, resulting in an effect of irregular pleating – crepon. Using the two directions of twist alternately breaks up this pleated effect, giving the overall random crinkled texture that is familiar in crepe fabrics. Excavations have revealed that these techniques have a long history in China; a piece from the Shang Dynasty (1600-1027 BC) shows the use of a single direction of twist, while an example of the classic crepe construction, with both directions of twist, dates from the Warring States period (475-221 BC).

If high-twist yarns are used in both warp *and* weft, then the interplay between different twist directions can produce distinctive textural patterns in the cloth. A 'tracking' pattern tends to appear when yarns of the same twist direction cross one another and this effect becomes very pronounced

Sample of a Japanese kimono fabric in which the yarn twist is reversed after several picks, causing the fabric to bend back and forth, creating a bolder texture than the classic crepe structure of 2S, 2Z. (Designer unknown. Gift from Margrit Waldron)

Same-twist yarn interactions produce a tracking pattern. Crepe wool 58/2 Nm, 32 epi, ppi, Z warp and weft.

Opposite-twist yarn interactions produce an undulating effect. Crepe wool 58/2 Nm, 32 epi, ppi, Z warp and S weft.

This scarf has broad stripes of S, Z and S twist yarn. When woven with an S twist weft, a central stripe of undulating texture is produced, where Z and S yarns cross, while the S × S interactions in the outer stripes produce a flatter fabric that forms a frilled edge. Warp and weft: Crepe wool 30 Nm.

if the yarns are highly twisted. By contrast, when S and Z yarns cross one another a more deeply textured, wavy effect is produced and this takes up more cloth than the flatter texture of the 'tracking' pattern. This difference in fabric take-up can be exploited to create frilled edges, seersucker effects and fabric shaping.

There are endless possibilities for creating textured fabrics using high-twist yarns in plain weave, and the topic is covered in more detail in my book *Weaving Textiles That Shape Themselves*.

VARIATIONS IN SETT

Cloth Setting

The yarn diameter can be used together with a cloth-setting formula (*see box*) to estimate the maximum possible sett for a yarn. As discussed in Chapter 2, the Ashenhurst formula is a quicker and more reliable method of estimating yarn diameter than the traditional technique of 'wrapping'. Also, because the wrapping technique flattens the yarns slightly, this gives an estimate of diameters/cm (or inch) that is approximately two thirds of that given by the formula, so that resulting cloth setting calculations will also be different. The issue of these different methods is discussed in detail in my book *Weaving Textiles That Shape Themselves*, but the basic point is that sett calculations based on the Ashenhurst formula are best regarded as maximums, while those based on wrapping will give 'average' setts, suitable for medium-weight fabrics. The cloth-setting formula takes account of the number of intersections in the weave so is generally applicable to all weave structures, not just plain weave, though some modifications may be needed for weaves with many long floats.

The maximum sett provides a useful and reliable reference point, but in practice most fabrics will need to be set lower than this. Upholstery fabrics might work well at about 90–95 per cent of maximum sett, while medium-weight clothing might be set at 60–80 per cent and scarves at 50 per cent or even lower. These reductions of maximum sett can be used to give a starting point for sampling, but it is important to cut off, finish and assess samples before deciding if this initial sett really is suitable. Once a satisfactory sett has been determined by sampling it is useful to record this as a percentage of maximum sett so that it can be used as a guide to future work. Examples of using percentage sett in this way will be given in Chapter 9.

Cloth-setting formula

$$\text{Sett} = \left(\frac{\text{No. of warp ends in a repeat}}{\text{No. of warp ends + No. intersections in a repeat}} \right) \times \text{yarn diameters/cm (or inch)}$$

Cover Factor

Although the cloth-setting formula is widely used, both by handweavers and in industrial textile production, an alternative calculation, the cover factor, is sometimes used, particularly in industry (see box). This gives a measure of how closely a cloth is set by indicating the fraction of available space in the cloth that is occupied by yarn. It is generally considered best to give the fractional cover factors for warp and weft individually because combining them to give a cumulative value does not give any idea of the relative importance of warp and weft yarns. This matters because the relationship between different densities of warp and weft can greatly influence the characteristics of the cloth.

However, a cumulative cover factor does give a sense of the overall density of the cloth which impacts on qualities such as porosity and the permeability to air and light. Until now this measurement has mainly been used for industrially produced textiles, but cumulative cover factor is starting to be used by textile historians and archaeologists, for example in the survey of the Hallstatt textiles by Karina Grömer and her colleagues, so it is worth understanding how it is calculated. The cumulative value cannot be derived by simply adding the warp and weft factors together because areas where warp and weft cross one another would then be counted twice, so allowance needs to be made for this (see box).

Fractional cover factor

c = cover factor, e = epcm (or epi), d = diameters/cm (or diameters/inch)
Warp cover factor: $c_1 = e_1/d_1$
Weft cover factor: $c_2 = e_2/d_2$

Cumulative cover factor

Cumulative warp and weft cover factor: $c = c_1 + c_2 - c_1 c_2$

BALANCED FABRICS

The linen fabrics shown here have the same yarns in both warp and weft and they are also *balanced*, that is to say there are the same number of threads/inch in both warp and weft. Broadly speaking, this means that the characteristics of the fabric – stiffness, flexibility, draping qualities – will be very similar both warpways and weftways, though because the warp has been under tension during the weaving process, the fabric will usually have a little less 'give' in the warp direction. However, these differences will be slight and so balanced fabrics work well in garments that are cut on the bias (that is, both warp and weft will stretch evenly).

Samples of linen 44 lea at two different setts in a balanced plain weave. On the left the fabric is set at 32 epi and ppi, which is 60 per cent of the maximum sett as calculated by the Ashenhurst formula. This gives a fairly open, softly draping quality suitable for scarves or lightweight clothing, though even lower setts could be used if aiming for a very delicate, transparent effect (examples will be given in Chapter 6). The closer weave is set at 44 epi and ppi, which is 83 per cent of maximum sett, giving a firmer quality that could work well for either clothing or lightweight furnishings.

Silk scarf, with a 'log cabin' colour-and-weave effect. The sett is 12 epcm in both warp and weft, but the yarn thickness varies. The black yarn is the same in both warp and weft, but the ecru yarn varies, with a fairly thick, rough-textured warp and a finer softer weft. This arrangement gives a good drape along the length of the scarf. (Designer unknown)

VARIATIONS IN WARP AND WEFT DENSITY

In contrast with such balanced cloths, fabrics may be woven with a predominance of either warp or weft and this will give them different characteristics in the warpways and weftways directions. The appearance of a cloth will also be changed, most obviously if different colours are used, since at the extremes the warp may completely cover the weft (warp-faced fabric), or vice versa (weft-faced fabric). Frequently the degree of warp or weft dominance may be less extreme, but in all cases there will be an impact on the physical characteristics of the fabric, which will generally fall into folds more easily in line with the higher density of threads since the fabric is likely to be stiffer in that direction. However this effect will be modified if different thicknesses of yarn are used in warp and weft, and the relative thickness

Detail of the 'log cabin' scarf.

In contrast with the 'log cabin' design, this silk fabric has a fine warp and a thicker, more softly twisted weft so the fabric falls into folds more readily across the warp than along its length. However, the width of this fabric is sufficient for it to be used for a garment with the weft running down the body. (Designer unknown)

and quality of warp and weft will then determine how the fabric will drape. If a relatively thick warp is combined with a fine weft then the fabric will generally have a good drape in the warpways direction.

Fabrics are most often used with the warp running

vertically. Curtains are usually constructed in this way because of the length required, and garments are generally cut so that the warp runs down the length of the body, so it is common for the warp to be more densely set than the weft. However, some thick, softly twisted yarns may be much easier to use as weft, and if these are combined with a fine warp the fabric will fall into folds more readily in the weftways direction. Such a fabric may still work well for garments if it is of adequate width.

Using fabric 'sideways' for garments has a long tradition in folk costumes in Europe and Scandinavia. Skirts were often woven using an unbleached linen warp that would be completely covered by a densely beaten, dyed wool weft, a technique that offers great flexibility of design since the widths and colours of stripes can be varied at will. These stripes, sometimes also ornamented by float patterns, would then run down the length of the body in wear. The clean edges at the selvedges also meant that the fabric did not necessarily have to be hemmed if the width of the fabric was appropriate to the height of the wearer, though a hem or tucks could easily be used to adjust the length if necessary.

The relative dominance of warp or weft may depend not only on sett and yarn thickness but also on the character of the yarns, particularly their stiffness. Tim Parry-Williams gives a good example of learning from nature when he describes his experience of harvesting and processing banana and ramie plants, while studying in Okinawa and observing the longitudinal fibres of the stems:

> I was quite struck by the fact that these 'bones' of the plants (that stood up against seasonal typhoons etc.) only ran vertically, and not both vertically and horizontally as in the warp and weft in weaving, which often employs the same material in both directions.

'Arai' scarf by Tim Parry-Williams. Ramie, paper, silk. Natural dyes. (Photo: Takao Oya)

'Shento' and 'Ishi' scarves by Tim Parry-Williams. Linen, floss silk, raw silk/linen, raw silk. Natural dyes. (Photo: Takao Oya)

CHAPTER 3: Structural Resources: Simple Gifts 43

On returning to Europe I chose to work with local plant fibre (linen) together with Japanese raw silk encountered in Okinawa, but placing the stiff linen fibre in the warp only, and working it with the fine silk weft. The focus was on creating a vertically draping cloth that could go from a wide width of at least 40–50cm to only a few cm when scrunched, and then return to the full width.

These initial experiments led to a whole series of scarves with various combinations of materials but all relying on the principle of a relatively thick, stiff, 'hard' warp combined with a fine, 'soft' weft to achieve a beautiful warpways drape.

Cramming and Spacing

An important way of varying the sett is to use stripes of different density across the fabric, either in the warp or weft direction. This can allow the effects of a strongly warp- or weft-faced setting, such as intensity of colour or smooth surface, to be used in occasional stripes without greatly affecting the overall draping qualities of the fabric. This may be done by using yarn of the same thickness throughout but at varying setts, by keeping the sett the same throughout and varying the thickness of the yarn, or by varying both yarn thickness and density. Attractive variations in colour or contrasts of translucency can be produced by these density variations when working with normal balanced yarns. Alternatively, contrasts of texture are possible if high-twist wefts are used, since only openly set areas will allow enough space for such yarns to create a crepon or crepe effect.

Cramming and spacing often works particularly well when used together with other effects, such as yarns of different thickness, colour variations and so on. Such a combination of effects is nicely shown in a fabric that was designed by Marianne Straub when she was working at Ethel Mairet's workshop 'Gospels' in Ditchling in the 1930s. This fabric uses a crammed and spaced warp with alternate wefts of thick undyed wool and fine dyed cotton. The cramming and spacing of the warp means that the dyed cotton weft is most clearly visible in the spaced areas creating a subtle stripe effect. The thick wool weft makes a fabric that drapes particularly well in the weft direction and the fabric was made into a jacket that was cut with the weft running down the body and sleeves.(See illustrations on page 46.)

Samples of crammed and spaced fabrics, showing the different translucencies of the fabric in the dense and open areas. Warp: Linen 60 lea, 44 epi and linen 40 lea, 66 epi. Weft: Hard silk 60 denier, 44 ppi.

This fabric by Margrit Waldron shows a subtle shading of colours between the crammed and spaced areas of the cloth. In contrast with the effect in plain weave, a band of twill at the bottom of the piece shows how this structure develops a gentle undulating effect due to the cramming and spacing.

A scarf by Berthe Forchhammer that uses a crammed and spaced warp crossed by a high-twist weft to create a contrast between smooth and textured areas of cloth. (Photo: Ole Akhøj)

It is interesting to note that another rather similar fabric, combining a fine warp with thick and thin wefts, was produced at the 'Gospels' workshop to be made into another jacket for the same customer, but this was cut with the weft running across the body and sleeves. This jacket, which is in the collection of the V&A Museum (T.34-1971), is also differently shaped, particularly around the neckline, presumably to allow for the different behaviour of the fabric when used in this way. The alternation of thick and thin yarns allows for many interesting effects and will be discussed in more detail later in this chapter.

Cramming and spacing can also be pushed to extremes by leaving definite gaps on the fabric. Various effects can result, ranging from a light, translucent quality to a highly textured fabric if the spacing is combined with a high-twist weft. The threads at the edges of the crammed areas may tend to fall off into the spaces to some extent, depending on various factors such as the texture of the materials and the density of the crammed stripes. This should not necessarily be seen as a fault because it can be used to good effect, either in monochrome or by using colour contrasts.

If the effect of ends falling off the edge of the stripes is not desired, then gauze (crossed warp) ends could be used to stabilize the threads at the edges of the spaces (see below for details of the gauze technique).

A jacket made from a fabric designed by Marianne Straub. Warp: Undyed cotton and wool, crammed and spaced. Weft: Thick, undyed wool and fine, dyed cotton. The use of a very thick wool weft results in a fabric that drapes particularly well when the garment is cut with the weft running down the body and along the length of the sleeves. (Crafts Study Centre, University for the Creative Arts. T.74.11. Photo: Loucia Manopoulou)

A detail of the crammed and spaced jacket fabric. (Photo: Loucia Manopoulou)

In this crammed and spaced scarf by Geraldine St Aubyn Hubbard, the dense packing of a silk warp combined with the texture of an unbalanced cashmere weft ensure a clean edge to the crammed stripes.

46   CHAPTER 3: Structural Resources: Simple Gifts

A linen scarf that uses cramming and spacing to create an open effect. At the edges of each stripe the warp threads fall into the gaps and since they are not being taken up by the weave their surplus length causes them to meander through these spaces. A contrasting colour emphasizes the effect. Warp: Linen 44 lea, stripes of 18 ends, 3 ends/dent, with 10 dent gaps, 18 dent/inch reed. Weft: Linen 44 lea, 30 ppi.

Samples of a textured crammed and spaced fabric, in the loom state and after wet finishing. Red accent threads at the edges of the crammed stripes randomly appear and disappear due to the three-dimensional nature of the cloth after finishing.

Warp: Linen 44 lea, stripes of 18 ends, 3 ends/dent, with 7 dent gaps, 22 dent/inch reed. Weft: Spun silk, 60/2 Nm, 30 ppi, crepe silk, 84 denier Z, 40 ppi.

SIMPLE COMPLEXITY

The basic fabric qualities discussed above can be developed in various ways, by using a wider range of yarn thicknesses, inlaying additional threads or using tension variations to manipulate the texture or density of the fabric. All these techniques have implications for the quality and drape of the cloth.

Accent Threads

One easy way to introduce variety into plain weave is with accent threads of different weight or textures. These may be of contrasting material or thickness to the main body of the cloth and can add interest without making a fine cloth too stiff or heavy. The French firm Rodier, working in the 1930s, produced some of the most dramatic examples of using heavy accent threads in this way, and several of these strikingly textured fabrics are shown in Ann Sutton's books *The Structure of Weaving* and *Ideas in Weaving*. Sometimes the accent threads were added in the weft, which is of course easily done, but there are some pieces in which very thick, slubby handspun yarns are used in the warp, which suggests that some reed wires were probably removed to make large enough dents to accommodate these thick yarns.

Inlay

Inlaying threads that are additional to the main cloth can arguably be regarded as a supplementary weft technique and therefore a compound weave. But examples are included here where the supplementary weft is inlaid with the plain weave structure, since in principle this is still plain weave and certainly also gives that visual effect. Other types of supplementary weft will be discussed in Chapter 4.

'The Hearts', a delicate fabric by Rezia Wahid, in spun silk, silk organzine and merino wool. Such fine inlaid details do not alter the soft drape of the fabric. (Photo: David Westwood)

The ground weave of this cotton dhaka cloth scarf is balanced, so the addition of the inlay threads makes it stiffer in the weft direction. In this case, as the scarf is relatively narrow, the weftways body given to the fabric works to its advantage. The inlay pattern has been carefully arranged to avoid the fabric becoming distorted by the additional inlaid threads. (Fabric collected in Nepal by Susi Dunsmore)

The impact of inlay on the quality of the cloth varies greatly depending on how it is done. With an inlay of fine yarn for small, isolated spot designs, it may have little influence on the overall drape of the cloth. By contrast, if the inlaid yarn covers all or most of the surface there will be a noticeable effect on the firmness and drape of the fabric.

Through Thick and Thin

A simple but very effective plain weave technique relies on the alternation of thick and thin threads, in either warp, weft or both, and this creates a fabric with a definite ribbed texture, as in the crammed and spaced design by Marianne Straub described above. The thick and thin alternation is most often used only in the weft and many handweavers refer to this as 'rep', although the confused nomenclature for ribbed fabrics leads Irene Emery to remark: 'the term *rep* has been used and defined in so many ways that it is almost devoid of meaning.' Some authorities would only include textiles in which there are alternations of thick and thin in both warp and weft but here I will use the term in the broader sense that includes structures with thick and thin alternations in only one direction. The 'thick' yarn may be a single thread but it is also common to use multiple fine threads to build up the required thickness, to improve the handle of the fabric.

Although this ribbed effect gives an interesting texture in itself, it can also be used to create a fabric with two different sides. If alternate threads in the warp are of different colours and the weft consists of alternate picks of thick and thin yarn, then each colour is pushed more to one side than the other. This technique is frequently used for rugs, especially in Scandinavia, and excellent examples can be seen in the book *Rep* by Swedish authors Catharina Carlstedt and Ylva Kongbäck. A classic approach is to use a fine, closely set

Linen rep rug by Angus Williams. Alternating colours in the warp are interchanged in blocks to create the design. (Photo: Angus Williams)

Detail of linen rep rugs by Angus Williams. The thick weft yarns used to give the rep effect create a rug that is stiff weftways and so rolls up easily along the length of the warp. One is shown here tied up for storage with a flat linen braid in the Japanese kumihimo technique. (Photo: Angus Williams)

warp that largely covers the weft, making the contrast between the different sides as strong as possible. This technique offers many possibilities for pattern through the interchange of colours.

It can also be interesting to set the warp less densely so the weft colours are clearly visible, as in the Swedish *glesrips* (openly set rep) technique. Some of the most beautiful examples of Swedish *ripsmatta* (rep rugs) use this technique, with the interplay of warp and weft colours allowing particularly subtle effects. A further possibility is to vary the warp density so the weft is visible in the open areas and hidden in the crammed sections, where the warp colour will show more intensely. Another technique, also used in Sweden, is to have alternating coloured warps of different thickness, so that the weft shows through the warp on one side but not the other, giving a fabric that is classic rep on one side and *glesrips* on the other. These various techniques offer many possibilities for stripe and check patterns producing contrasts of colour and fabric quality.

Most weavers are familiar with this 'thick and thin' technique for robust textiles such as table mats and rugs, but the same principle can work equally well for lighter weight fabrics such as blankets, garments or even scarves. In fact, 'thick and thin' offers a good example of the possibilities of using basic principles to create fabric qualities that differ greatly from those normally associated with a particular technique or structure. More examples of this idea of 'playing against type' will be picked up in the next chapter.

Although a colour alternation in the warp, with thick and thin yarns in the weft, is perhaps most common, the arrangement could of course be turned to employ a similar strategy with alternating colours in the weft and the thick and thin alternation in the warp. A further possibility is an arrangement that satisfies the tighter definition of rep, as a fabric with thick and thin alternations in both warp and weft, and that also has the fine warp yarn more tightly tensioned than the thick warp, thus creating an especially strong ribbed effect on one side of the fabric.

Erica de Ruiter has developed an especially surprising and imaginative way of using rep that enabled her to create an effect of ribbing or soft pleating. For this she used the true rep construction of thick and thin in both warp and weft, but arranged this in narrow stripes that reverse the sequence of thick and thin in the warp. The thick weft running under

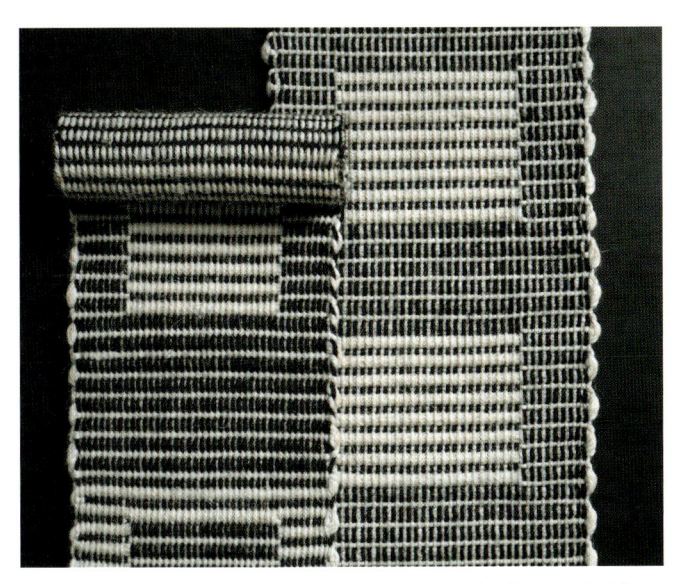

Rep samples using different setts. Warp: Black mohair 4/5 wc and white wool 4/5 wc. Weft: Cotton 8/8 Ne and mohair 4/5 wc used singly for the fine weft and with multiple threads for the thick weft. On the left the sett is 20 epi and the warp almost covers the weft. On the right the sett is 16 epi and the weft is clearly visible, softening the contrast between the different coloured blocks.

These lightweight fabric samples in silk have alternating colours in the warp, with thick and thin yarns in the weft to create double-sided fabrics. Where the warp is closely set, with a strong contrast between the yarn thicknesses in the weft, the ribbed nature of the fabric is noticeable and the handle quite crisp. Where the sett is more open, with only a modest difference in weft thicknesses, the thick/thin alternation is less obvious and the fabric softer and more flexible. Nevertheless this small contrast in weft thicknesses can still achieve a separation of colour between the two sides.

Left: Warp: Spun silk 60/2 Nm, 48 epi. Thick weft: Spun silk 60/2 Nm × 4. Thin wefts: Spun silk 60/2 Nm × 2, 26 ppi; spun silk 60/2 Nm, 28 ppi; spun silk 120/2 Nm, 30 ppi; spun silk 210/2 Nm, 32 ppi.

Right: Warp: Spun silk 60/2 Nm, 40 epi. Thick weft: Spun silk 60/2 Nm. Thin wefts: Spun silk 120/2 Nm, 36 ppi; spun silk 210/2 Nm, 38 ppi; silk grenadine 40/44 denier, 40 ppi.

the thick warps tends to push one face of the fabric forward, so alternating stripes of the two faces cause the fabric to be pushed back and forth into soft pleats. This was carried out in fairly heavy cotton but as with other rep structures it could be used for a variety of different weights. See the Bibliography for details of her article 'Magic Pleats – from eight shafts to two'.

Tension Variations

Almost all the variations of plain weave discussed so far could be woven using a single warp beam. Exceptions might be extremes of cramming and spacing or the use of very heavy accent threads, as in the Rodier textiles described above, since these could possibly cause tension difficulties. The most strict definition of rep would also fall into this category, as it would need to be woven with the fine warp yarn running from a separate beam at a tighter tension than the thick yarn, to maximize the ribbed texture.

Seersucker

However, the use of two differently tensioned warps can be a strategy in itself, and the classic example is seersucker, in which stripes of yarn are run alternately from separate beams at different tensions. The tightly tensioned stripes will remain flat, while the lightly tensioned ones will take up more yarn, creating a crinkled stripe. The term derives from Persian words meaning 'milk' and 'sugar' – referring to the smooth quality of the stripes woven from the high-tension beam and the textured surface of the slackly tensioned stripes. This effect can be achieved entirely in plain weave and with normal-twist yarns, but other options include using more complex weave structures, high-twist yarns, or both.

A classic seersucker produced by tension variations will form a firm fabric, but if the contrast in shrinkage between high-twist and normal-twist yarn is used then this will produce a fabric with considerable elasticity. This technique can be applied to create weftways as well as warpways seersuckers and works particularly well if the high-twist yarns

Andreas Möller's 'Shadow boxes' fabric is shown here while still on the loom. (Photo: Andreas Möller)

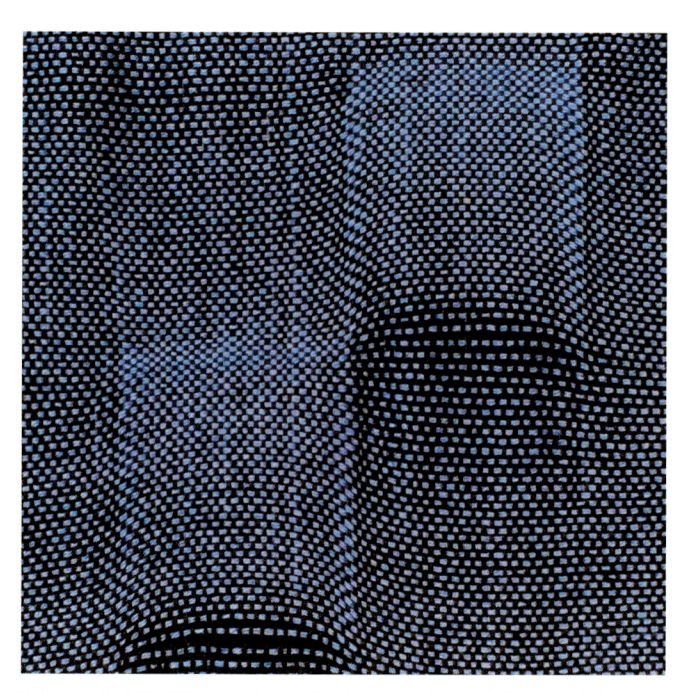

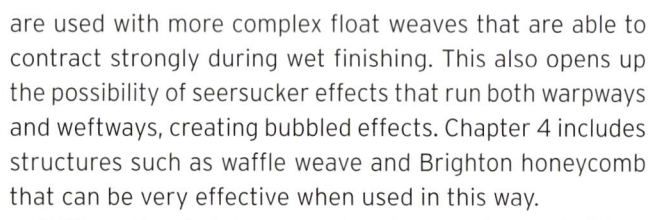

This detail of the 'Shadow boxes' fabric shows the variations in cloth density that create the shadow effect. (Photo: Andreas Möller)

are used with more complex float weaves that are able to contract strongly during wet finishing. This also opens up the possibility of seersucker effects that run both warpways and weftways, creating bubbled effects. Chapter 4 includes structures such as waffle weave and Brighton honeycomb that can be very effective when used in this way.

Differential shrinkage produced through yarn twist or weave structure tends to create a relatively elastic fabric. However, the same principle can be used to make a seersucker with a firm quality by using a yarn that fulls easily for the flat stripe, combined with one that is resistant to fulling for the puckered stripe. Finishing the fabric by heavy milling will then create a firm but textured fabric, and this differential response to fulling can be used for a seersucker effect that runs both warpways and weftways to create a bubbled texture. Liz Williamson has worked extensively with this technique and there are beautiful examples in her article 'Fulled Seersucker Scarves' and also in the book about her work by Grace Cochrane.

Other Tension Variation Techniques

Seersucker is a classic differential tension fabric, but there are less conventional ways of exploiting tension variations that are particularly suited to the flexible nature of hand-weaving. Peter Collingwood devised an ingenious method of creating a weft distortion with a system of rocker sticks to vary the tension of different sets of warp yarns.

He described this technique in an article for the *Journal of Weavers, Spinners and Dyers* that has recently been reprinted (instructions for this system can also be found in Marianne Straub's book *Hand Weaving and Cloth Design*). Because the weft can be beaten down more easily on highly tensioned threads, the density of the fabric becomes varied in a block arrangement. Ann Sutton has experimented with a similar idea but with even simpler equipment by inserting a broomstick over and under groups of warp threads behind the heddles and pushing it back to rest on the back beam to temporarily tension some bands of threads more than others. After weaving a certain amount, the broomstick can be reinserted under different groups of threads (*see her book *The Structure of Weaving*, pp. 50-51*).

Andreas Möller has devised another intriguing technique that he calls 'shadow boxes', which not only creates an extremely attractive fabric but also provides an excellent example of reflective practice. When a thread got caught up accidentally and caused unevenness in the fabric he did not simply dismiss this as a mistake but realized it could be put to good use as a deliberate strategy. For this technique some blocks of yarn are threaded through heddles on two different shafts. If both shafts are raised and lowered together then the fabric weaves plain as normally, but if these shafts work *against* one another then the threads are put under tension, so that the weft can be beaten down more closely on that section of the cloth. Once the normal lift is resumed, the warp in these blocks becomes slack so that the weft cannot be beaten so closely. This tension variation results in an alternation of densely and loosely picked sections of cloth, creating the shadow effect. Detailed instructions for this technique can be found in Andreas' article in *Vävmagasinet*.

INTERPLAY OF STRUCTURE AND COLOUR

Colour is one of the characteristics most immediately obvious in textiles, often the major feature of the design, so it is important to consider how the variations in cloth quality described above interact with colour. Ideally the fabric should have a good handle and drape, but without in any way conflicting with the impact of the colour, rather if possible supporting or enhancing it. The classic situation of a balanced plain weave is ideal for using different colours in warp and weft, creating an effect that is very different from that produced when the same colour is used for both. This works well even if relatively similar shades are used, for example a pink-red for the warp and an orange-red for the weft; these colours crossing one another create a livelier effect than if an intermediate shade of red had been used for both.

This way of mixing colours is specific to weave, though some suggestion of a similar effect can be achieved through printing colours over one another or overlaying washes of watercolour. An interesting watercolour painting by Paul Klee was included in the 2018-19 exhibition of the work of Anni Albers at the Tate Modern, and the caption commented on the influence of his watercolour technique on Albers:

> Anni Albers had taken Paul Klee's class on colour theory at the Bauhaus, yet she said she was more influenced by his paintings than his teachings. Albers's notes from his classes, displayed nearby, show how she followed his exercises in composition and tonal variation. But it was the way Klee mixed together layers of watercolour on paper that had the most impact on Albers's own designs.
> Exhibition caption accompanying Klee's 1929 *Measured Fields*

When the colours used for warp and weft are far apart on the colour circle, dramatic iridescent (shot) effects can be produced. The precise result depends not only on the colours chosen, but also on fibre, yarn twist, relative thickness of warp and weft, sett and weave structure. Silk is classically used for a shot effect because of its lustre, but the technique can also work well with fabrics that have less gloss (mercerized cotton, linen) or even those that are matt (unmercerized cotton, wool). With these materials the contrast of colours can produce an attractively soft, 'dusty' effect rather like the bloom on a plum. There will also be differences in the visual impact between softly draping, loosely woven fabrics that tend to give a soft shimmering effect and the classic tightly woven, stiff taffetas used for evening wear in which contrasting colours dramatically shoot out depending on the angle from which the fabric is viewed.

As well as the classic situation of a relatively balanced weave with yarns of similar thickness but contrasting colours in warp and weft, there are many possible variations. For example, if warp and weft are of very different thickness this will affect both the drape of the cloth and the way that a shot effect can be achieved, because a very fine weft will probably need to have a much more intense colour than a thicker warp yarn if both colours are to show equally.

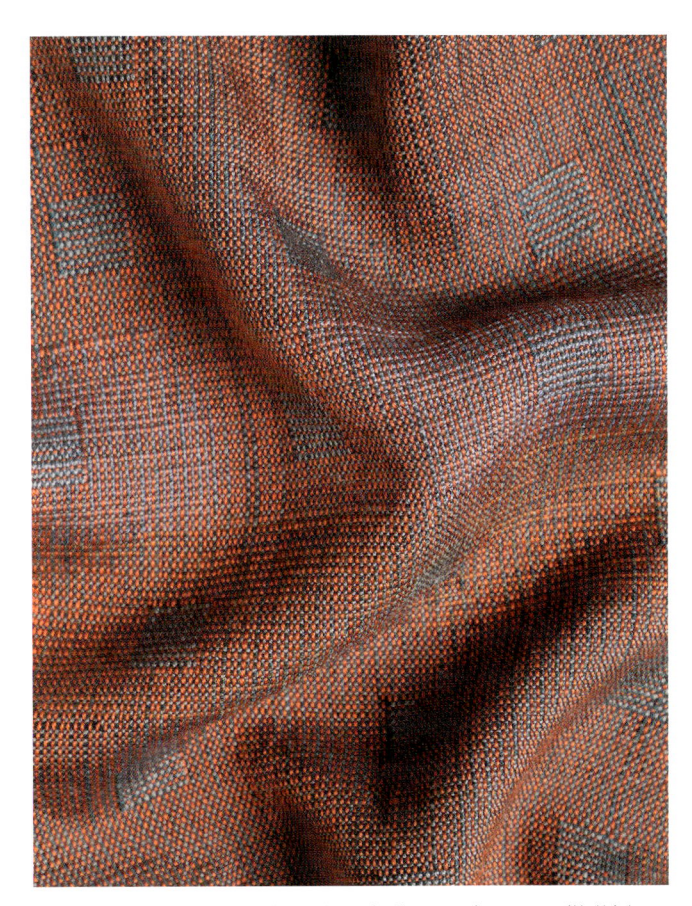

This silk fabric with alternating colours in the warp is woven with thick and thin wefts. The warp is sufficiently openly set that both of the warp colours are visible, producing an iridescent effect, and the piece is patterned with blocks of the reverse face of the cloth. Warp: Spun silk 60/2 Nm, alternating rust and slate, 40 epi. Thick weft: Spun silk 60/2 Nm × 2. Thin weft: Spun silk 210/2 Nm, 32 ppi.

A particularly interesting effect can be produced by the technique, discussed above, of alternating strongly contrasting colours in the warp and then weaving with thick and thin wefts, to create a fabric that is different on the two sides. If this is done with the warp quite widely spaced, then each of the two warp colours will show through faintly from the other side. Carried out in a fine weight, particularly with a glossy yarn such as silk, this can result in a fabric that is both iridescent and double sided. Also with an openly spaced warp the weft will be visible, so variations in the colour of the weft can be used to emphasize one or other of the warp colours.

Although iridescence is most frequently associated with plain weave, good results can also be produced with other structures. Bobbie Irwin gives a detailed and beautifully illustrated account of the many possibilities.

GAUZE

I want finally to discuss a special structure that is neither plain weave nor a float weave or compound weave, the topics to be covered in the next chapter. Unlike other structures that rely on different arrangements of raised warps, gauze uniquely employs *crossed* warp ends. This allows the construction of a very open cloth that is nevertheless extremely stable and so is particularly associated with delicate, translucent effects. However, it does not necessarily have to produce this type of cloth and many variations are possible.

Gauze is sometimes also referred to as 'leno' and there is some disagreement about the use of these terms. Some authors use them indiscriminately while others make a distinction, using gauze for fabrics that are entirely crossed warp and leno to cover various 'fancy gauzes'. Emery suggests that historically gauze may have been applied to silk fabrics (possibly after the Arabic *gazz*, meaning floss silk), while leno may have referred to linen or cotton, though such a clear distinction has fallen out of use. Of the current definitions of leno she feels the most useful is that of gauzes that also include areas of plain weave, though she also suggests that it is not particularly helpful to have two terms that can be applied to the same structure, and that gauze should be the preferred term.

Setting Up Gauze

Traditionally, the crossed warps of gauze have been achieved with special half-heddles, called *doups,* but although this works well these heddles have to be made by hand, which is quite time consuming. Also, in my experience, they tend to wear out, which is very inconvenient partway through a warp. An alternative method with beads is quicker to set up and not subject to wear so this is the technique described here. When aiming for a delicate effect it is common to produce gauze in a single colour to emphasize the lacelike quality of the fabric, but it is of course possible to use different coloured yarns. This can give a variety of interesting effects and is also helpful for anyone new to the technique, as a way of keeping track of the ground and whip threads.

The set-up where the whip threads (forming the crossing) are pulled up seems to be the most frequently used but I have recently experimented with the alternative method where the whip threads are pulled down, which has some advantages. The whip threads tend to become rather tight during the formation of the shed, and this means that when they are pulled up the ground (or standard) ends are relatively slack and do not form a firm base to the shed. This can cause difficulties in weaving, especially if the gauze units are widely spaced, and the problem is not really solved by tightening the whole warp as this can cause breakages and a poor shed.

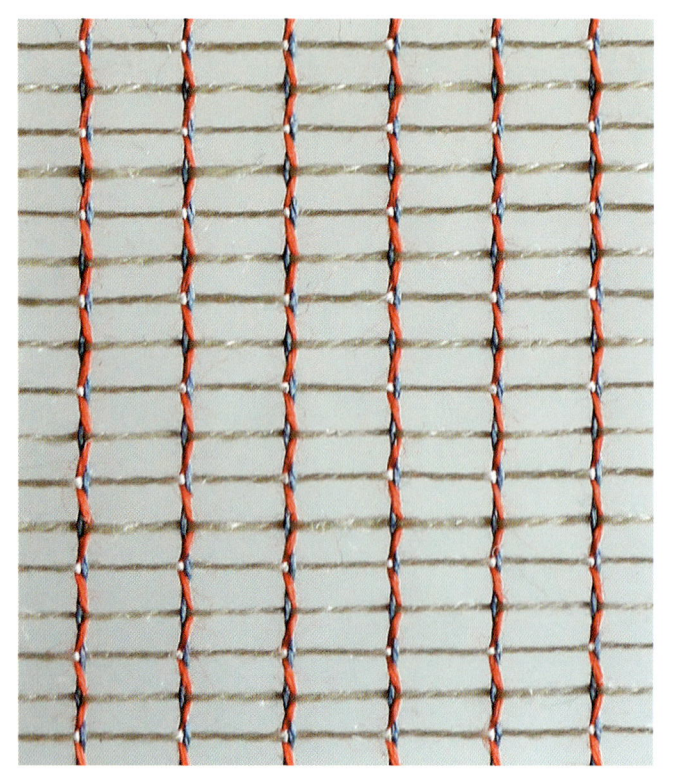

The structure of gauze, showing the crossing of the warp ends.

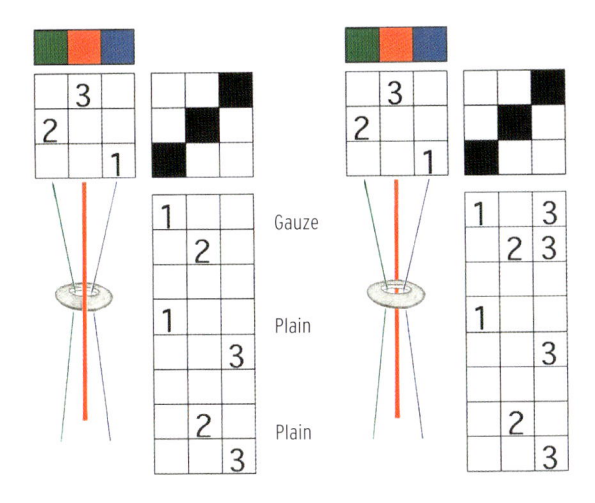

Two alternative set-ups for gauze weave, with the whip threads pulled up (left) or pulled down (right).

In contrast, if the whip ends are pulled *down*, then as they tighten they form a firm base to the shed. This set-up requires the whip ends to lie *over* the ground ends rather than under them and for the ground ends to be raised during the formation of the crossed sheds. A further variation in set-up is possible if the intention is to weave only plain gauze and not to include any plain weave picks. In this case, given that the ground ends do not need to be raised and lowered, they can remain in the same position throughout the weaving, with the whip ends simply moving back and forth across them. So it works well and simplifies the threading if the ground ends are not threaded at all. Separate warps can be made for the ground and the whips, and the ground ends are then run from a separate beam, brought in at a higher level than the whip threads, and passed between and under them.

With this arrangement it is also easy to have the ground ends at a slightly higher tension. This helps them to resist the pull of the whip threads (which can otherwise reduce what is already quite a small shed) but it does mean that there will be a difference between beating on an open shed (when the tensions will be equalized) and on a closed shed (when the crossing threads will be slacker). Beating on a closed shed will cause the crossing threads to bend around the ground ends and allow the weft to pack down more closely than when equal tension causes the crossing and ground threads to bend equally around one another.

Using Different Weights of Yarn

If the same thickness of yarn is used for both ground and whip ends then the combined whip ends will be thicker than the ground ends. The effect can be evened out either by doubling the threads for the ground ends or by using a thicker yarn for these ends. However, though this is usually advised when aiming for a classic, delicate gauze effect, breaking this rule and having different thicknesses for the two sets of threads opens up additional design possibilities. The warp material obviously needs to be carefully chosen to be strong enough to withstand the crossing process but within this limitation a wide variety of weights and qualities of cloth are possible. As with all textiles, a wider range of options are possible for weft, and very different effects can be produced according to the character of the weft yarn, even when the material and spacing of the warp remain the same.

Although the classic form of gauze uses fine yarns in both warp and weft to create an open and delicate fabric, it is interesting to experiment with thicker yarns and also to vary the spacing between gauze units. The stability provided by the crossing warp means that the warp can be quite widely spaced and so can be relatively inconspicuous compared with the weft, while still keeping the fabric cohesive. Gauze can also work well in giving stability to a very smooth yarn, allowing a more open sett than would be practicable in plain weave.

This simple cotton window netting is typical of the lightweight, translucent quality that many people associate with the term 'gauze'. (Designer unknown)

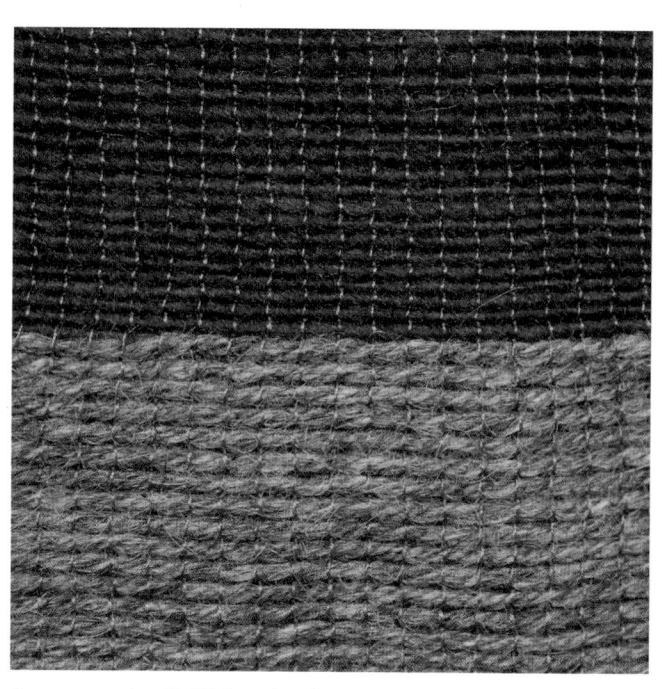

A gauze sample with thick wool wefts. Although the warp yarns are fine, these thick wefts create a heavy fabric with a very different character from the window netting. Warp: Grounds ends: Spun silk 60/2 Nm. Whip ends: Spun silk 120/2 Nm. Wefts: Wool 4 Nm, 11 ppi and 1.2 Nm, 7 ppi.

This scarf by Mariana Eriksson uses a heavy space-dyed silk yarn and this material gives a fabric that is very different from more typical, delicate gauzes. With this extremely smooth, glossy yarn the gauze structure allows a stable fabric to be produced with a more open sett than would be possible with plain weave. The space between the gauze units gives great flexibility to the fabric, creating a luxurious scarf with excellent draping qualities.

Seersucker with Gauze

The open structure provided by gauze is excellent for weftways seersuckers, and combinations of high-twist and normal yarns in the weft can produce either bold or subtle effects, depending on the contrasting properties of the two sets of yarns.

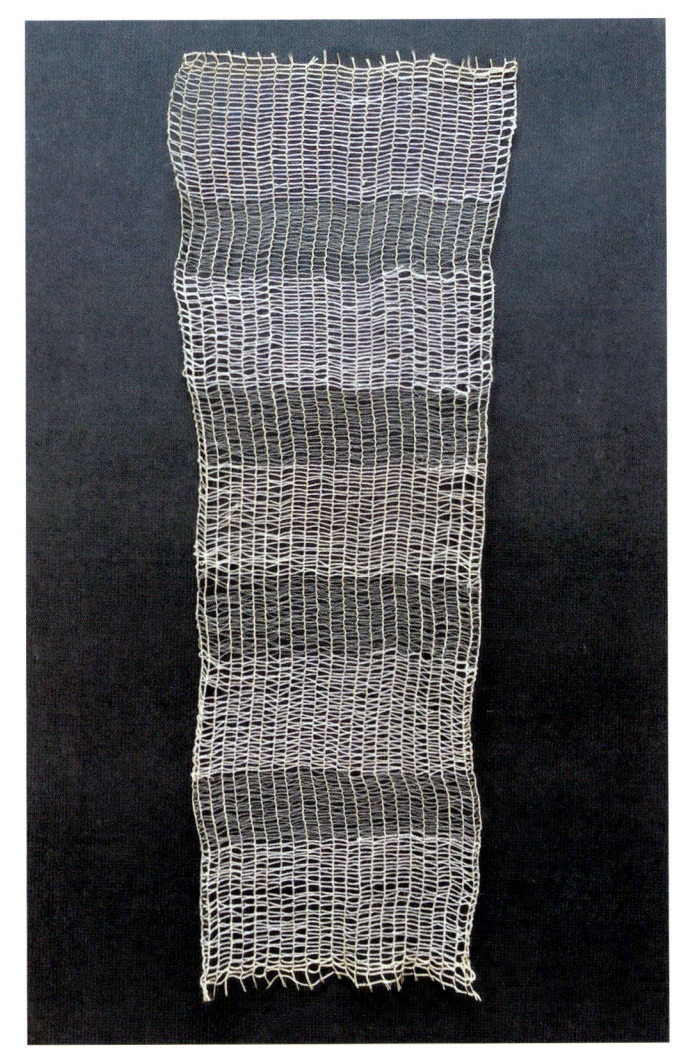

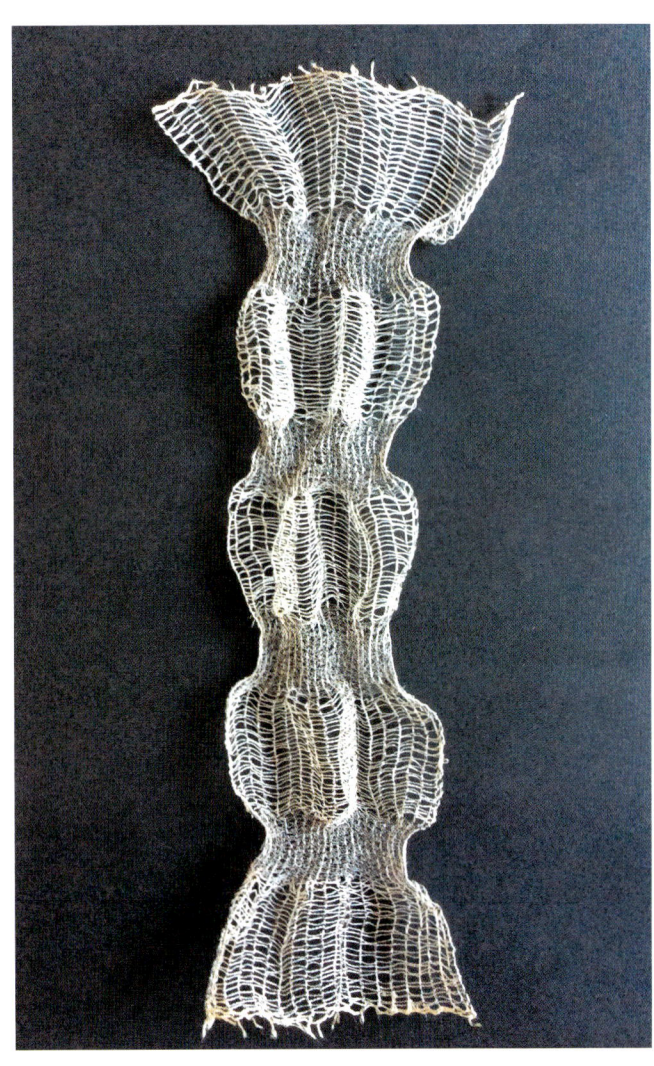

Samples of gauze seersucker, showing the loomstate fabric on the left and the finished fabric on the right.

Warp: Ground ends: Silk/steel 82/2 Nm. Whip ends: Tussah 120/2 Nm. 5 gauze units/inch. Weft: Crepe silk 40/44 denier, 24 ppi, combined with: ramie 60 lea, 21 ppi; cotton/brass 20 Nm, 21 ppi; silk/steel 82/2 Nm, 20 ppi.

Making the Most of Colour

It can be helpful to use different colours for the various threads to keep track of the threading, but this can also produce interesting effects in the fabric. Because the threads are *crossing*, not twisting round one another, the colours may show differently on the two sides, depending on the thickness and spacing of the weft. The effect may be so subtle as to be unnoticeable or it may be very striking, definitely giving a double-sided fabric – examples will be given in Chapter 7. If using colours in this way, remember that if you wish to set up a double-layer gauze (either to create a wider fabric than the loom width or to produce a tube) then one layer must have crossing threads pulled *up* and the other *down* for the colour effect to remain consistent.

Gauze with a Twist

Although, as has already been mentioned, the warp ends in gauze are not twisting round one another, twist can have an interesting impact in the sense of twist in the yarn itself. The open structure of gauze allows great freedom of movement, so high-twist yarns can create varied textured effects, including crepon pleating, depending on the character of the yarn. However, even normal single yarns may be sufficiently unbalanced to move within the structure during wet finishing and can create interesting undulating effects that will be shown in Chapter 8.

Mirrored Gauze Units

The simplest set-up for gauze is to use a series of identical units, but an alternative arrangement is to reverse the direction in which the whip threads move so that successive gauze units mirror one another. This is done simply by reversing the threading sequence, so that if the first unit is threaded 1,3,2 then the next will be 2,3,1 and so on. If using a set-up where the ground ends have not been threaded at all, as described above, then it is simply the sequence for the whip threads that is reversed: 1,2 followed by 2,1 and so on.

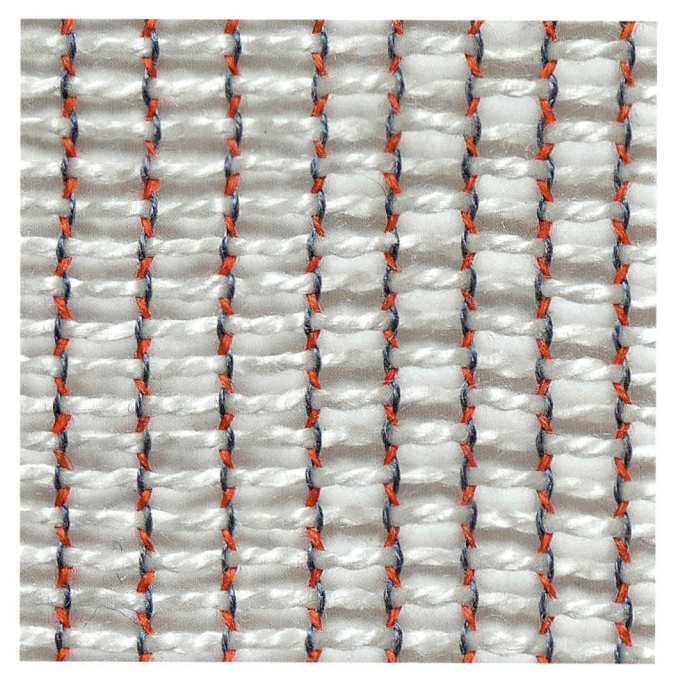

This sample has been set up with regular gauze units on the left and mirrored units on the right, and shows how the mirrored units tend to push the weft alternately to one side of the fabric and then the other. Warp: Ground ends: Spun silk 60/2 Nm. Whip ends: Spun silk 120/2 Nm. 6 gauze units/inch. Weft: Spun silk 16/2 Nm, 14 ppi.

The interplay of structure and material becomes particularly important here because with some weft materials there is little difference to be seen between these two arrangements, while in other cases the difference is very noticeable. With linen, for example, the opposing pull of the mirrored units appears to be insufficient to overcome the stiffness of the material and the general effect of the fabric tends to be similar to that with an arrangement of identical units. In contrast, with softer materials such as silk the texture of the fabric changes considerably and the opposing twists of the mirrored units may push small loops of weft out of the fabric, creating a slightly raised, 'pebbly' texture on both sides of the fabric. This texture contrasts with the smoother effect given by regular units and also causes more take-up of weft, giving a stronger weftways contraction of the fabric.

Other combinations of yarn can also produce surprisingly different effects from the two types of arrangement. If the whip ends are substantially thicker than the ground ends then the effect is different again, with the whip ends tending to slide together where they bend towards one another, especially if they are at a slacker tension than the ground ends. The mirrored structure may then become very obvious, almost producing a honeycomb effect.

Russian Cords

There are many possible variations on the gauze structure, but probably the most surprising of all is the technique of Russian cords. The idea of running the whip ends at a slacker tension than the ground ends has already been mentioned, but Russian cords push this difference in tension to extremes, producing a fabric that is completely different in appearance from the normal open gauze effect. Fine whip ends, running at a slack tension, pass back and forth over tightly tensioned, thicker ground ends (often multiple fine threads rather than a single thick thread). As the whip ends are beaten down they completely cover the ground ends. On the reverse of the fabric, the whip ends are only faintly visible, giving an extreme example of gauze that is different on the two sides, although this is not a case where both sides are intended to be used – the reverse is definitely the back.

A sample of Russian cords by Amelia Uden. (Gift from the designer)

The reverse side of the Russian cords sample.

At first glance this fabric seems completely unrecognizable as gauze, being totally different from the open, delicate fabrics that generally come to mind when gauze is mentioned. It exemplifies the way that factors such as yarn thickness and warp tension can be varied to create fabrics that are vastly different in appearance from normal expectations while working from what is, in simple interlacement terms, the same weave structure. This sets the scene for the next chapter in which this approach of 'playing against type' will be applied to some other weave structures to show what a rich resource they provide for creating widely varied qualities of fabric.

A gauze unit showing the principle of Russian cords, which depends on whip ends at a very light tension passing back and forth over tightly tensioned ground ends. (After Watson, *Advanced Textile Design*)

CHAPTER 4

Structural Resources: Beyond Plain Weave

A design on paper cannot take into account the fine surprises of a material and make imaginative use of them.

Anni Albers, *On Designing*

Moving beyond plain weave, there are two basic approaches to producing more complex structures. The first is to allow yarns to pass over more than one warp or weft thread, producing a *float*, and this simple strategy generates a huge range of possibilities. The second strategy is to bring in one or more additional elements. This may involve supplementary threads that occur in only limited areas of the cloth, the overall doubling of one or other of the elements or the construction of a true double cloth with two sets of warp and weft. Visually these various techniques offer wide possibilities for design, but they all also have implications for the substance and character of the cloth.

I am not setting out to give a detailed survey of weave structures, since there are many fine texts already available. For example, William Watson's *Textile Design and Colour* remains a classic, while an excellent recent treatment is Sharon Alderman's *Mastering Weave Structures*. The Bibliography gives details of these and other useful books on weave structure. My aim is rather to make a selection of some traditional groups or 'families' of weaves and show how each has the potential for producing a wide range of different cloth qualities, depending on material, yarn thickness, sett and so on.

As in the case of plain weave, even simple variations in yarn thickness can transform a structure, both in appearance and substance, from what is often perceived as the 'classic' form in which it is most frequently woven. Rather than putting together a detailed catalogue of individual weaves, I want to look at what can potentially *go on* in a particular type of structure. If there are floats, what can they do in a weave? If some elements of the cloth are doubled, how can this play out?

MESSING ABOUT WITH FLOATS

As yarns are released from the constraints of plain weave, floats make the individual character of the yarns more obvious, with any special qualities more clearly revealed. Yarns and their properties can be a source of inspiration for design but weavers frequently comment that it is hard to make a fabric as beautiful as the yarn! Float weaves alleviate this problem to some extent; the texture of the yarn is more visible in these structures than within the close intersections of plain weave and the lustre of a glossy yarn is much better displayed. Floats assist shrinkage in the case of high-twist or elastomeric yarns and fulling in the case of woollen yarns. Also, free from the constraint of plain weave, yarns can shift position to create fabrics that differ greatly from the appearance of the weave draft.

The Development of Float Weaves

It is common in textile textbooks to introduce the three basic weaves as plain weave, twill and satin (in that order), and this naturally leads the reader to see twills as the next degree of complexity after plain weave and tends also to suggest that this was the first step in the evolution of float weaves. However, Irene Emery suggests that plain weave patterned by floats may have been a very early step on from plain weave. It is also possible that different lines of development may be characteristic of different areas of the world. William Willetts, in describing some early Chinese textiles that are in plain weave patterned by floats, points out that although some of these floats are in a twill arrangement no early examples have been found of genuine twills, with the first evidence for true twills in the Far East dating from the second half of the sixth century AD.

Further to the west, twills are found much earlier than this and it has been suggested that the technique originated in Austria among the Hallstatt people, since the earliest twills excavated from the salt mines in this area date from the Bronze Age. However, although the technique may well have been spread by this group of people, Elizabeth Barber points to even earlier examples of twills, from Turkey in the fourth millennium BC and Georgia in the third. She suggests that the origins may lie in Anatolia in the fourth millennium BC, but also raises the possibility of multiple origins of twill as a loom-woven fabric, since by this time the twill interlacement had already been widely used for mats.

These different developments in weave structure probably relate to the various looms that were in use, which naturally facilitated different techniques. These variations are interesting in themselves and perhaps also provide more nuanced ways of viewing the evolution of textile structures than the conventional 'first past the post' view of the history of technology. However, for ease of explanation I will stay with convention by discussing twills and satins first, before moving on to plain weave patterned by floats and some traditional weaves that include relatively long floats.

With all these structures the different ways that floats can be part of a weave structure have an important impact on fabric quality. In some weaves, such as twills and satins, *all* the ends or picks are floating throughout the structure, but in others only *some* ends or picks form floats while the others weave more tightly into the fabric, for example the alternating float weaves. In this second type of structure it is possible to use different yarns for the floating ends or picks, so that the floats show off the quality of a special, perhaps more expensive material to best advantage, for example the high gloss of a lightly twisted silk yarn. Or high-twist yarns may be used for the floating ends or picks to allow them to shrink easily, with 'normal' yarns for the more closely interlaced threads, a combination that works well in creating textured effects.

TWILLS

Twills are characterized by clear diagonal lines of warp and weft floats, and can be *even* twills, where warp and weft pass over an equal number of threads, as in the classic 2/2 twill, or *uneven* twills where warp floats predominate on one face and weft floats on the other, the simplest being 1/2 twill. The structure of twill makes a fabric that is generally more flexible than plain weave and, given that threads can be pushed closer together, potentially warmer. Several interacting factors are involved in determining exactly how prominent the twill lines appear, as explained in detail by Robinson and Marks in their useful book *Woven Cloth Construction*. To summarize there are four possible combinations (*see* box) with two shown in bold that are relevant in most situations. The others will only come into play when either warp or weft is strongly dominant, whether in the case of warp-float or weft-float twills or because of the sett.

If the fabric is turned over the direction of the twill will be reversed while the yarn twists will, of course, remain the same, so that the twill line will be more distinct on one side of the fabric than the other. This effect is noticeable also in fabrics such as herringbone or diamond twills in which the twill lines are reversed, because if the yarn twists remain the same throughout the fabric the twill lines will also be more or less distinct in different parts of the design. In the case of a straight twill that also uses varied yarn twists to create shadow stripes or checks, it will not merely be differences of light reflectance that will be visible (as with plain weave) but also variations in the prominence of the twill line.

Although twist-twill interaction is the major factor in creating a prominent twill line, the character of the yarn also plays a part with coarse-spun or soft-spun yarns tending

TWIST/TWILL INTERACTIONS

1) **Twill line opposite to warp twist, warp and weft opposite twists: Distinct twill**
2) Twill line opposite to yarn twist, warp and weft the same twist: Prominent warp twill
3) Twill line the same as yarn twist, warp and weft the same twist: Prominent weft twill
4) **Twill line the same as warp twist, warp and weft opposite twists: Indistinct twill**

to show the line more clearly than fine or hard-spun yarns, and plied yarns tending to emphasize it more than single yarns. These various factors mean that in some fabrics the difference between the two sides of the cloth is obvious while in others it may be very subtle. Also, very high-twist yarns provide an exception to the normal situation, since the extreme curling of these yarns creates a marked twill effect when the direction of yarn twist is the *same* as that of the twill line.

The Origins of Twill Weaves

It seems likely that 2/2 twill, the simplest of the even twills, predates the uneven twills. To modern eyes the simplest uneven twill, with a 1/2 interlacing, might appear to be the next step in complexity after plain weave because only one extra shed is required to produce it, but the archaeological record does not seem to bear this out. Margrethe Hald raises precisely this issue regarding textiles from Danish bogs and burials, pointing out that in spite of a natural expectation that three-end twill would be the first step after plain weave, such twills do not occur in Denmark until the tenth century AD. There are some earlier finds of 1/2 twill, for example from Bronze Age Hallstatt and from Birka in Sweden, but none that predate the earliest known 2/2 twills.

Elizabeth Barber suggests that 2/2 twill is actually the most logical development from plain weave when working on the warp-weighted loom because it is easy to produce four sheds by splitting each half of the plain weave shed in half again. By contrast 1/2 twill requires three sheds, 'a much less obvious step from a 2-shed loom, especially one that depends upon balanced sets of weights.' At one time it was suggested that the late development of three-end twills was because they would be impossible to weave on the warp-weighted loom, but experiments at the Lejre Experimental Centre in Denmark have shown that it is as easy to weave 1/2 twill as 2/2 twill on this loom.

When working with 2/2 twill, patterning is possible not only with colour but also by using different directions of yarn twist to produce shadow stripes and checks. By the Iron Age (AD 100–300) such spin patterns were in use in various countries across Scandinavia and Europe. Striking examples from Denmark can be seen in Margrethe Hald's book, and the textiles excavated from the Hallstatt salt mines include many spin-patterned pieces that have been described in great detail by Karina Grömer and her colleagues. Anna Nørgaard is a specialist in the reconstruction of early textiles and has produced some beautiful examples.

The development of the uneven 1/2 twill offered a further possibility for patterning – weavers seem to have been quick to grasp the effectiveness of *turning* the weave to play off the different surfaces against one another. The effect may be more than simply visual because when the different faces are used in very narrow stripes an attractive ribbed texture emerges, reminiscent of pleating. Such fabrics, using crossways 1/2 and 2/1 stripes, have been found in Germany, Scandinavia, Switzerland and Latvia, with dates ranging from the fourth to the eleventh centuries AD. The German textile archaeologist Hundt who studied these fabrics in detail coined the term *Rippenköper* (literally 'ribbed twill') for this structure though some textile historians have now begun to use the term 'barred damask'. Finds in Roman Egypt have recently pushed back the date of this technique to the second century AD. These fabrics will be discussed in detail in Chapter 5.

After the eleventh century AD, three-end twills become much more common, but although they are sometimes herringbone or diamond twills they use only one face of the weave. Even though experiments with the warp-weighted loom have shown it to be suitable for weaving three-end twills, some writers persist in suggesting that the increased use of the structure was due to the introduction of the treadle loom. However, others consider that the mediaeval treadle loom with its counterbalanced mechanism would itself have been unsuited to weaving uneven twills, though this difficulty really applies to the weaving of uneven four-end twills on a four-shaft loom. An arrangement of three shafts with a system of one single and one double pulley can give good sheds for 1/2 and 2/1 twills – details of this set-up are given in Erica de Ruiter's book *Weaving on 3 Shafts*.

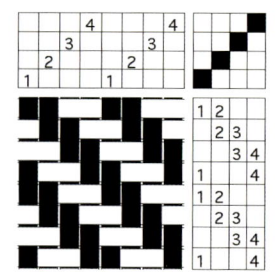

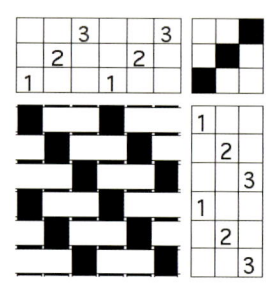

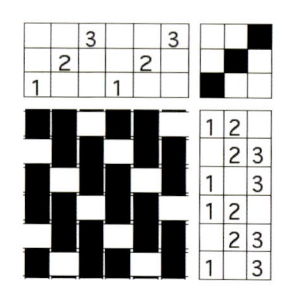

Drafts of 2/2 and 1/2, 2/1 twill. The three-end twills might seem 'simpler' to modern eyes, but current knowledge suggests that 2/2 twill predates them.

This richly coloured fabric by Anna Nørgaard is a reconstruction of a piece that dates from about 700BC, from a tomb in Verucchio, Italy. The fabric is 2/2 twill and has reversals of Z and S spin after every six threads in both warp and weft. It is finished with a decorative tablet woven border. (Photo: Ole Akhøj)

Rippenköper draft showing the reversing structure of 1/2 and 2/1 twill.

It is interesting that just as three-end twill as an overall weave becomes more common the reversing structure of the *Rippenköper* weave seems to disappear, but perhaps this was because it would have required six treadles rather than just three. It is also possible to speculate that there might have been an earlier stage when three-end twill was woven on a two-shaft treadle loom, combined with a shed stick for the third shed. This would allow 1/2 twill to be woven, but not 2/1 twill, so *Rippenköper* would not be possible. A well-known early representation of a two-shaft treadle loom shows a fabric being woven that is generally interpreted as plain weave (presumably on the basis that it would have to be) but it actually looks remarkably like a diamond twill!

CHAPTER 4: Structural Resources: Beyond Plain Weave

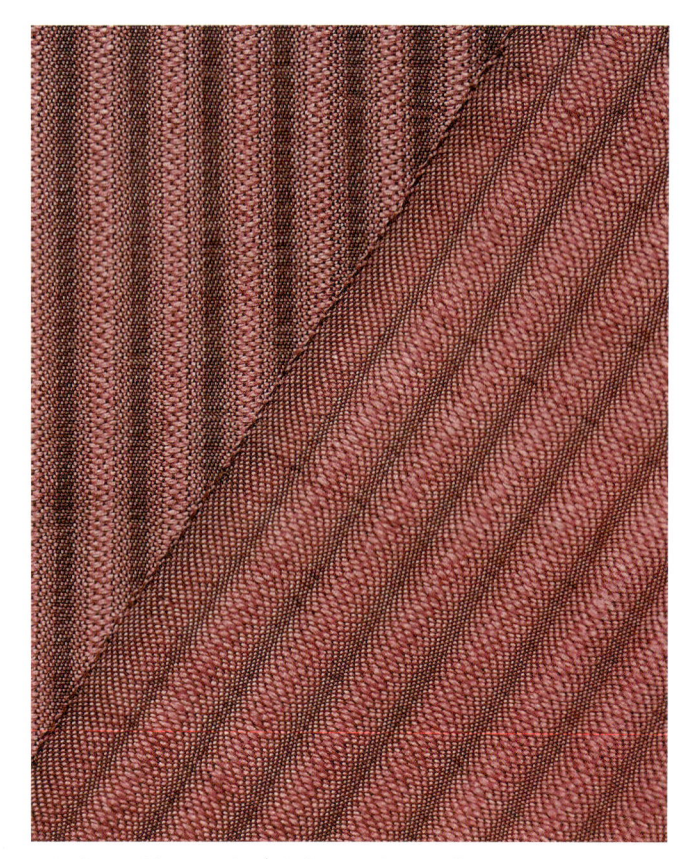

This silk scarf is woven in 1/2 twill with slightly different colours in warp and weft, giving a subtle colour difference between the two sides. The crammed and spaced arrangement causes the intensity of the weft colour to vary and also creates the illusion of a gentle curve as the twill line interacts with the varied spacing. With a fine firmly twisted warp and a thicker, lightly twisted weft, the scarf is stiffer in the weftways direction. Another view of this piece, showing its interesting *'Rippenköper'* border, is given in Chapter 5. (Designer unknown. Lent by Margrit Waldron)

Harris tweed in a herringbone design is a classic use of 2/2 twill, creating a warm, hardwearing fabric. Both warp and weft are melange yarns where the wool fibres have been dyed before spinning, giving a very attractive 'heather mixture' effect. (Designer unknown)

Cloth Quality in Twills

Many different weights of fabric can be produced in twill, from fine and delicate to tough and hardwearing, making it second only to plain weave in the range of cloth qualities that are possible.

SATIN/SATEEN: BREAKING THE TWILL LINE

It is possible to break the twill line while working on only four shafts – the uneven versions of broken twill are sometimes referred to as four-end satin and sateen to draw attention to their relationship to the satins. The smallest true satin repeats on five ends and so provides a greater contrast between warp-float and weft-float surfaces and this naturally becomes more extreme in satins drafted on a larger number of shafts. Satin is also more effective than broken twill in avoiding a twill line, being constructed through a rearrangement of the binding points, but as it is not possible to entirely suppress it the principles described above regarding twist/twill interactions will still apply – to reduce the twill effect, the yarn should have the same twist as the direction of the incipient twill. This will produce a very smooth surface, and traditionally this has often been emphasized by the choice of yarn, with lustrous yarns such as linen or silk being chosen.

Fabric qualities can vary greatly depending on the function of the cloth, ranging from crisp, closely set fabrics for table linen to softer, more fluid fabrics in silk for dress fabrics or scarves. If aiming to use the warp-float (satin) face of the cloth, the warp can be more closely set than the weft to emphasize this smooth surface, while for a weft-float (sateen) fabric the weft can be the more closely set. A classic use of the structure is to turn the weave to play off

This exceptionally fine wool and silk shawl in 2/2 twill has a beautiful drape and achieves almost the gloss of a satin, particularly where the black silk warp is crossed by stripes of a fine, rust-coloured wool. (Designer: Sharon Fisher. Woven in Nepal)

Detail of the twill shawl.

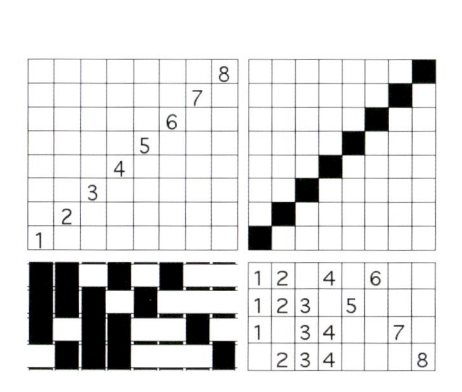

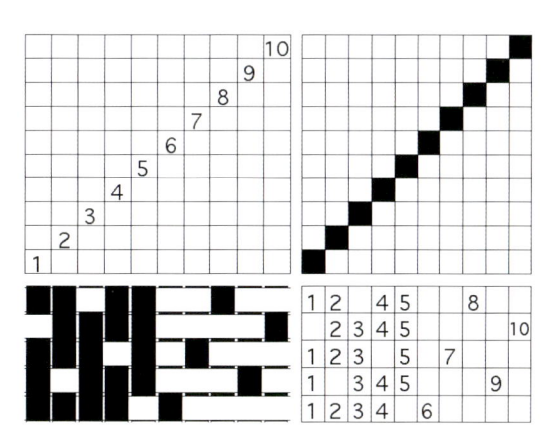

A comparison of the structures of broken twill (four-end satin and sateen) and five-end satin and sateen.

CHAPTER 4: Structural Resources: Beyond Plain Weave

A scarf in eight-end regular satin/sateen with black silk warp and white silk weft. As the weft is slightly more closely set than the warp, it is the white sateen face that is the glossiest, and the play of light on this surface is enhanced by the way that the black warp shows through faintly at the intersection points. A fairly close sett gives the piece quite a crisp handle. (Designer unknown)

A scarf in eight-end irregular satin/sateen, with ecru silk warp and red wool weft. The rich colour of the weft showing faintly through the muted silk warp creates an attractive, slightly iridescent effect. The sett is relatively open, giving a soft, fluid character to the fabric. (Designer unknown)

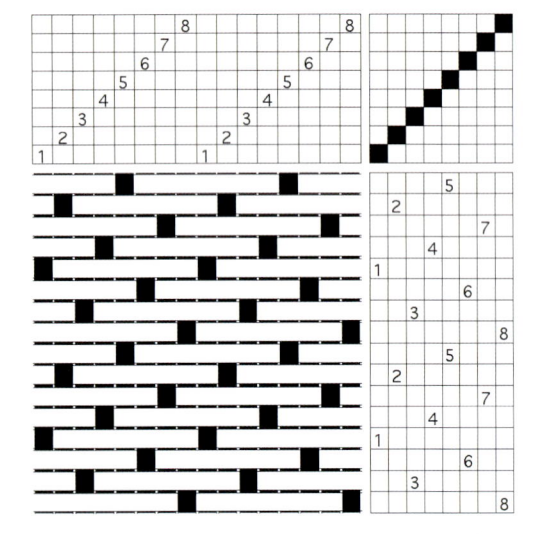

Draft of eight-end regular sateen. It is more convenient to weave a fabric with the sateen face uppermost so that fewer shafts need to be lifted.

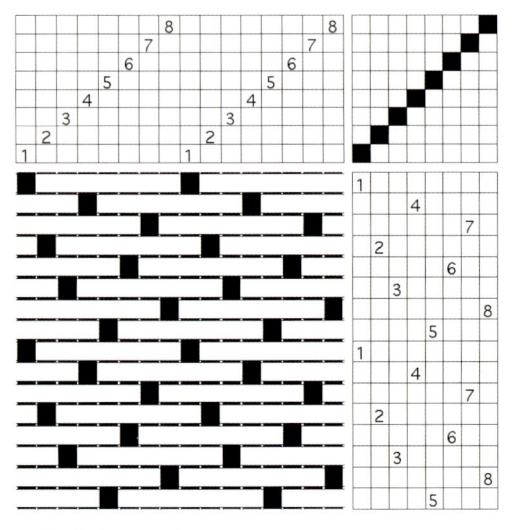

Draft of eight-end irregular sateen.

66   CHAPTER 4: Structural Resources: Beyond Plain Weave

The contrast between the two scarves shown here provides a good example of the way that material and sett can alter the character of a weave. The black and white scarf conforms to the classic idea of satin with closely set silk in both warp and weft to give highly glossy surfaces. The red and ecru scarf gives a very different effect by bringing in wool as well as silk, so that one side is matt and has a softer, warmer feel than the other. The fabric is quite openly set, which allows the weft colour to show through on the warp-float face of the fabric, and also gives the scarf a softer drape compared with the relatively crisp handle of the silk scarf. The difference in character between the two pieces would have been noticeable even if both had been in a regular satin, but the red and ecru scarf is further moved away from a classic effect by the use of an irregular satin.

Though frequently associated with glossy materials such as linen and silk, satin and sateen are weave structures that can be carried out in any material. The combination of wool and silk used in the red and ecru scarf gives an attractive effect of a glossy surface on one face and a matt effect on the other, while using wool for both warp and weft produces a soft, warm fabric suitable for winter scarves.

An interesting issue arises when combining blocks of satin and sateen in a chequerboard arrangement. It is desirable to make a clean cut between adjoining weaves but some arrangements produce tiny squares of plain weave at alternate corners where the blocks join, creating small

A sample of six-end satin/sateen in wool. Warp and weft: High-twist woollen merino 14.5 Nm, 32 epi, ppi. It can be seen how a high-twist weft used in a satin weave tends to cause the selvedge to roll up. This reaction applies also to uneven twills and can form the basis for warp-float/weft-float pleating, which will be discussed in Chapter 5.

Draft showing the two faces of six-end satin/sateen.

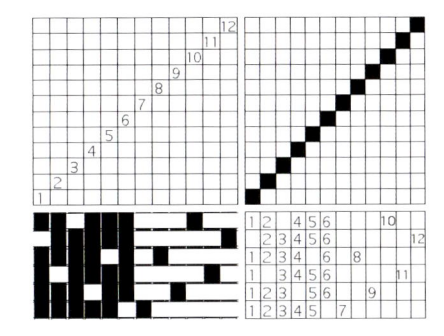

Top: Blocks of satin/sateen drafted so as to avoid pinholes.

Bottom: A draft of satin/sateen that causes pinholes to form. Is this really 'incorrect'?

the two faces against one another as damask, often using the same colour in warp and weft so it is only the play of light on the different surfaces that reveals the design. In this case the fabric can be more evenly set between warp and weft to maximize the play of light on both warp- and weft-float surfaces.

It can also be interesting to use contrasting colours in warp and weft because although the relatively long floats create a clear difference between the two faces, the yarns do not completely conceal one another. Even if one of them is dominant, a contrasting colour in the other element will show through at the intersection points, and with a suitable choice of colour and sett this may actually serve to emphasize the lustre of the dominant surface, as in the black and white silk scarf shown here. The effect of a bright colour showing through a darker or more muted shade can also be interesting, sometimes giving an almost iridescent effect.

CHAPTER 4: Structural Resources: Beyond Plain Weave 67

holes in the fabric. This is often considered a fault but these tiny 'pinholes' scattered across the fabric can give a most attractive effect – a good example of how unhelpful it is to be too rigid about what is the 'correct' way to do things. This effect occurs also with uneven twills, but tends to be more noticeable with the smoother surfaces of satin/sateen.

Textured Weaves on Satin Bases

The scattered binding points of the satin weave can be used as a base for building up small-scale overall textures by adding extra intersections or by rearranging twills in a satin sequence. Some of these structures retain something of a twill line and are classified as corkscrew twills but others have a more random effect and this provides one method of building up structural crepe weaves. Ann Sutton, noting the fine, slightly irregular surfaces that tend to be produced, calls this group of structures 'granites', while Nisbet, emphasizing their usefulness to the designer, rather charmingly refers to them as 'fancy weaves of great utility'.

ALTERNATING FLOAT WEAVES

One *float weave* which apparently exemplifies minimum deviation from *plain weave* has been widely and variously used. Its seemingly unnamed structure is based on *alternation* – alternation of uniform 3/1 with uniform 1/1 interlacing in both warp and weft, and alternation in the alignment of the 3-span warp floats on one face and of the 3-span weft floats on the other. This undoubtedly represents an early departure from the *plain-weave* formula and may be the prototype of many *plain-weave* derivatives.

Irene Emery, *The Primary Structures of Fabrics*

Although some individual structures within this group have traditional names, Irene Emery could find no name for the general principle of this type of structure and so adopted the term 'alternating float weaves' to cover the whole category. These weaves appear to predate twills in some parts of the world, and it certainly could be argued, as Emery does, that they offer the simplest possible deviation from plain weave. John Becker has made a compelling case that textiles of this type that have previously been regarded as requiring complex drawlooms could have been woven with simple two-shaft looms combined with pattern sticks, which makes it plausible to suggest that this group of structures may be very old.

Han Damask and Associated Weaves

An alternating float weave, well-known from the Han Dynasty in China, depends on warp floats passing over three weft threads and is commonly known as Han damask. Irene Emery points out that in some ways this term is problematic because the structure does not conform to the most widely used definition of damask – an uneven twill or satin that is turned to create a design from the contrasting warp- and weft-float faces of the weave. But in its historical context it was clearly used in a similar way to create a fabric that relies on the different reflective qualities of the surface to define the design.

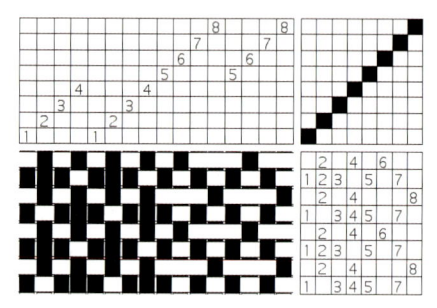

Structure of Han damask, showing warp-float and weft-float faces. Areas of the warp-float face were used in Han Dynasty China to create a design that stood out in contrast with plain weave areas of cloth. The structure can be woven with only three shafts for each face, but it is often convenient to spread it onto four.

When there are warp floats on one face, weft floats are inevitably formed on the other and either set can be contrasted with plain weave to create the design depending on yarns and sett. In the Han period fabrics were relatively warp-faced and so it was the warp floats that showed up clearly to form the design, but present day Chinese minority people such as the Miao use the same structure in fabrics that are balanced or slightly weft dominant and so it is the weft floats that create a clear design. The structure may have three-span floats, as in the original Han damask, or five-span floats, and both work particularly well with lightly twisted silk weft, because the yarn becomes compressed on plain weave picks while spreading on the float picks, producing a glossy design on a relatively matt background. William Willetts suggests that in the Han period silks were probably woven in the gum, thus providing adequate strength and cohesion for the warp, while after degumming these almost twistless yarns would spread to emphasize the floats.

This Miao fabric uses an alternating float weave with three-span floats. This shows an effective interplay of material and structure as the weft of almost twistless silk spreads out on the float picks but is compressed on the plain picks, giving a good contrast between an almost matt background cloth and a glossy pattern. (Designer unknown. Photo: Gina Corrigan)

Draft of the weave structure of the three-span alternating float design.

Chinese minority silk fabric in an alternating float weave with five-span floats. (Designer unknown. Gina Corrigan Collection)

Draft of the weave structure with five-span floats.

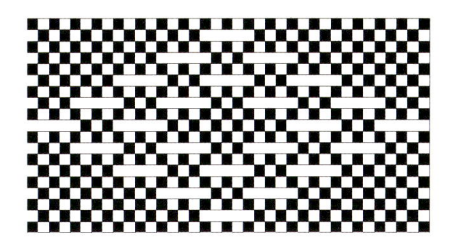

As well as producing these fine silk cloths, the Miao also use an alternating float weave to produce much heavier fabrics for wedding blankets. The striking contrast in character between the two types of cloth provides an excellent example of how a structure, as drafted on point paper, can create widely different fabrics depending on the materials and relative weights of the yarns that are used. Martin Conlan of Slow Loris Textiles (see Online Resources) showed me these interesting wedding blankets and asked if I could identify the structure. At first glance the impression on the face of the fabric is of plain weave with the warps doubled, but on turning the fabric over an intriguing arrangement of warp threads interlacing with curving wefts is revealed. I was initially perplexed, but after some thought and experiment was surprised (and amused) to realize that the structure was one that I already knew extremely well – it was only the use of thick and thin wefts that had made it difficult to recognize.

CHAPTER 4: Structural Resources: Beyond Plain Weave

Miao wedding blanket, showing the weft-float face of the fabric. (Designer unknown. Photo: Martin Conlan)

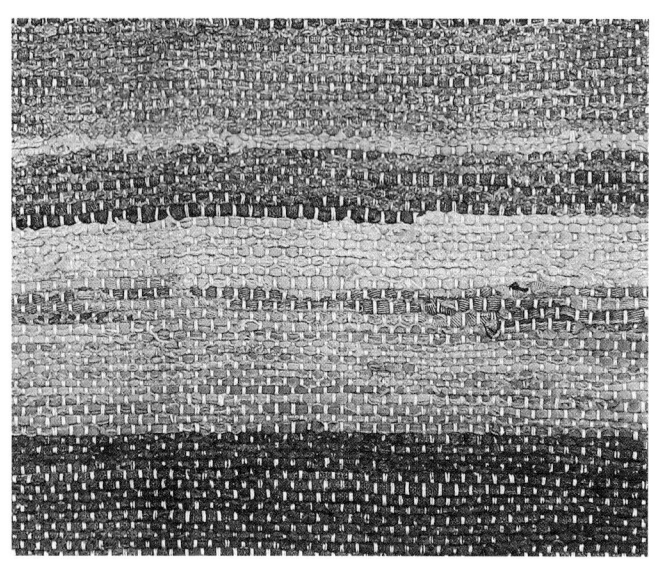

Detail of the weft-float face of the Miao wedding blanket. (Photo: Martin Conlan)

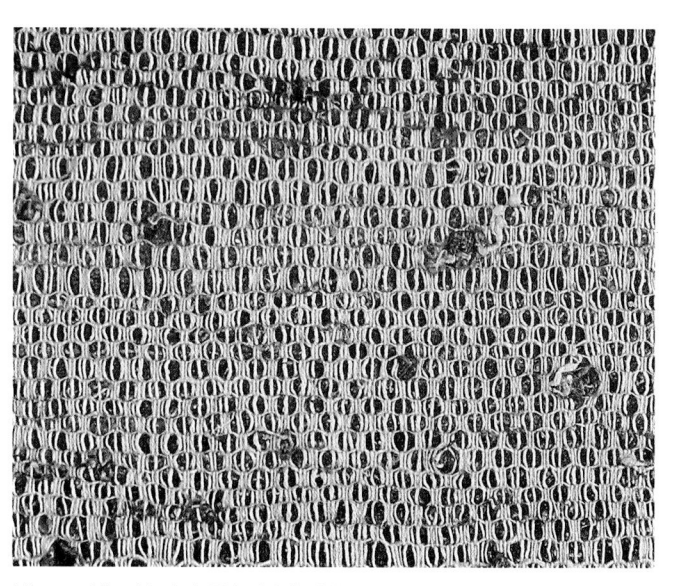

Miao wedding blanket. This detail of the warp-float face of the fabric shows the distortions of the cotton warp and weft. (Photo: Martin Conlan)

These fabrics are woven in exactly the same five-span alternating float structure that is used to pattern one of the fine silk fabrics shown above, but using a cotton warp and a thin/thick alternation in the weft, with a fine cotton yarn for the plain weave picks and thick rag strips for the float picks. This combination causes extreme distortions of both warp and weft on the back (warp-float face) while allowing warp threads to slide together on the weft-float face of the fabric, so that the warp ends appear to be doubled. Some blankets have the five-span floats covering the whole surface while others have patterns that are produced when selected ends are pushed to the weft-float face of the cloth.

Sample of the structure of the wedding blankets, showing the weft-float and warp-float sides. This small sample, trying two different thicknesses of rags as weft, was woven to check that I had understood the structure. The thicker rags gave a result closer to the effect seen in the Miao wedding blankets.

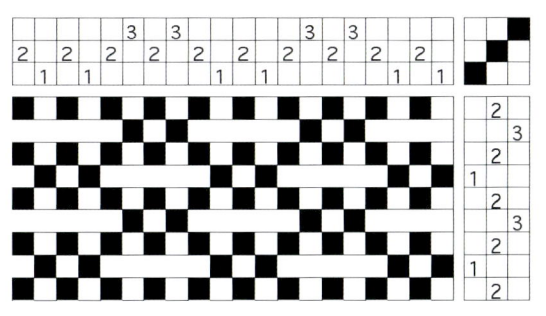

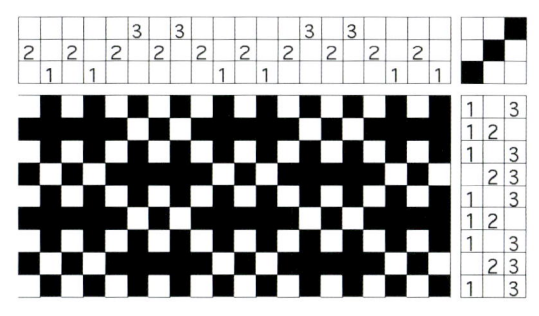

Drafts of the weft- and warp-float faces of the Miao wedding blanket.

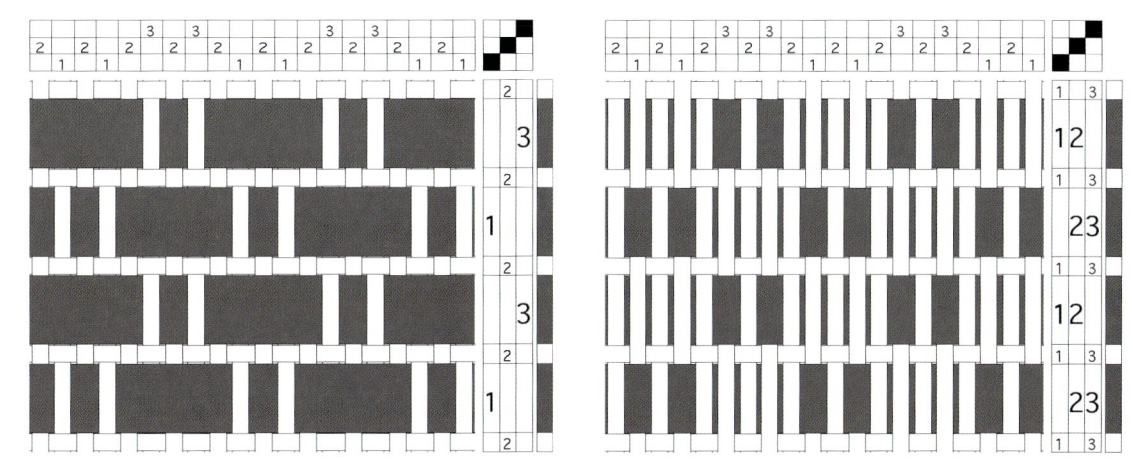

Thread diagrams of the two sides, showing how the thick floating weft dominates the surface of the fabric and also leaves the plain weave picks free to shift position on the reverse of the fabric.

CHAPTER 4: Structural Resources: Beyond Plain Weave

Two different weights of fabric and arrangements of colour in five-span alternating float weave.

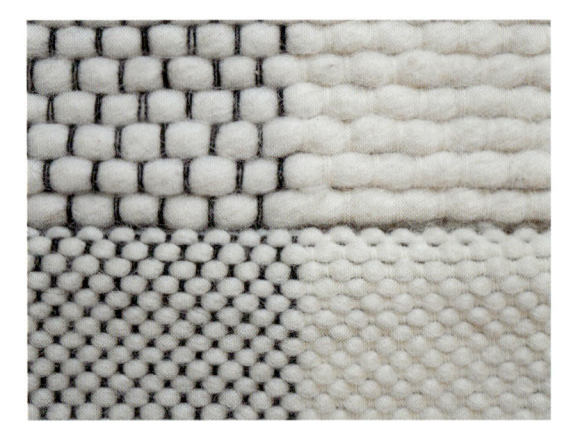

Top: Warp: High-twist woollen merino 14.5 Nm, half black, half white, 20 epi. Weft: Felted wool 0.0165 Nm, white (float picks) and high-twist woollen merino 14.5 Nm, black (plain picks) 6 ppi.

Bottom: Warp: High-twist woollen merino 14.5 Nm, half black, half white, 28 epi. Weft: Wool 1 Nm, white (float picks) and high-twist woollen merino 14.5 Nm, black (plain picks), 12 ppi.

Warp-float faces of the same fabrics.

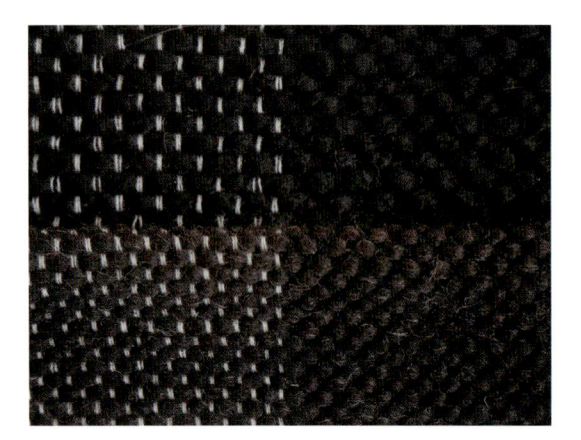

Top: Warp: High-twist woollen merino 14.5 Nm, half black, half white, 20 epi. Weft: Acrylic 0.55 Nm, black (float picks) and high-twist woollen merino 14.5 Nm, white (plain picks) 6 ppi.

Bottom: High-twist woollen merino 14.5 Nm, half black, half white, 28 epi. Weft: Wool 1 Nm, natural black (float picks) and high-twist woollen merino 14.5 Nm, white (plain picks), 12 ppi.

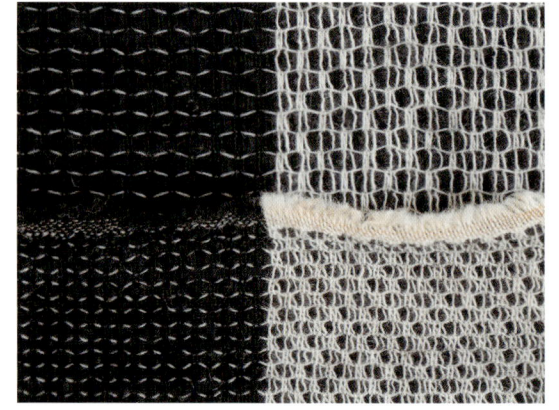

Warp-float faces of the same fabrics.

Many different effects can be produced on this thick and thin principle by varying the weight of yarn and the arrangement of different colours. If the plain weave picks of fine yarn are of a contrasting colour to the thicker yarn, they tend to be barely visible on the weft-float face of the fabric, but form an interesting distorted weft effect on the reverse.

A similar strategy of using thick and thin yarns can be carried out warpways, with thick yarn for the float ends and a fine yarn for the plain weave ends, once again forming a fabric with two very different sides. It can also be woven on a very different scale from the original wedding blankets, using the same principle but making a much finer cloth. It can work well for the 'thick' yarn to be built up from several finer threads used together, especially if a relatively soft drape to the fabric is required, and this allows the blending of different colours for a richer effect. Also, as well as being used for fabrics where one face of the structure is used throughout, a ribbed or pleated effect can be created by

Alternating float weave with five-span floats running warpways. Warp: Spun silk 60/2 Nm × 3 (thick yarn), spun silk 60/2 Nm (thin yarn), 48 epi. Weft: Spun silk 60/2 Nm, 40 ppi. The contrast between the blue-green of the thick float ends and the bright red of the thin warp and weft creates an iridescent effect.

Close-up of the five-span float weave, showing both faces. Another view of this fabric is shown in Chapter 7.

Huckaback fabric woven in allo, the Himalayan giant nettle, an ideal material for these spot weaves in their classic form as towels or table linen. (Woven by Nepalese weavers for Susi Dunsmore)

Draft of huckaback as woven in the Nepalese cloth.

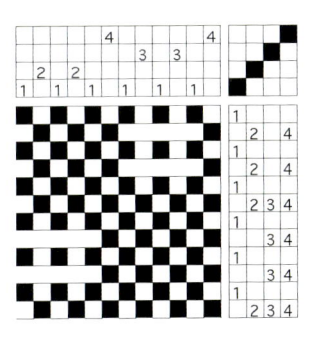

using narrow stripes of the two faces, and examples of this technique are shown in Chapter 5.

Spot and Lace Weaves

In spite of its long history Han damask is probably less well known than other alternating float structures that are familiar to handweavers in the form of various spot and lace weaves, under names such as huckaback, Bronson, mock leno, Swedish lace and so on. These all depend on the creation of spots formed by floats on alternate ends and picks, but the effect varies depending on how these spot units are placed. Some structures have both warp-float and weft-float spots while others have warp floats on one face and weft floats on the other, so can produce double-sided fabrics if contrasting colours or materials are used in warp and weft. Although they rely on the movement of threads to create their effects, some spot arrangements produce a textured surface while others create a lacelike effect. Huckaback, for example, uses a chequerboard arrangement of plain weave and spots whose floats create a slightly raised texture, making a highly absorbent fabric, so it is a classic construction for towels and teacloths.

Mock leno is the same on both sides while Swedish lace has weft floats on one face and warp floats on the other so could be used to create a cloth that is different on the two sides.

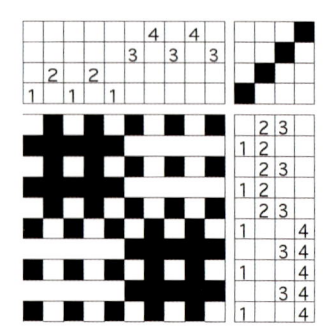

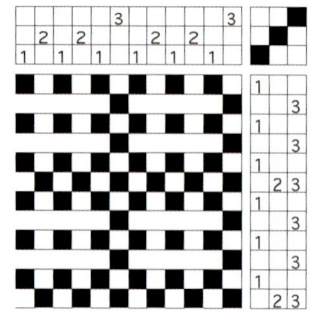

Mock leno.

Swedish lace.

Three different weights of linen fabric in mock leno are shown here. The coarsest one is a tea towel that uses three-span float units but with the floating ends and picks doubled, emphasizing the floats. The very open sett allows the floating threads to shift and create a slightly rippled effect in both warp and weft. The medium weight fabric would be suitable for either clothing or curtains and has contrasting colours in warp and weft. It uses five-span float units rather than three-span and the closer sett gives a crisper handle than the tea towel and means that the float picks do not ripple in the same way. The finest and most closely set piece is a man's shirting fabric, which uses three-span float units and creates a very lightweight, well-draping cloth. (Designers unknown)

This cotton fabric from Yunnan in China forms a pattern on a plain weave ground that is rather similar to the Miao alternating float weaves in silk, but here the pattern is built up using a variant of Swedish lace, with rectangular rather than the usual square spots. The pattern shows up most clearly on the warp-float side of the fabric. (Designer unknown)

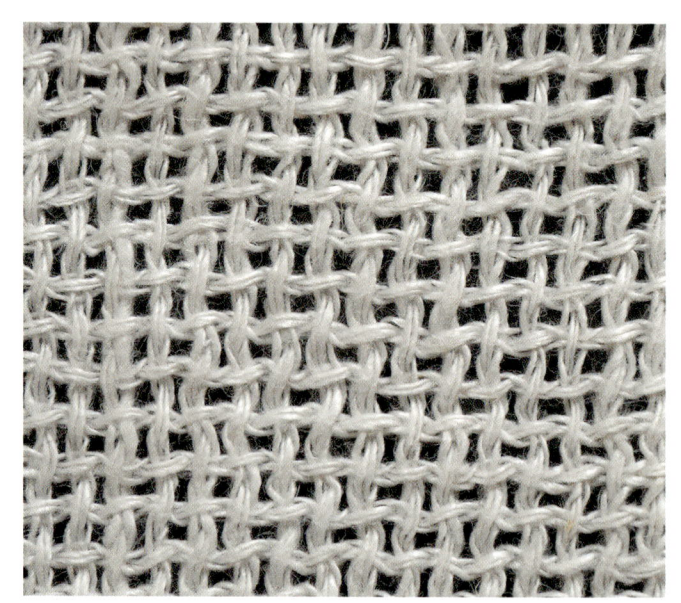

Detail of the tea towel, showing the rippled effect of the floating ends and picks.

Mock leno (or huck lace) uses similar spot units but with a chequerboard of warp-float and weft-float spots. This switch from warp to weft floats creates openings in the cloth forming a lacework effect that can produce a translucent and delicate cloth. Classic mock leno has warp floats and weft floats on both sides so forms a fabric that is the same on both sides even if different colours are used in warp and weft. In contrast, the variant known as Swedish lace uses similar spot units but with warp floats on one face and weft

Rita Beales made extensive use of Swedish lace for table mats woven with her handspun linen yarn, producing exquisitely delicate pieces that play off the lace weave against blocks of plain weave. The open weave Swedish lace relaxes more than the plain weave, introducing gentle curves into the fabric, which Rita Beales has emphasized with contrasting threads around the border of the piece. (Crafts Study Centre, University for the Creative Arts. T.81.14. Photo: David Westwood)

floats on the other, so if different colours or yarn qualities are used for warp and weft the fabric will be different on the two sides. The lacework effect is produced because single ends and picks interlace in plain weave between the spots.

Although these weaves are most frequently applied to items that make the most of their lacelike qualities, especially table linen and curtains, the openwork effect is a good structure for trapping air, especially if woven in wool. This gives a very different character of fabric, suitable for items such as scarves and shawls. These structures also offer scope for other variations through combining yarns of different weights because some ends and picks always weave plain while others are always floating.

FURTHER FLOATS

There are many other traditional float weaves that have the potential for very varied effects. In some structures all the threads are floating at some point but with others only certain threads float, while the rest weave closely into the fabric, so there is the possibility of using different colours, weights or qualities of yarns to emphasize the floats. In other structures, even if all threads are floating to some extent, the length of the floats varies and so once again there is the possibility of emphasizing the longest floats by varying the colour, material or yarn twist.

Although my general aim is to stress the flexible nature of each weave structure and its ability to create different cloth qualities, some of the traditional structures that include relatively long floats do tend to create rather definite effects. There are still possibilities for working with different materials and yarn thicknesses, but there is not quite the same scope for varying their character as with simpler weaves. Whatever the material or weight of fabric, structures with very long floats are likely to produce strong textures, thread distortions or both.

Waffle Weave and Brighton Honeycomb

Waffle weave provides a good example, as it has a somewhat assertive character with a grid-like form that cannot easily be escaped. I used to teach a course where students were asked to choose a single structure and experiment with it for several weeks, aiming to discover all the different possibilities it offered. Waffle weave is so striking in its appearance that students would frequently pounce on it with delight, only to return a week later in despair asking to pick an alternative. In spite of their best efforts waffle weave had remained determinedly itself!

Having said this, there are still *some* possibilities for variations in fabric quality. Although fine, balanced yarns will certainly show the characteristic grid-like structure they may create a relatively thin and lightly textured cloth, especially in an open sett, while with unbalanced yarns the shrinkage of the floats tends to pull the two surfaces apart to form a thicker spongy cloth. However, a different quality can be given to the fabric through the character of the yarn, for example by using a very stiff yarn such as paper or by exploiting very high-twist yarns so that the crinkling of the floating threads can become a feature in itself, creating a very elastic fabric.

A beautiful example of waffle weave using high-twist yarn in a very open sett can be seen in a book issued by the Nuno Corporation, *Fuwa Fuwa*. Because such a fabric will shrink considerably, waffle weave with high-twist yarns can also work particularly well if played off against firmer structures

These two waffle weave tea towels show an interesting contrast of qualities. The openly set linen in the background shows the characteristic grid structure but the fabric is almost flat, giving a pattern of glossy floats rather than a three-dimensional effect, while the more closely set piece is a typical example of an inexpensive cotton tea towel. In both cases the long floats create good absorbent cloths that function well. The linen towel has single yarns in a balanced cloth at 16 epi and ppi. It can be woven on five shafts, threaded as a point draft, and repeats on eight ends and picks. The cotton towel has a plied warp and singles weft. It could be woven on the same threading but has a weftways repeat of only six threads. The different settings of warp and weft, 24 epi and 18 ppi, ensure that the effect is still a square grid. (Designers unknown)

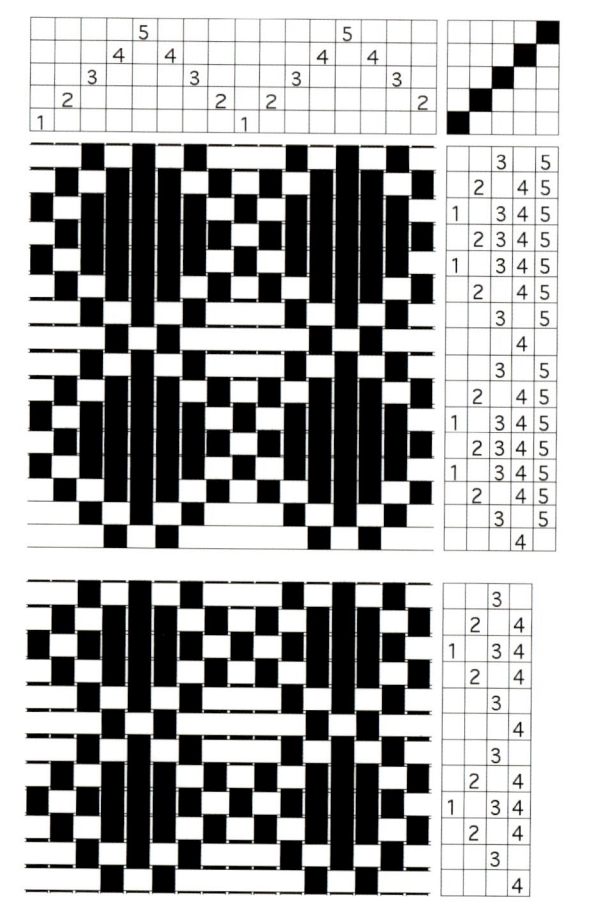

Drafts for the two tea towels. Top: Linen towel. Bottom: Cotton towel. Clearly there are only slight differences in the structure of the two pieces so it is the choice of material and sett that mainly accounts for their different qualities.

This is still recognizably waffle weave but the use of paper yarn in an open sett has given it a very different character from usual. (Designer: Lotte Dalgaard. Photo: Sanne Krogh)

and balanced yarns, for example to create seersucker effects. Also, precisely because this is a structure where only *some* threads have very long floats, different yarns can be used for these floats to emphasize the structure. If this is carried out on only one face or with different colours or textures on the two faces it will create a fabric that is different on the two sides.

This weave was traditionally known as honeycomb in England, though its grid-like structure is much better captured by the term waffle as used in the US and Scandinavia (*vaffel, våffel*), where the term honeycomb is instead applied to a type of distorted weft weave (*see below*). However there is another structure, Brighton honeycomb, which seems to better justify the name as it has a less regimented look, with a staggered arrangement of cells. It needs a minimum of eight shafts, though versions on twelve or sixteen shafts give more striking effects. This is another structure that tends to shrink strongly so can be played off against more stable structures but it differs from waffle by having two very different sides. It also provides interesting distortions of the longest warp and weft threads, which can be emphasized with colour contrasts – an example will be illustrated in Chapter 8.

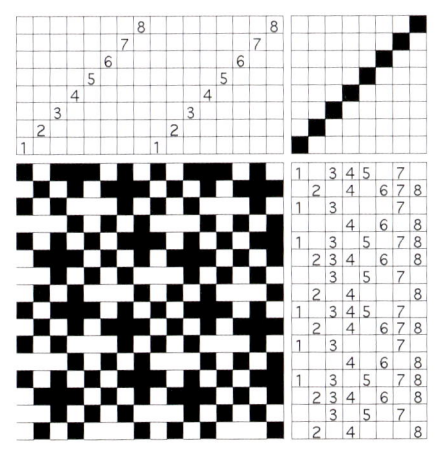

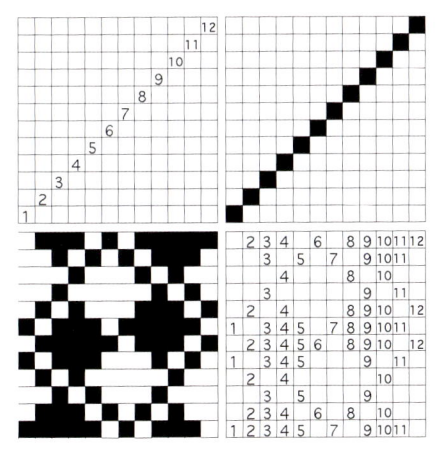

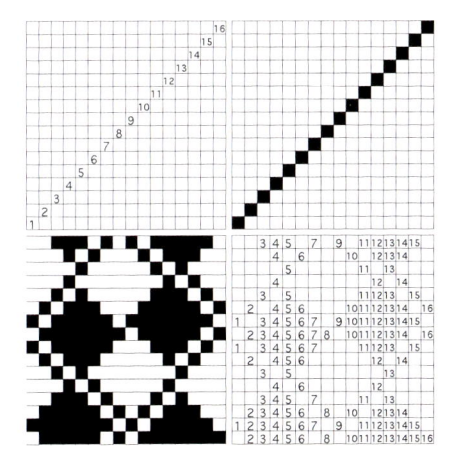

Brighton honeycomb on eight, twelve and sixteen shafts.

CHAPTER 4: Structural Resources: Beyond Plain Weave

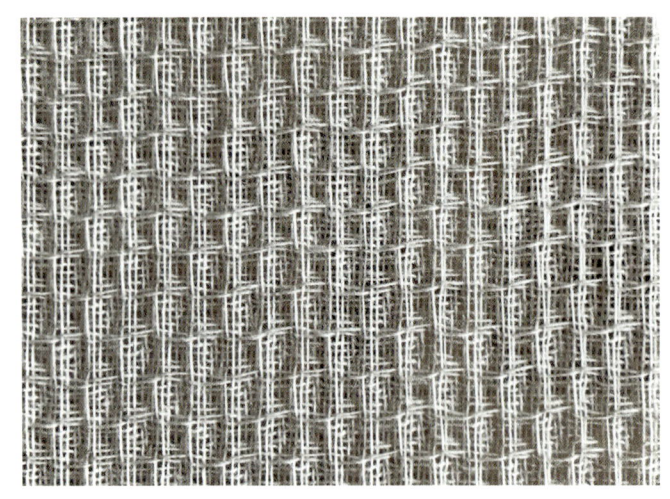

This twelve-shaft Brighton honeycomb has been photographed while still on the loom. Warp and weft: High-twist woollen merino 14.5 Nm, S, 36 epi, ppi.

The sample of twelve-shaft Brighton honeycomb after finishing.

A comparison of Brighton honeycomb samples, showing the effect of having the same or different directions of twist in warp and weft. Warp: High-twist woollen merino 14.5 Nm, S, 36 epi. Weft: High-twist woollen merino 14.5 Nm, top: S, bottom: Z, 36 ppi. The cellular nature of the weave shows up more clearly with the same twist in both warp and weft. Using opposite twists softens the effect, and also causes the fabric to show some curling at the corners, which can be a problem with many types of cloth when opposite twists cross one another.

Honeycomb (Distorted Weft Weave)

Honeycomb is another structure that seems at first sight to have quite an assertive character, from which an easily recognizable cellular effect will necessarily emerge, but Stacey Harvey-Brown has experimented widely with this weave and provides excellent examples of its flexibility, showing the importance of understanding the interplay of structure and material (see her book *Honeycomb Hybrids*). The use of high-twist yarns can also give a very different character to the weave, as seen in the work of Lotte Dalgaard.

These fabrics by Stacey Harvey-Brown show two versions of honeycomb. At the top is a classic honeycomb with bold outlining threads that emphasize the cellular effect. Below is a variation without outlining threads that gives an impression similar to huckaback, which she calls 'honeyhuck'. (Photo: Stacey Harvey-Brown)

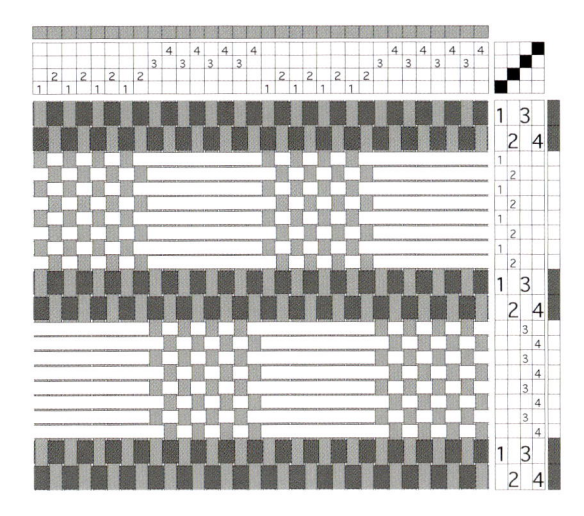

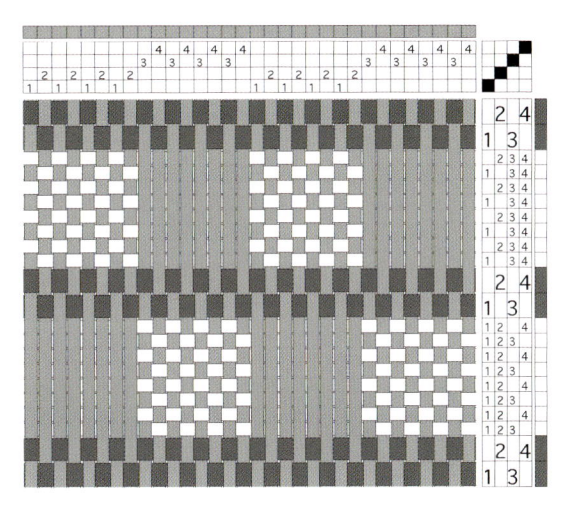

The classic honeycomb structure, showing the two faces. The warp-float face is generally regarded as the right side of the fabric though it is usual to weave it with the weft-float face uppermost as this requires fewer shafts to be lifted.

CHAPTER 4: Structural Resources: Beyond Plain Weave

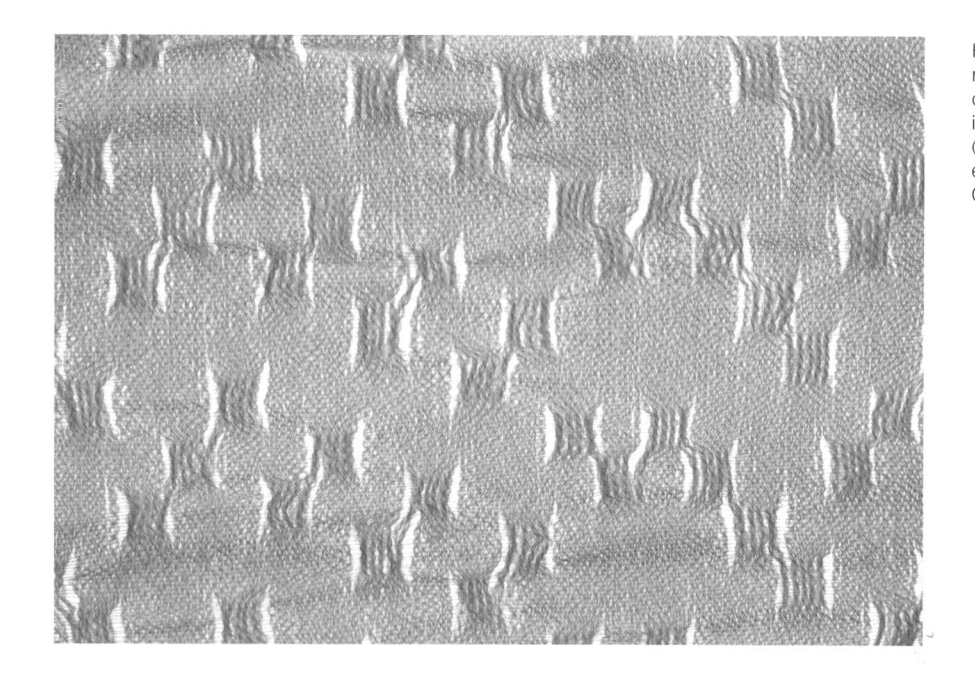

Here Stacey Harvey-Brown uses a monofilament weft across a cotton warp to create a fabric with a translucent quality that is quite different from a classic honeycomb. (Photo: Stacey Harvey-Brown) Another example of this type of fabric is shown in Chapter 6.

'Mussels', a highly textured honeycomb fabric by Lotte Dalgaard. This lightweight, flexible fabric in linen, wool and crepe wool has been designed for clothing. The selvedge, which can be seen running diagonally across the picture, is incorporated into the garment design. Instructions for weaving this fabric, together with a view of the finished garment, designed and made by Elisabeth Hagen, can be seen in *Thread Magic* by Lotte Dalgaard and Paulette Adam. (Photo: Karl Ravn)

Deflected Double Weave/False Double Weave/Integrated Cell Weave

These various names have been applied to a style of construction that combines floats and plain weave in a very specific way. There are two sets of differently coloured yarns, in both warp and weft, and each colour interlaces *only* with itself while floating over or under the other set. This principle was originally developed as a way of increasing the scale of colour-and-weave effects without losing fabric cohesion. As William Watson explains, 'where a colour of warp is intersected by the same colour of weft, that colour will appear on the surface whatever the weave is, which enables plain or other firm weave to be employed in those places to give the cloth the necessary strength'.

Initially classed simply as a special colour-and-weave technique, this method of construction was later labelled integrated cell weave or false double weave, since some structures create a cellular effect while others give the impression of double cloths. The floating threads often show extreme deflections during wet finishing, creating bold curved motifs. A further possibility is to use two sets of threads with different shrinkage, allowing strongly textured surfaces to emerge.

The structures produced with this highly adaptable principle of construction were known by various names until Madelyn van der Hoogt introduced the term deflected double weave to cover the whole group and this has been widely adopted. The method is exceptionally good at creating pattern and, as Watson points out, this is because the cloth is firmly woven at certain places and this makes it possible to produce relatively large-scale designs. A wide range of fabric qualities is possible, from delicate to robust and with varied degrees of integration between the two sets of yarns. *See* the Bibliography for articles by Madelyn van der Hoogt and Vicki Masterson and a book by Marian Stubenitsky.

A jacket fabric in deflected double weave by Denise Kovnat. A contrast in properties between the two sets of yarns causes the floating threads to deflect strongly. (Photo: Denise Kovnat)

Here Denise Kovnat uses deflected double weave in a completely different way with very loose integration between the two sets of interlacing yarns. The fabric is then given a wet finishing treatment that is sufficient to stabilize the two cloths, while allowing them to remain independent but interlocking. (Photo: Denise Kovnat)

COMPOUNDING THE SITUATION

A compound weave has more than one set of elements in either the warp or weft direction, or in both. Such structures offer many possibilities for varying the colour or texture on the two sides and for creating pattern by transposing the surfaces. However, bringing in an additional set or sets of elements inevitably has implications for the substance of the cloth, and the impact will vary greatly depending on whether the additional element is used only in some areas of the cloth or throughout the structure.

Doubling One Set of Elements

In general, having an extra warp or weft will tend to make the fabric firmer, either warpways or weftways, allowing it to fold more easily in that direction. This particularly applies to fabrics with complementary warps or wefts and backed or double-faced cloths where the two elements are present throughout the cloth, but supplementary yarns that are used only intermittently may also impact upon the handle and drape of the fabric. It is worth bearing this in mind at an early stage because it may be possible to mitigate any unwanted

This linen fabric has an extra weft that weaves only in blocks, with surplus yarn cut away to leave fringes on one side of the fabric. Although the extra weft is quite heavy the overall drape of the fabric is good, particularly weftways, and the fabric is wide enough to be cut in this direction for garments. (Designer unknown)

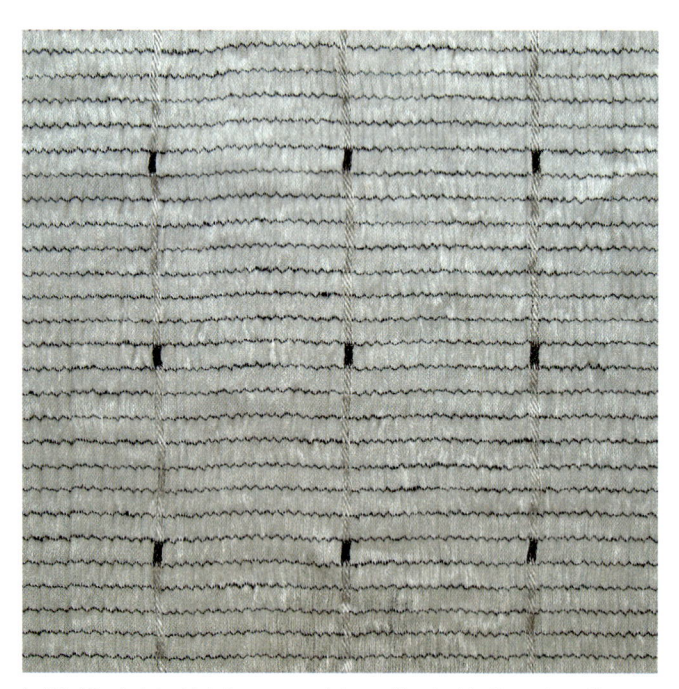

In this 'Spot-stripe' fabric, narrow stripes of backed twill create pattern but are only used intermittently, so the delicate quality of the cloth is retained.

firmness by using very fine yarns for the double elements and thicker/stiffer yarn for the single part of the cloth.

Weft patterning with supplementary yarns is often referred to as brocading but this is a somewhat ambiguous term as it is not clear whether it should apply to extra wefts that run all the way across the warp or only to those used intermittently. Irene Emery comments that: 'there is probably no type of extra-weft patterning that has not, at one time or another, been referred to as "brocading".' Intermittent, spot-type brocading may not greatly affect the handle of the cloth but extra wefts that run right across the fabric will obviously do so.

A supplementary yarn that is present throughout the fabric will increase the weight of the cloth – hence the traditional use of supplementary weft structures such as 'summer and winter' and overshot for bedcovers. This firmness can also be useful in other situations where the fabric needs to have a good amount of body, as can be seen in the work of Deirdre Wood who uses backed cloths for her wall pieces (examples are given in Chapters 7, 8 and 9).

Moorman Technique

Moorman is a special extra-weft technique that was developed by Theo Moorman to allow her to produce figurative pieces that did not have the same effect or take the same time as tapestry. Her work is characterized by a delicate

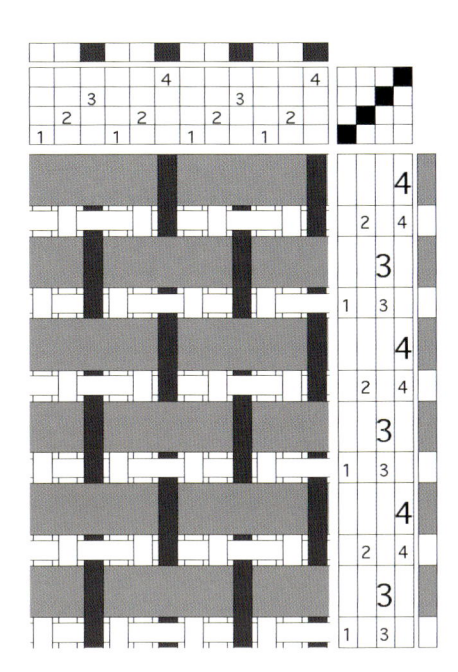

Draft of Moorman structure.

This mat by Mariana Eriksson uses the Moorman technique in a very unusual way. Mariana's article in *Vävmagasinet* gives details of this piece and also describes other innovative ways of using the Moorman technique. (Photo: Håkan Lovallius)

translucency with images lying on a fine plain weave ground, tied down by warp threads that are additional to the main structure. However, just as with many traditional weaves, the basic principle can be used very differently. Mariana Eriksson is well aware how attractive the Moorman technique can be in its original form, and has used it for delicate figurative pieces, but she has also put it to work in a variety of other ways so her work provides an excellent example of the idea of 'playing against type' with a well-known weave structure. Mariana's sturdy mats could not be more different from Theo Moorman's delicate wall hangings but they are using the same weave structure.

DOUBLE CLOTHS

Creating two complete layers offers the chance to make a firm hardwearing cloth or a thicker, warmer fabric, but more delicate qualities are also possible. Whatever the weight of cloth, an important issue is whether large areas of fabric can remain as separate layers or whether these should be joined together for greater stability. This is often a matter of scale – a scarf may work well with the two layers remaining separate but with a larger piece it may be better to bring them together. This can be done by interchanging the layers, which gives good opportunities for pattern, but the two cloths can also be stitched together by allowing a warp end of one cloth to interlace with a weft thread of the other. With cloths woven in twill or other float weaves a careful placing of the stitching points will allow them to be concealed by floats. If both cloths are plain weave it is not strictly possible to cover the stitching points but, depending on the colours used, they can be successfully hidden.

Although having two complete layers can potentially make a thicker or heavier cloth, many other qualities are possible. Because the layers support one another the sett of each cloth can be opened out considerably, even to an extent that would be unstable in a single-layer fabric, to give softly draping fabrics suitable for lightweight scarves or shawls. In this case there are also good opportunities for allowing one colour to show through another, which can give attractive effects. For example, a bright colour in one layer can give an almost glowing effect when viewed through a relatively dark layer, while its brightness will be muted by an overlay of a pale colour.

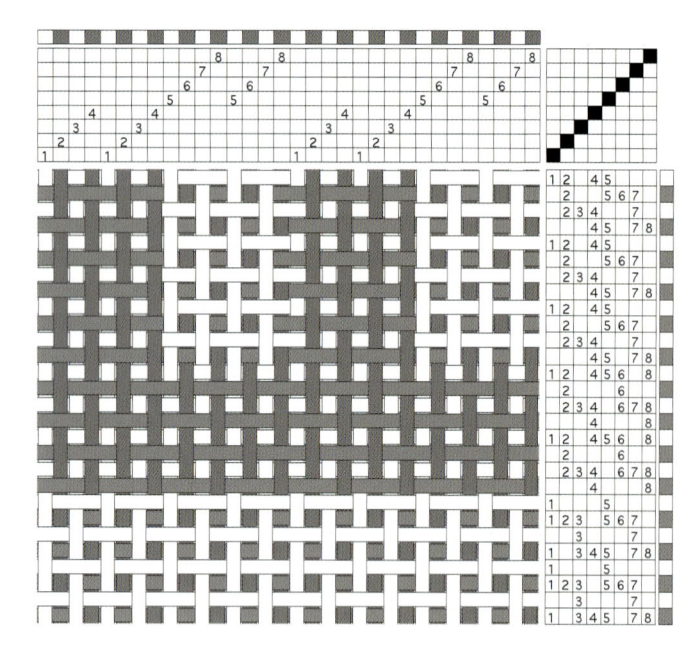

This draft of a double plain weave cloth shows the layers of cloth interchanging both warpways and weftways. Very varied effects will result from mixing different colours.

This softly draping wool shawl uses both interchange and stitching techniques to bind the cloths together. The warp has alternate ends of pale and dark grey and is intersected by several different weft colours to give various colour mixes. Vertical and horizontal stripes result from interchanging the layers both warpways and weftways, and these are played off against large plain areas where the two cloths are linked by stitching points. Both cloths are plain weave and so technically these points cannot be concealed by the structure, but the careful use of colour makes the stitching points invisible. (Designer unknown)

The effect of allowing one cloth to be seen through the other may be enhanced by varying the weight and/or density of the two cloths, with a very fine open cloth overlaying one that is more firmly set. Chapter 6 gives some examples of translucent or transparent cloths that could be used in this way as part of a double cloth. Another possibility with double cloths is to combine shrinking and non-shrinking layers to create textured effects and some examples of this strategy are given in Chapter 7. Further variations can be introduced by allowing the two layers of cloth to weave together at certain points to form a single layer, resulting in an increased density of cloth. The design potential of such single-and-double fabrics is very great both in terms of visual effect and cloth quality and some of the possibilities will be explored in Chapters 7 and 8.

Double Cloth Combined with Floats

As well as designing with traditional float weaves, floats can be positioned freely within a fabric to obtain specific effects, either in terms of displaying the yarn quality or using the contracting power of the yarn to create texture. Although floats can obviously be used in this way in single-layer or backed cloths they work particularly well in double cloths, and Junichi Arai was a master of this type of strategically placed float. Ann Sutton perfectly captures his approach:

Another scarf, again with a predominantly wool weft, in a double plain weave with triangular patterning, pleats and folds itself symmetrically, out from the centre, to create pockets of warmth in its sculptural surface. Strong weavers have ground their teeth when they discover that such spectacular pleats are created simply by omitting certain ends in order to allow the energies from the overspun weft of one cloth to erupt at that point.

Ann Sutton, *Journal of Weavers, Spinners and Dyers*

Lightweight linen scarf in double cloth patterned with blocks of uneven twill. The bright red warp is faintly visible through, but muted by the ecru warp and grey weft. Warp: Linen 40 lea, red and ecru, 48 epi. Weft: Linen 60 lea, pale grey, 48 ppi.

A scarf by Junichi Arai. Gaps left in the warp create weft floats so that the shrinkage of the magenta cloth throws the black cloth into folds. (Ann Sutton Collection)

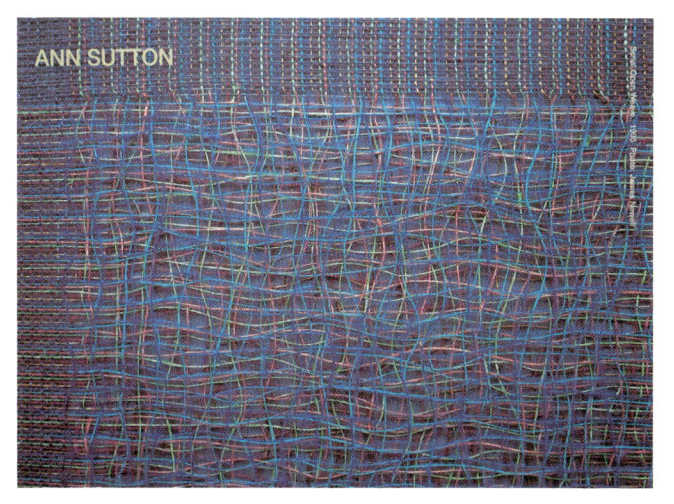

Ann Sutton pushes the idea of multilayer cloths to extremes in her series 'Six Layers of Linen, Rotating', part of her exhibition *No Cheating*. A single layer of multi-coloured cloth at the borders of each square of fabric separates into six layers, with different colours coming to the surface in rotation. The firmly woven linen of the single cloth breaks into exuberant ripples as it separates into layers. A detail of one of the pieces from this series, photographed by James Newell, was used for the exhibition invitation card that is shown here.

TRIPLE AND BEYOND

The simplest way to move beyond two layers is to insert objects within pockets of double cloth or introduce a third set of threads that remains enclosed between the two layers of cloth or only interlaces with them in places. Beautiful examples of both of these techniques have been produced by the Nuno Corporation: in 'Feather Flurries', feathers are trapped between two layers of transparent silk (this fabric is illustrated in Chapters 6 and 10), while in 'Slipstream', paper yarns stay mainly enclosed between the layers but then weave in occasionally, binding the two layers together. Illustrations of these and other Nuno fabrics can be seen in the book *Suké Suké*.

It is also possible to introduce further complete layers of cloth. As in the case of double cloths, the same number of layers does not have to be maintained throughout the fabric, and varying the number of layers will create interesting contrasts of cloth quality between areas with different densities. Junichi Arai was highly inventive in this way, moving from two layers to four within a single warp to produce tubular, reversible cloths and even bags that could be cut ready-made from the loom without stitching (*see my book Weaving Textiles That Shape Themselves* for an example). Ann Sutton has chosen to go even further, with experimental pieces that move from one layer to six.

CHAPTER 4: Structural Resources: Beyond Plain Weave **85**

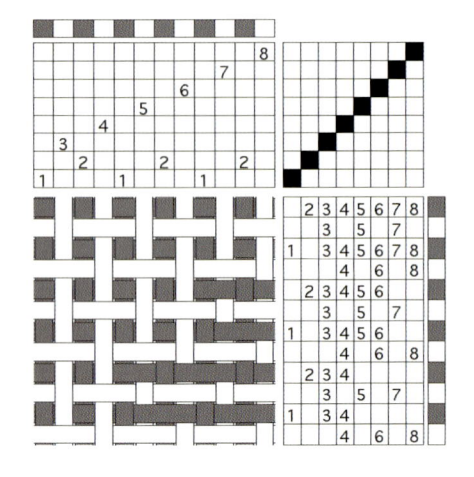

THREADING DRAFTS AS A RESOURCE

Many traditional systems of threading are aimed at making best use of a limited number of shafts, a good example being the 'tied weaves' where two shafts are used to 'tie down' other threads to give variation to the structure. Because the aim is generally to achieve more pattern blocks within a single weave structure these additional shafts are often described as 'pattern shafts', but this type of threading can also be a resource for efficiently combining different qualities of cloth.

Double Two-Tie Weaves

A particularly useful threading is that used to produce double two-tie unit weaves, in which two 'pattern' shafts are needed to create each block. This system exploits the fact that different structures can sometimes have two intersections in common. For example, double plain weave has two intersections in common with 1/3 or 3/1 twill. This is certainly efficient at creating blocks for more complex patterns but can also be useful in creating variations in density and texture within a single piece of cloth, a technique that works particularly well for fabric shaping. Examples of the combination of double cloth and twill used in this way will be given in Chapter 8.

Combining Structures on the Same Base Weave

Stripes of different weaves can be combined without using any more shafts, simply by varying the threading. For example if a straight threading is weaving twill then a different structure can be created alongside using the same shafts differently arranged. The technique of creating 'granites' or corkscrew twills by rearranging twills on a satin base has already been mentioned, so combining a straight and sateen threading can produce stripes of the two weaves without requiring any extra shafts. Although the different visual effect is often the most obvious concern with such rearrangements, there can also be an impact on the cloth quality.

Network Drafting

This complex system of drafting is well beyond the scope of this book but it is just worth noting that although it is frequently aimed at expanding the range of pattern possibilities it can also be used to vary the character of the cloth in different parts of the fabric. Structural variations that result in some parts of the cloth being more firmly woven than others have obvious possibilities for textural effects and fabric shaping.

Drafts of double two-tie threading used to combine 1/3 twill and double weave. These two structures have every alternate thread in common, so this style of threading can give three blocks on eight shafts, rather than the two that would be possible if each of these structures were threaded on four shafts. Extended to more shafts this system will give five blocks on twelve shafts and seven blocks on sixteen shafts. If threaded with contrasting colours in both warp and weft, the result will be a double cloth with contrasting colours on the two sides, while the twill areas will have hairline stripes running in different directions on the two faces.

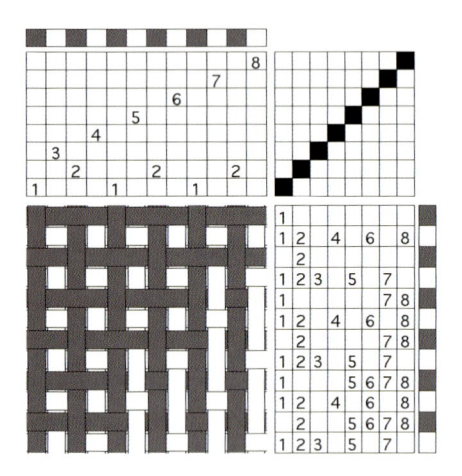

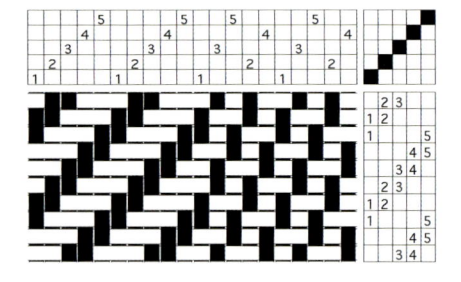

A five-end twill can be rearranged to give stripes of corkscrew twill without requiring more shafts.

A wool and silk fabric combining two differently threading sequences to give stripes of a five-end straight twill and a corkscrew twill that has a slightly firmer quality and a faintly granular surface.

CHAPTER 4: Structural Resources: Beyond Plain Weave

TEXTILE ANALYSIS AS A RESOURCE

Much can be learnt from examining existing textiles and seeing how other designers have used materials, setts and structures. Often the weave structure may be easy to see, particularly with a linen tester, but sometimes it may be worth making a more detailed analysis by picking apart a fabric swatch. It is less easy to be precise about yarn counts and setts, but you can usually learn enough to use as a starting point for your own experiments. Remember that the sett of the yarns as originally woven will be less than in the finished fabric because of the relaxation of the yarns during finishing. This is difficult to judge precisely, but the contraction that will have taken place in a woollen fabric that has been heavily milled will obviously be greater than that in a fabric that appears simply to have been washed.

Distinguishing Warp from Weft

If there is no selvedge on the fabric that you are analysing, it may be impossible to be certain which set of threads is warp, but there are several clues to look for:

1. The warp has to take greater stress than the weft so it follows that:
   a) If one set of threads is plied and the other single, the plied yarn is more likely to be warp.
   b) If one set is more firmly twisted, this is likely to be warp (though crepe yarns are an exception).
   c) If one set is stronger, it is likely to be warp.
2. During both weaving and finishing, the weft is usually allowed to contract more than the warp. Consequently warp threads often appear straighter than weft, and the cloth will usually feel slightly springier in the weft direction. Also any reed marks that remain visible obviously indicate warp.
3. Aspects of the design may help to distinguish warp and weft. As it is efficient to introduce different coloured threads while making the warp, stripes frequently run in the warp direction. Fabrics are most often used with the warp running in a vertical direction, so if a design 'reads' better in one direction this is likely to be warp. For example, in a twill fabric, the twill line is likely to incline towards the warp direction. In checked fabrics the length of the check is likely to be slightly greater in the warp direction.

Obviously none of these rules of thumb can be completely relied upon and not all clues may point the same way. Some yarns such as linen are frequently used as singles in both warp and weft so in this case the presence of stripes may be a safer, though not conclusive, indicator of warp direction. All these guidelines are more reliable when analysing industrial power-woven fabrics, where speed and ease of manufacture are of great importance. With handwoven fabrics, a respect for tradition or a desire to obtain particular effects regardless of the time involved may carry greater weight. For example, fabrics woven for traditional folk costumes, particularly those intended for skirts, have often been woven 'sideways', allowing colours and widths of stripes to be easily varied.

Analysing the Weave

The method adopted will depend on whether or not it is possible to obtain a small swatch that can be sacrificed. If so, the structure can be found by taking the cloth apart, thread by thread, and recording the intersections of warp and weft on point paper or as a computer draft. Unless the cloth is very coarse, a linen tester or magnifier will be necessary. The linen tester is particularly useful, as its graduated sides will also allow you to record the sett.

Pull away a few threads of both warp and weft so that a small fringe is left on each side to prevent threads falling off accidentally. If possible, isolate one repeat of the weave and mark it with tacking threads or pins. If you cannot easily identify a repeat, then you will need to record thread intersections until a repeat of the sequence becomes obvious. If the cloth is not balanced then it is usually easier to see the structure by removing the threads that are more densely set. Use a needle to loosen the first pick (or end) so that you can clearly see the interlacing and record this using normal weave notation. When you have recorded all the intersections for one thread, remove it from the repeat you are working on but it is best to leave it still attached to the rest of the cloth. This makes it easier to find your place again if you are interrupted. Work your way through the swatch until it is clear that a repeat has been completed or until you have recorded enough that the structure has become obvious to you.

Analysis and Synthesis

Of course you may sometimes wish to analyse a fabric where there is no swatch available that can be destroyed. In this case it is necessary to adopt an approach that is as much synthesis as analysis. By combining what can be seen of the weave intersections together with your knowledge of weave structures, a judgment can be made about the probable structure and a provisional draft built up. This must then be carefully checked against the fabric and revised if necessary until there are no inconsistencies.

Finishing techniques applied to the piece can make it difficult to see the structure. Heavy milling is an obvious one, but I had particular difficulty with a piece from the Chinese minority group the Dong, as the right side of the fabric was finished with a heavy glaze that obscured the weave structure. Fortunately this was not applied to the back, making it just possible to see that the design was built up from five-span spot units. However, it still took two attempts to determine the structure because my first draft, though superficially resembling the general effect of the fabric, did not correctly tally with the number of spot units in a repeat.

When analysing an old textile, it is well worth examining it thoroughly for any places that are already damaged or worn, as it is often much easier to see the structure in such areas – the textile analyst is probably the only type of person that is pleased to see wear in a textile! In difficult cases, especially with weaves where the threads move considerably during finishing, it may be desirable to weave and finish a replica sample to be absolutely certain that you have understood the structure correctly. I did this in the case of the Miao wedding blankets described earlier in this chapter.

The warp-float and weft-float faces of a Dong fabric. It may seem surprising that having taken the trouble to weave this design people should choose to glaze the fabric so heavily but the weave creates a subtle texture that is very attractive when the fabric is made into garments. (Designer unknown) *See* the Bibliography for details of the book edited by Ruth Smith that describes these Chinese minority textiles in detail.

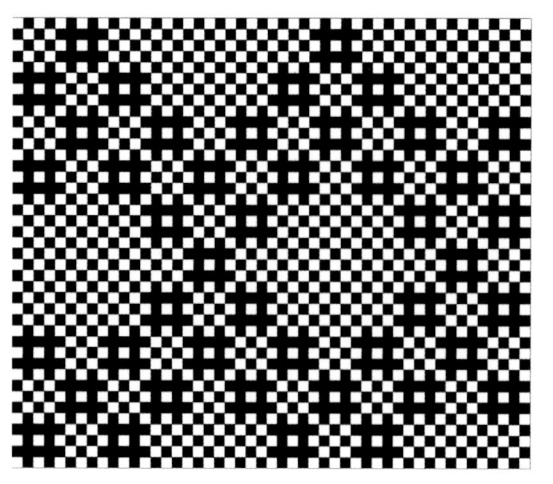

Drafts of the warp-float and weft-float faces of the Dong fabric.

Yarn Twist and Diameter

It is easy to see the direction of twist and whether a yarn is single or plied, if necessary using a linen tester. Judging the diameter is more difficult, especially with fine yarns, so quite powerful measuring equipment is necessary to do this accurately (a digital microscope is obviously worthwhile for anyone intending to do a great deal of analysis). For general purposes, a visual comparison with yarns of known count will usually give a rough guide.

The amount of twist may also be relevant, but in most standard fabrics this will not vary all that much. If trying to make a replica or similar fabric, standard yarns of appropriate thickness will probably be suitable, though weft yarns are often more lightly twisted than warp yarns so this is worth checking even if warp and weft appear to be similar. The main situation where assessing the twist angle becomes important is where a high-twist yarn has clearly been used, such as fabrics where there is a crepe or crepon texture or obvious crinkling of the yarns. Twist angle can be measured with a protractor, using a linen tester or magnifier for fine yarns, and although it is not possible to be precise, even a rough estimate will be useful in choosing yarns to make a similar fabric. If enough yarn is available a short section can be untwisted to count the turns and this information used to calculate the twist angle. For more information on these detailed aspects of yarn twist see my book *Weaving Textiles That Shape Themselves*.

Identifying Fibres

Identifying textile fibres accurately is a complex process requiring specialist chemicals and equipment, so beyond the scope of this book. A good account is given in Marjorie Taylor's *Technology of Textile Properties*.

Historical and Archaeological Textiles

These obviously come under the category of pieces that must be tackled by synthesis as much as analysis, though not always merely because of their value. Many ancient textiles are preserved through being mineralized, so if they are highly textured or folded only part of their surface may be visible and being rigid they cannot be opened out. This is the case with the *Rippenköper* fragment that is shown in Chapter 5, making it difficult to be certain of the number of threads in each stripe. Detailed analysis of such fabrics is a specialized task for archaeologists, but their work is a wonderful source of information and inspiration, and projects where archaeologists and weavers collaborate in producing replicas can be very rewarding.

ANOTHER APPROACH TO DESIGN

This short survey has looked at some well-known structures, showing some of the variations in cloth quality that are possible depending on material, yarn thickness and sett. Effectively this is designing by asking the question: what can I do with this structure? But by approaching the design process from the other direction, with an idea already in mind, a different question can be asked. Given the resources of material and structure there is usually more than one way to achieve an effect, sometimes multiple possibilities, so the question then becomes: why should I choose this solution rather than another? The choice will impact not only on the visual effect, which is frequently the driving force behind the initial design idea, but also on the substance of the cloth. This approach to design will be explored in the next section of this book by looking at several different fabric qualities.

PART 3

Designing for Fabric Qualities

One of the distinguishing features of the good designer is his ability to *converge from a wide base* on a good choice.

Michael French, *Invention and Evolution*

Rather than taking inspiration from material and weave structure, the designer may start with a particular quality of fabric in mind, perhaps based on observational studies or determined by the practical demands of a brief. This can be a productive approach, given a willingness to consider various options rather than rushing too quickly to a conventional solution. Light, open fabrics do not necessarily have to be mock leno and double-sided fabrics do not have to be double cloth. Four fabric qualities have been chosen here: ribbing/pleating, translucency, double-sided textiles and those that 'go off-grid'. Although these are considered separately for clarity they are obviously not mutually exclusive – pleated fabrics lend themselves well to double-sided effects and translucent gauzes may spontaneously develop pleats – so there will be some cross-referencing between chapters. When designing with a particular end in view the weaver needs to be flexible, freely combining traditional structures or even starting from scratch and working from basic principles of weave construction. A classic textbook by Nisbet has the title *Grammar of Textile Design*, which nicely captures the sense that once such fundamental principles are understood one can 'say' anything.

This gauze scarf is openly set to give a lightweight, translucent fabric, but there are additional effects. An unbalanced mohair weft spirals its way through the fabric, creating crepon pleating and also forcing the contrasting stripes out of the horizontal into a zigzag path. The ground and whip threads are different colours so the fabric is also very subtly double-sided, with the natural tussah whip threads showing up more clearly on one side than the other. This one piece consequently shows all four of the characteristics to be discussed in this section.

CHAPTER 5

Fold Here

One could almost redefine biology as the natural history of deployable structures.

Julian Vincent

RIBBING AND PLEATING

Ribbed and pleated structures are widespread in the natural world and possess various useful characteristics, including a large surface area combined with compactness, strength with economy of material and, in many cases, deployability. All these qualities work well in man-made structures, including textiles, so not surprisingly traditions of pleating extend back over millennia. The earliest technique appears to be the imposition of pleats on fabric that has already been woven but the alternative approach of creating self-pleating textiles may possibly go as far back as ancient Egypt (see the Bibliography for details of my article on this topic). Certainly by the second century AD the *Rippenköper* fabrics, with their finely ribbed surfaces, were well established. When considering the possibilities of more complex pleating, there are both natural and man-made sources of inspiration, ranging from the 'natural origami' of unfolding leaves to the elegance and sophistication of the origami tradition itself.

The possible effects range from gentle ridges to deep pleats, and a choice of technique will depend on the function of the cloth and the qualities required – should it be finely ribbed but relatively firm or does it need to be a genuinely deployable structure, with deeper pleats that are free to unfold? Even if deep, deployable pleats are chosen, these can vary in character with some techniques giving a softly rounded effect while others can create a sharper edge, closer to the effect of an imposed pleat.

SOFT PLEAT EFFECTS

Crepon Pleating

The simplest form of woven-in pleating is the crepon texture that forms when a high-twist yarn crosses a normal-twist yarn. This works well in plain weave, though other structures such as twill or satin could be used, and the result is an irregular, tree-bark effect rather than sharp-edged pleating. Depending on the scale and character of the yarns, textures can range from finely crinkled fabrics with moderate flexibility to large-scale pleating giving a highly elastic fabric. Though crepons are frequently woven with the normal-twist yarn in the warp, they can be turned so there is high-twist in the warp and normal-twist in the weft, so the pleating runs across the fabric. The topic is discussed in more detail in my book *Weaving Textiles That Shape Themselves*.

These two crepon fabrics were woven on the same warp but using different high-twist yarns as weft. Warp: Linen 100 lea, 20 epcm. Wefts: Left: Linen crepe 32/2 Nm ('Scatto'), 10 ppcm. Right: Silk crepe 40/44 denier, 20 ppcm.

Amplitude and Pitch in Yarn Spiralling

The crepon effect develops when high-twist yarns release their energy by spiralling their way through the fabric, disturbing the surface in the process, and the precise effect that results will depend on both the pitch and amplitude of such spirals. The steepness of the pitch will be determined by the amount of yarn twist, while amplitude depends on both the thickness and stiffness of the yarn. Stiffness, in its turn, depends not only on the character of the fibres themselves but also on their degree of alignment. Soft woollen yarns spun from short, fine fibres will form small spirals while the parallel alignment of longer, thicker fibres produces stiffer worsted yarns that form wider spirals. The thickness of the yarn itself is also relevant since a thick yarn, even if soft, simply does not have the space to form a very small spiral (in absolute terms) though it may well be small in relation to the yarn thickness. These characteristics, together with the sett, will determine whether a particular high-twist yarn will be able to create crepon effects with a normal-twist warp of any particular thickness.

Results are obviously not completely predictable simply from the known characteristics of the yarn, which is why sampling is so important, but these properties can suggest roughly what to expect. For example, the high-twist woollen merino 14.5 Nm that is used for a number of samples in this book forms a spiral of rather small amplitude *relative to its thickness*, but with a steep pitch due to its very high twist. So it is forceful enough to form crepons when crossing fairly fine warp yarns, but is less successful with yarns thicker than itself because such small spirals become lost in the structure of the fabric rather than disturbing the surface. Sett is also relevant because an open warp allows this lively yarn to release its energy by forming small crinkles between the warp ends rather than pleating up the fabric. In contrast, a moderately twisted worsted yarn, such as alpaca/wool 24 Nm, is stiff enough to make very wide spirals of low pitch that create attractive crepons in open weaves, while this yarn lacks the force to work well in a closer weave.

This complex interplay of factors also explains why yarns of different character and thickness may sometimes match up in surprising ways. When high-twist yarns of opposite twist are used in warp and weft they generate spirals running at right angles to one another and the result is an overall undulating texture (as described in Chapter 3), but this does not *always* require yarns of exactly the same thickness and character. A fine, stiff worsted yarn that makes a spiral that is large in scale, relative to the fineness of the yarn, may turn out to be of similar amplitude to that made by a thicker woollen yarn (where the spiral is only 'small' relative to the yarn thickness), so the two may work well together. The woollen merino 14.5 Nm and crepe wool 30 Nm provide an example of this kind of unexpectedly effective combination.

Crepon Effects in Gauze and Lace Weaves

Gauze allows the warp yarns to be quite widely spaced and only certain types of weft will give a crepon effect in such open cloths. The general principles outlined above suggest that stiff, slightly unbalanced yarns should work well in this situation and this proves to be the case – lightly twisted worsted yarns of mohair or alpaca/wool produce fairly large-scale crepon effects. By contrast, softer high-twist yarns that work well in plain weave do not produce a crepon at all – instead they tend to form small kinks between the gauze units and may even ply back on themselves to produce something closer to a bouclé effect. Similar principles also apply to the lace weaves, which can form large-scale crepons when a normal-twist warp is crossed by a fairly stiff, moderately unbalanced weft.

In this gauze scarf the weft yarns of alpaca/wool and mohair are relatively lightly twisted but are still sufficiently unbalanced to create a large-scale crepon effect in the open structure of the gauze. Warp: Ground ends: Tussah silk 68/2 Nm. Whip ends: Tussah silk 120/2 Nm, 5 gauze units/inch. Weft: Alpaca/wool 24 Nm and mohair 24.8 Nm, 18 ppi.

A sample of Swedish lace showing a crepon effect with several different yarns. Warp: Spun silk 60/2 Nm, 32 epi. Weft: Mohair 24.8 Nm, 36 ppi; alpaca/wool 24 Nm, 48 ppi; crepe wool 27.5 Nm, 48 ppi.

Ribbed/Pleated Structures

An effect of ribbing or soft pleating can be produced with various structures, but depends on a careful use of yarn properties such as thickness, stiffness and twist, and also a close attention to sett. Structurally the simplest approach is to use plain weave in reversing rep stripes, an ingenious technique devised by Erica de Ruiter (described in Chapter 3) but a wider range of fabric qualities is possible with structures where warp floats predominate on one face and weft floats on the other. Narrow stripes of the two faces, running either warpways or weftways, tend to produce a ribbed texture though usually wet-finishing will be required before the effect becomes obvious. This technique has a long history in the form of the *Rippenköper* fabrics that are constructed with weftways stripes of uneven three-end (occasionally four-end) twill, with the earliest pieces excavated so far dating from the second century AD.

I have a special interest in these fabrics, having accidentally produced a pleated fabric from this type of structure many years ago whilst still a beginner at spinning and weaving. My fascination with this effect has influenced much of my subsequent work in textiles and I have discussed the principles involved in detail in my book *Weaving Textiles That Shape Themselves*. I expected there would be a considerable history to such a striking effect and so was surprised at first to trace it back only as far as the nineteenth (possibly eighteenth) century in the form of a warpways ribbed fabric called dimity. Only later, when invited to replicate a *Rippenköper* fabric, did I discover that twills had been used in this way, at least in a weftways direction, for almost 2,000 years.

Rippenköper

Noortje Kramer, an archaeologist working in the Netherlands, asked me to make some samples to replicate the effect of some early textiles with a ribbed surface. These were to be displayed as part of an exhibition entitled 'Beautiful Pleats', covering the history of pleating in a variety of forms both woven-in and imposed. Noortje sent me a photograph of a *Rippenköper* fabric dating from about AD 600 to work from and I was intrigued to discover that this technique was used from the second to the eleventh centuries, after which it seems to have completely fallen out of use. Fabrics constructed on the same principle, but with the ribbing running warpways, do not seem to have appeared until the eighteenth to nineteenth centuries. In my initial efforts to trace a history I did not look back far enough, not having anticipated a gap of 700-800 years!

The majority of *Rippenköper* so far excavated have a structure of 1/2 and 2/1 twill, suggesting that it was the uneven nature of three-end twill that gave rise to the idea of turning the weave to use both faces. It might be assumed that only later would this principle be applied to four-end twill but I have stopped expecting weavers, either in antiquity

This *Rippenköper* fragment was analysed by the textile archaeologist Johanna Banck-Burgess. It dates from about AD 600. (Photo: Johanna Banck-Burgess)

These samples of *Rippenköper* are based on the structure of the fabric dating from about AD 600. Warp: High-twist woollen merino 14.5 Nm, 22 epcm. Weft: Wool crepe 27.5 Nm, 13 ppcm. Reversing stripes of 1/2 and 2/1 twill.

Sample before finishing.

Samples after wet finishing, comparing different pickings and directions of twill.

CHAPTER 5: Fold Here 95

Rippenköper sample with variations in the width of the ribs. The original fragment of fabric shows ribs of varying width but as the piece is so small one cannot exclude the possibility of this being a mistake. However, Noortje Kramer was interested in the idea that this could be deliberate and asked for a sample to show how such variations would look in a larger piece of fabric.

stripes of different widths within the same fabric, which as well as changing the texture can be used to vary the shape of the fabric, a strategy that will be discussed in more detail in Chapter 8.

Contemporary Fabrics Using the Ribbed Effect

Satin/sateen and Han damask can also be used to give a ribbed or pleated effect. Naturally, each structure will give a different character to the texture and using them in combination offers further ways to vary the quality of the cloth. Three-end twills necessarily create a twill line, but on four ends this can be avoided by using broken twill, while if more shafts are available, satin/sateen will give an even smoother surface. Results vary from fine ribbing to a more distinctly pleated effect depending on the materials and width of the stripes.

This silk scarf is woven in 1/2 twill and also uses cramming and spacing. A ribbed effect is created at the borders, through reversals of the structure, with stripes of 2/1 and 1/2 twill. The alternating stripes are of different width, with repeats of 16 picks and 20 picks, giving an effect of narrow ridges on one face and slightly wider ones on the other. (Designer unknown. Lent by Margrit Waldron)

or in the present day, to do the obvious thing. Finds at Mons Claudianus, a Roman stone-quarry in Egypt, dating from AD 110–160, already include four-end as well as three-end *Rippenköper* (see the Bibliography for details of a useful article by Martin Ciszuk). These fabrics are of excellent quality, suggesting that such techniques may already have been in use for some time. It seems surprising that, with a four-end *Rippenköper* appearing so early, there have been few further finds of this structure, with the majority of later examples being three-end twills.

Although most *Rippenköper* so far excavated use straight twills, reversing only with the turn of the weave, a few have been found where the ribbed texture is combined with point twill. Carolyn Priest-Dorman (see Online Resources) refers to one from Switzerland that also alternates weft-float stripes of nine picks and three picks, combined with warp-float stripes of three picks. These pieces seem to offer interesting examples of attempts to vary the texture and appearance of the fabric and support the suggestion, made by Noortje Kramer, that variations in stripe width seen on the *Rippenköper* fragment from AD 600 may have been intentional.

Given the limitations of the looms available the ribs of the *Rippenköper* inevitably run across the warp but with adequate shafts the equivalent structure can of course be used warpways. Also there are many possibilities for using

This detail of the border of the scarf shows the reversal of the twill structure.

Dress fabric using five-end satin and Han damask for alternate stripes. The linen and silk warps were separately tensioned and a pronounced ripple is produced by the contrast of these different materials. A loomstate sample is shown on the right. Warp: Satin: Linen 25 lea, 22.5 epcm. Han damask: Alternate ends silk noil 20 Nm and tussah silk 68/2 Nm, 10.8 epcm. Weft: Tussah silk 34 ppi (13.4 ppcm). In this case the pleated effect results from the contraction of the tussah weft, because although this yarn is not high-twist it is slightly unbalanced and the strong natural shrinkage of tussah fibre is also helpful.

A wool scarf with narrow stripes of 1/3 and 3/1 broken twill. Warp: Lambswool 12.5 Nm, 36 epi. Weft: High-twist woollen merino 14.5 Nm, 28 ppi. The shrinkage of the high-twist weft yarn creates an effect of soft pleating.

This silk scarf has stripes of four-end broken twill and Han damask, giving a smooth surface on one face and a slightly textured effect on the other. A customer remarked on this combination of smooth and textured surfaces, saying that it was good to have a silk scarf that did not easily slip off. There is some contrast between the different types of silk because tussah shrinks more strongly than cultivated silk, but this gives only a slight ripple to the pleating. Warp: Broken twill stripes: Spun silk 40/2 Nm, 60 epi; Han damask stripes: alternate ends of silk noil 20 Nm and tussah 68/2 Nm, 36 epi. Weft: Tussah silk 68/2 Nm, 34 ppi.

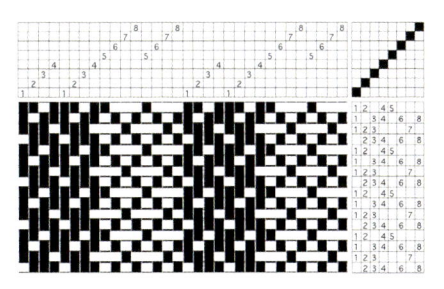

Draft showing stripes of 3/1 broken twill and Han damask.

CHAPTER 5: Fold Here

Samples of soft pleating in alternating float weaves with thick and thin yarns running warpways. Warp: Spun silk 60/2 Nm × 3 (thick yarn), and spun silk 60/2 Nm (thin yarn), 48 epi. Weft: Silk tram 200/220 denier, 40 ppi.

Left: Han damask. Right: Five-span alternating float weave.

This sample shows the two faces of a five-span float weave, woven with thick and thin weft yarns. Warp: High-twist woollen merino 14.5 Nm, 32 epi. Weft: Jacob wool 1 Nm (float picks) and high-twist woollen merino 14.5 Nm (plain picks), 16 ppi. The central section shows how narrow stripes of the two faces produce a ribbed effect.

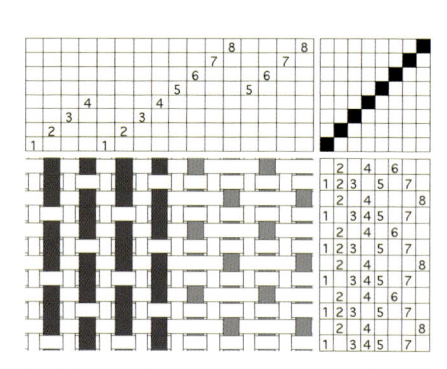

Draft for Han damask, emphasizing the thicker float ends.

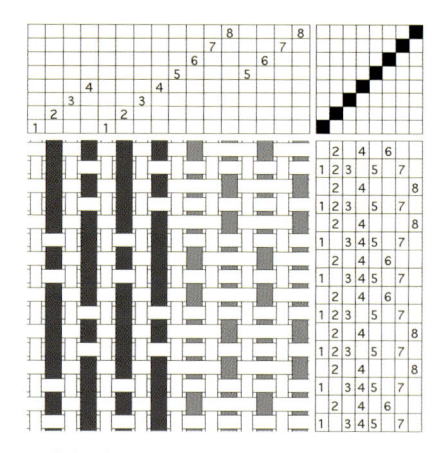

Draft for five-span alternating float weave.

In the pieces shown on the previous page all the yarns in the Han damask stripes are of roughly similar weight, but a very different effect is produced if the thickness of the yarn is varied. The Miao wedding blankets described in Chapter 4 are woven using thick rags for the floating picks and a fine yarn for the plain weave picks (though these fabrics use five-span floats rather than the three-span floats of the Han damask). Alternating float weaves that use thick and thin yarns in this way have a relatively smooth surface on one side of the cloth and a slightly textured surface on the other. Narrow stripes of the warp- and weft-float faces of the cloth provide another variation on the ribbed or pleated effect, which works well over many weights and qualities of fabric. The same principle can also be used with the thick and thin alternation in the warp rather than the weft. Although a single thick yarn can be used for the thick ends or picks it also works well to use multiple strands of a finer yarn and this has the added advantage that colours can be mixed in the 'thick' yarn.

Because these alternating float weaves require only three shafts and one of these is a plain weave intersection, it is possible to obtain a ribbed effect on only four shafts. With a suitable choice of yarns a narrow stripe of the float weave will curl into a rib even when combined only with plain weave stripes and this effect can be strong enough to pull in the edges of the plain weave stripes so that there is an effect of soft pleating on both sides. This echoes the structure of the courgette flower shown in Chapter 1. Not surprisingly such pleating does not form quite so easily as when using both faces of Han damask but is a useful option for anyone working on only four shafts. The plain weave stripes need to be fairly soft and flexible – with firmer cloth the effect tends to become a series of Han damask ridges projecting from a flat surface.

A pleated effect produced with stripes of Han damask and plain weave. Warp: Han damask stripes: Spun silk 60/2 Nm × 3 (float ends) and spun silk 60/2 Nm (plain weave ends). Plain weave stripes: Spun silk 60/2 Nm. Sett: 20 epcm. Weft: Spun silk 120/2 Nm, 20 ppcm.

Warp-float face showing the Han damask stripes.

Reverse of the cloth, showing the plain weave stripes.

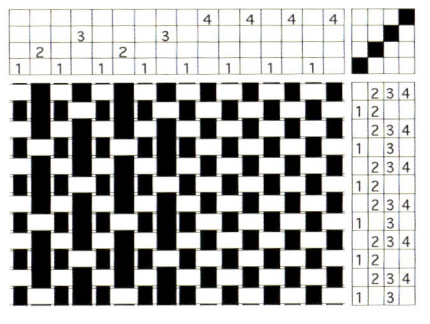

Four-shaft draft for Han damask and plain weave.

This silk and linen scarf has a striped effect created by the reversal of the pleats. The weft colour remains the same throughout so this is a 'structural' stripe that disappears when the fabric is stretched to its full width. Warp: Linen 77 lea, 72 epi and spun silk 60/2 Nm, 54 epi. Weft: Spun silk 210/2 Nm, 48 ppi.

A ribbed or pleated effect offers plenty of scope for variation, most obviously by using different colours for alternate stripes so the fabric will be double sided. Once two colours are in place another easy variation is to reverse the structure, bringing the 'back' colour to the face. This will produce a stripe running across the fabric, even if the weft colour remains the same, though a change of weft colour could also be used at this point to further vary the effect.

All the examples shown so far have the ribbing or pleating running either entirely down the warp or across it but an interesting further development is to combine the two. Wendy Morris has designed a piece with a chequerboard arrangement of warpways and weftways pleats, producing a striking effect that relies on a similar principle to ribbed entrelac knitting. As the opposing blocks of pleats pull against one another attractive curves emerge within the fabric, so this piece is illustrated in Chapter 8.

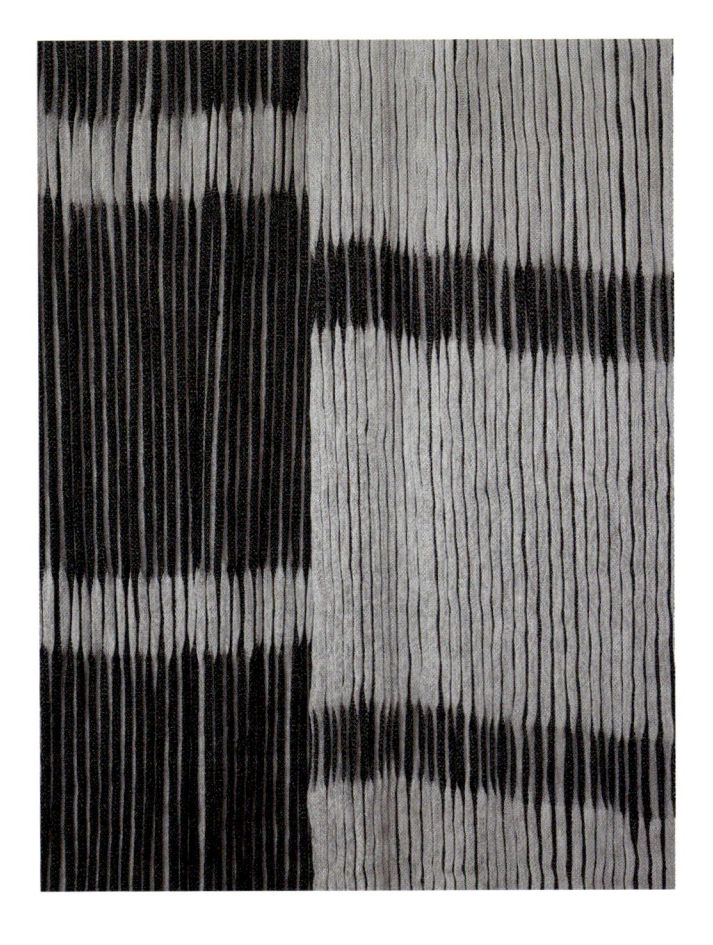

CHAPTER 5: Fold Here

'Saimaa' scarf fabrics by Andreas Möller, woven on a wide loom to create reversing weftways pleats that will run lengthways when worn as a scarf. Andreas also outlines the edges of the pleats with narrow stripes of weft cord and 1/3 twill in contrasting colours so that gentle curves emerge when the fabric is cut from the loom and wet finished. The structure creates an interesting texture even when there is a less bold use of colour, as in the white and grey colourway. (Photos: Andreas Möller)

See Andreas' project in *Vävmagasinet* for the instructions for this scarf.

An interesting article by Loescher (see Online Resources) describes another way of using the warp- and weft-float faces of a fabric to create pleats. These pleats lap over one another, rather in the style of knife pleats but with a softly rounded effect rather than a sharp edge. These are clearly relying on the same principles as the soft pleats made with warp-float and weft-float twill stripes, but using a gradual transition from warp-float to weft-float, for example a gradation of six-end twills – 1/5, 2/4, 3/3, 4/2 and 5/1. This is a nice idea but does need rather a lot of shafts, so for many handweavers it would be easier to carry out weftways.

Cords

In traditional Bedford cord the same yarn is used for both weaving and floating picks, with the weft pick that weaves into one cord floating under the next. The natural relaxation of the floats during wet finishing contrasted with the firm structure of the surface combine to create a corded structure. Depending on the yarn and sett the cloth quality can vary from a firm, faintly ribbed texture to a cloth with large, softly rounded cords, particularly if wadding ends are added to make the cords more prominent. Another way to emphasize the texture is to use high-twist or elastomeric yarns as weft so that the floats contract more strongly. However, if crepe yarns are used in the classic Bedford cord structure they will tend also to disturb the surface of the fabric, giving crinkled rather than smoothly rounded cords, so a modified cord structure can be used with some picks weaving into the cords while others float.

Although cords can give a pronounced rib effect and may have some degree of elasticity, particularly if woven with high-twist or elastomeric yarns, they cannot in themselves produce pleating that can be unfolded, like the warp-float/weft-float structures described above. However they can work exceptionally well in producing fabrics with sharp-edged pleats when combined with plain weave or other 'flat' structures.

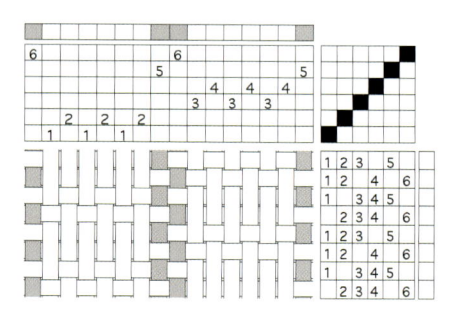

In a traditional Bedford cord all the picks are both weaving and floating.

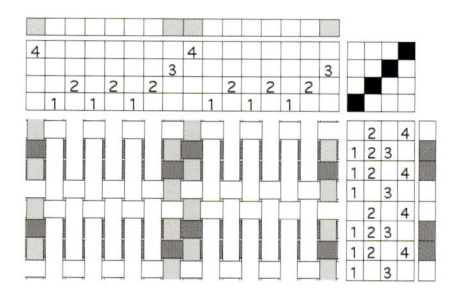

An alternative structure with separate weaving and floating picks allows a normal yarn to be used for the weaving picks and a shrinking yarn, either crepe or elastomeric, for the floating picks (shown in grey).

SHARP-EDGED PLEATS

These require a combination of structures, with flat areas to form the sides of the pleats and a series of 'hinges' to make the fabric fold sharply back and forth. There are several structures that can act as hinges, all relying on floats that form alternately on one side of the fabric and then the other, which will shrink during wet finishing. So the twills, satins and alternating float weaves, described above for soft ribbed effects, can all work in this way, with reversing twills being particularly effective because of the longer float that is created. This reversal also tends to produce a sharper edge, though the visual impression of sharpness can usefully be enhanced through a careful choice of colours shading from dark to light (or muted to bright) to emphasize the apex of the ridge. Cords are another option and are particularly good at creating a really sharp edge when a crepe or elastomeric yarn is used for the float picks. The sides of the pleats can be any structure that will remain flat, with plain weave and 2/2 twill being probably the most useful, though warp-faced compound tabby can also work well.

These combinations of structure can form deep pleats similar in appearance to imposed pleats but with the advantage of being permanently woven in, though a potential problem is achieving an attractive quality of fabric while maintaining sufficient stiffness to sustain the pleating. This is a particular difficulty with a lightweight fabric and I ran into this problem when basing a design on the dragonfly wing and aiming for a light, translucent effect. Fortunately, the pleated structure of the wing already incorporates the design solution to this problem in the form of small crossways struts that reinforce and stiffen the pleats, as illustrated in Chapter 1. It was only necessary to acknowledge that nature had got there first and accept the lesson.

The various structures that can be used for the flat sides of the pleats tend to be suited to different materials. For example, plain weave works particularly well with stiff yarns such as linen or silk/steel, especially when aiming for a delicate effect, but in the case of silk the softness of the material can make it more difficult to achieve enough body to hold the pleat. Of course there is still the option of using struts to support a plain weave fabric, but an attractive alternative is to use other structures such as twill or warp-faced compound tabby to form a slightly thicker fabric that has enough body to sustain the pleating.

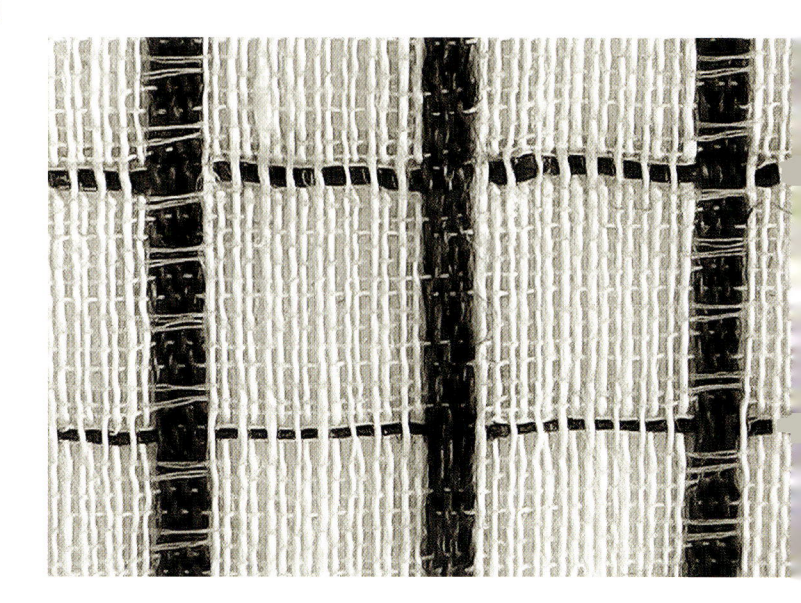

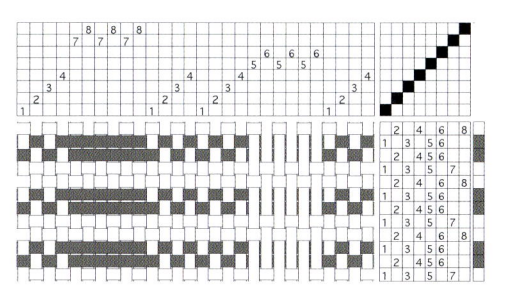

A detail of the pleated fabric in the loomstate, showing how the crepe silk weft floats over one cord and then under the next.

Dragonfly pleat scarf. Warp: Linen 44 lea (pleats), 48 epi, linen 40 lea (cords), 72 epi. Weft: Hard silk 60/66 denier and crepe silk 40/44 denier, S+Z, 48 ppi. Plain weave sides to the pleats are combined with cords that cause the fabric to fold back and forth. The cords are woven with separate plain and floating picks, so that the stable hard silk yarn can be used for the plain picks and the high-twist silk for floating picks that will shrink during wet finishing to form the pleating. Crossways 'struts' of heavier linen are laid in at intervals alongside a plain weave pick of hard silk to stiffen the pleats.

Draft of plain weave combined with reversing cords, using separate plain weave and floating picks (shown in grey).

CHAPTER 5: Fold Here 101

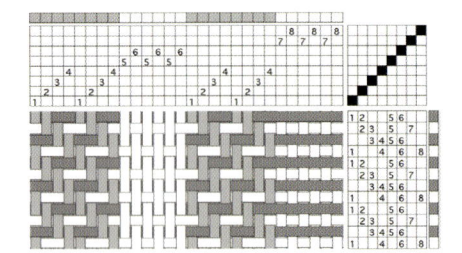

Draft for twill pleats. Picks of crepe silk are shown in grey.

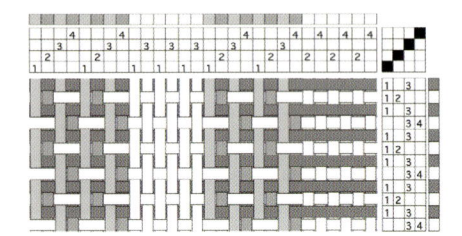

Draft for warp-faced compound tabby pleats. Picks of crepe silk are shown in grey. As the shafts used for this weave can be differently arranged to create the cord weave this structure can be woven on four shafts.

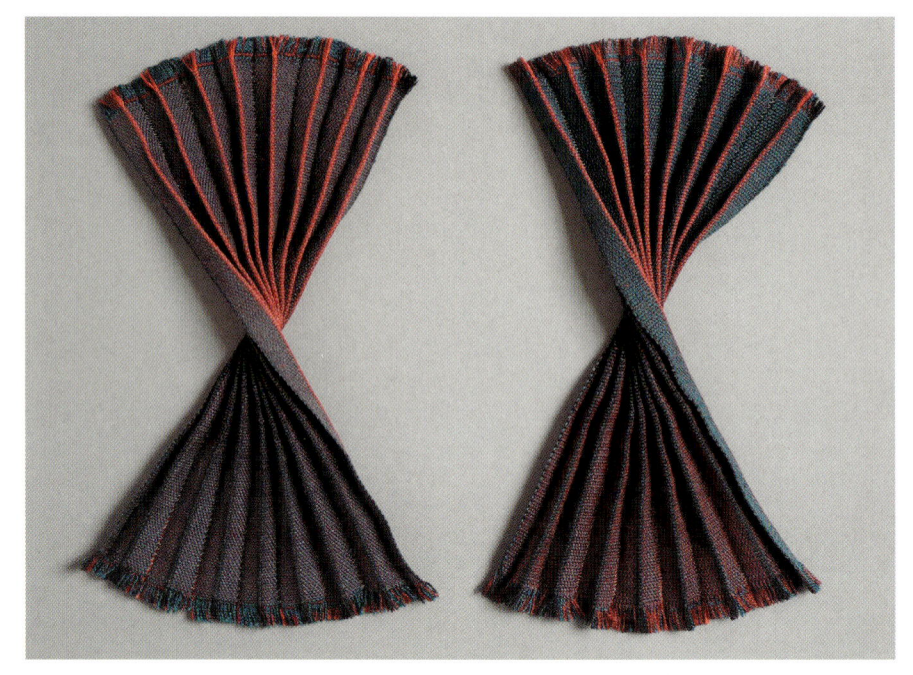

Pleated samples, showing two different flat weaves combined with reversing cords. Warp: Spun silk 60/2 Nm. Pleats: 80 epi, alternate ends of petrol and maroon. Cords: 60 epi, alternately red and black. With alternating colours on the cords, both samples are different on the two sides but the contrast is increased in the case of the warp-faced compound tabby as this structure causes the pleats themselves to be differently coloured on the two sides of the cloth.

Left: Pleats of 2/2 twill. Weft: 52 ppi, with picks of spun silk 60/2 Nm alternating with crepe silk 60/66 denier, S for the float picks.

Right: Pleats of warp-faced compound tabby. Weft: 48 ppi, with picks of spun silk 60/2 Nm × 2 alternating with crepe silk 60/66 denier, S for the float picks.

Accordion Pleats

This simple style of pleating works extremely well for both scarves and garments and examples are shown here using various different combinations of yarns and structure. If 2/2 twill is used for the sides of the pleats then this part of the cloth will be the same on both sides (apart from a subtle difference that could arise from twist twill interactions) though it is still easy to produce a double-sided fabric by alternating the colours on the 'hinges' that form the edges of the pleats. However, the pleats themselves can also be different on the two sides if alternate colours are used in the warp together with a double-sided weave, such as plain weave with thick and thin wefts, or warp-faced compound tabby.

When using high-twist wefts to create pleating it is advisable to use the *same* direction of twist as has been used for the warp yarn as this reduces curling at the corners of the fabric. If this still causes problems then using both S and Z twist wound together on the same bobbin can be a solution. This can also be a useful strategy if a high-twist yarn creates any unwanted texture on the sides of the pleats, which may happen with very high-twist yarns. In parts of the cloth where the crepe yarn is held down firmly by the weave the opposing twists will 'fight' and so be prevented from forming any texture, but where they are free to float their capacity for contraction will be unimpaired.

Clearly there are many ways of creating a woven pleat so it is worth keeping your options open and experimenting with different combinations of material and structure before making a final decision. There are also endless possibilities for varying the colour of both the sides and edges of the pleats.

A self-pleating silk shawl by Wendy Morris, woven in a combination of straight and point twill. This designer uses various different structures for her pleated fabrics, with flat weaves such as plain weave, 2/2 twill or crepe weave for the sides of the pleats and with warp-float and weft-float point twills to create the peaks and troughs. (Photo: Wendy Morris)

Detail of self-pleating shawl by Wendy Morris. (Photo: Wendy Morris)

This scarf uses linen in plain weave for the sides of the pleats, while the reversing cords are of silk. All the yarn is run from one beam. During wet finishing the silk relaxes more than the linen, giving a rippled effect to the pleats. Contrasting colours on the sides of the pleats emphasize the three-dimensional effect while alternating colours on the cords create a double-sided fabric. Warp: Linen 40 and 44 lea (pleats), 48 epi, spun silk 60/2 Nm (cords), 72 epi. Weft: Crepe silk 40/44 denier, S+Z wound together (float picks); hard silk 60/66 denier (plain picks) with extra picks of linen as 'struts', 48 ppi.

CHAPTER 5: Fold Here 103

A scarf constructed with knife pleats by Wendy Morris. (Photo: Wendy Morris)

Different Styles of Pleating

Other styles of pleating can be constructed on the same principle with different arrangements of hinges and flat areas. For knife pleats, alternate sides of the pleats need to be of different widths so that the pleats can lie flat, but the alternation of warp-float and weft-float hinges remains the same as for accordion pleats. However, to produce box pleats the sequence of hinges also needs to change so that two warp-float stripes are followed by two weft-float stripes. It is well worth experimenting with paper models to try different proportions of folds before embarking on woven samples – Paul Jackson's books on folding and pleating are extremely helpful.

PLAYING ABOUT WITH PLEATS

Inserting Extra Folds

It was weaving pleated scarves in linen that first gave me the idea of smaller pieces to be worn like jewellery but, although linen is an excellent yarn for some shapes, a silk/steel yarn manufactured by the Italian firm Loro Piana has proved even better for many pieces. It has intermediate properties between textiles and wire, being relatively soft and flexible but having the 'memory' of wire. This has meant that pieces with pleats created through yarn and structure can be given additional folds to create chevron effects running across the original pleats.

I have experimented with various arrangements of the chevron effect, folding some pieces into double layers and twisting others to form Möbius strips and trefoil knots. All have been woven as a single layer of fabric and joined at the selvedges; in principle they could be woven as tubes but this seems unnecessarily complicated when an inconspicuous join is so easy to make. If the cord stripes alternate between a bright and a dark colour and the dark colour is used for the selvedges, then these can be sewn together to closely resemble the dark cords on the rest of the piece.

If contrasting colours are used also on alternate sides of the pleats this works well in emphasizing the pleated effect. Although these pieces can be woven on a minimum of six shafts it is worth spreading the warp that forms the sides of the pleats on to four shafts even if using plain weave – this avoids crowding of the heddles on densely set pieces and also leaves open the option of weaving other structures such as twill or warp-faced compound tabby.

The Möbius strip is a mathematical curiosity that is created by giving a strip a half turn before joining the ends together, forming a structure with only one side and only one edge. It has become a popular form in textiles, especially in knitting where it can be produced without a join, and it also works nicely in woven textiles, but in this case the edges do need to be joined. Using a strip that is pleated complicates the situation a little because the half turn means that one side of a pleat must be dropped in order to keep the pleating consistent. This can raise some interesting problems in terms of arranging colours, which will be discussed in Chapter 10.

Another construction method for jewellery is to assemble pieces from smaller sections of pleated fabric to make more complex shapes. I have experimented with this technique using various numbers of sections but have generally found that assemblages of three sections are the most flattering to wear, particularly for small items such as bracelets.

This group of neckpieces shows how the silk/steel yarn can be folded to give a chevron effect. Warp: Silk/steel 82/2 Nm (pleats) and spun silk 60/2 Nm (cords). Weft: Crepe silk (float picks) and linen (plain picks).

This chevron neckpiece is folded over to form a double layer. Warp: Silk/steel 82/2 Nm (pleats) and spun silk 60/2 Nm (cords). Weft: Crepe silk and linen.

The pleated fabric can be given a half turn to form a Möbius neckpiece. Warp: Silk/steel 82/2 Nm (pleats) and spun silk 60/2 Nm (cords). Weft: Crepe silk and linen.

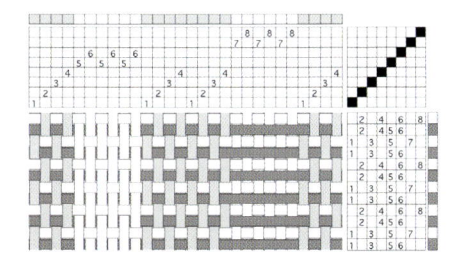

Although a weave draft similar to that for the dragonfly pleat scarf can be used for jewellery, an alternative structure is useful for making a stiffer, firmer fabric. Jewellery pieces do not need to be as soft as scarves and there is an advantage in making a more robust fabric that will resist crushing. The cord weave is combined with half hopsack, with a stiff yarn such as linen or paper for the plain picks and a high-twist yarn for the floating picks.

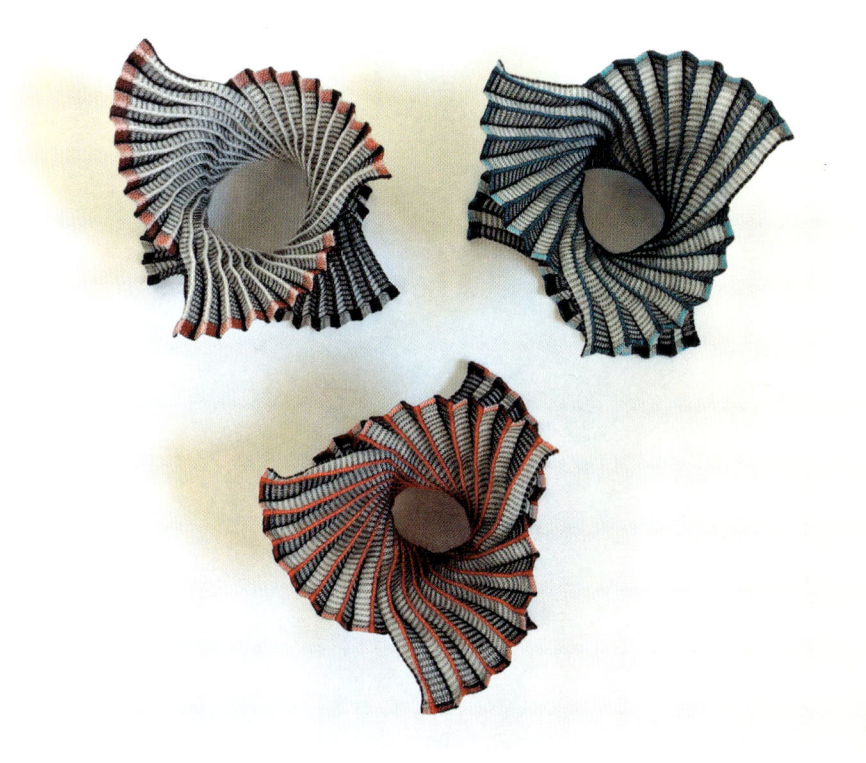

These triple spiral bracelets are assembled from offset sections of pleated fabric. Warp: Silk/steel 82/2 Nm (pleats) and spun silk 60/2 Nm (cords). Weft: Crepe silk and polyester reflective yarn.

CHAPTER 5: Fold Here

WOVEN ORIGAMI

Experimenting with multiple folds gave some of my neckpieces rather an 'origami' look, and my interest in the origami tradition was further piqued when I realized that diagonal folds could be produced by relying solely on vertically arranged mountain and valley folds, as this made it possible to use a loom with relatively few shafts. Weavers with more shafts or thread-control looms could obviously arrange for diagonal pleats to be woven in, which would give greater direct control of the structure. However, it is extremely interesting, especially to a former biologist like myself, to simply 'seed' the situation with a limited number of stress lines and then let natural forces play themselves out. This echoes the situation in plant leaves where certain initial stress lines cause complex folds to emerge spontaneously.

Creating origami effects by such simple means relies on a classic origami fold where a conflict between mountain and valley folds is resolved through V-shaped diagonals, as described in Chapter 1. The fact that the diagonals simply emerge rather than being imposed means that the origami effect can be produced without a metal content to the yarn, though the attractive stiffness of the silk/steel yarn still makes this a useful warp option.

When folding a large piece of paper it is necessary to insert all the vertical and diagonal folds (and make all the vertical folds into universal folds) before the pleating can begin and this can take some time. But when weaving, once the mountain and valley folds have been woven in, the diagonal folds that resolve the structure will emerge spontaneously during wet finishing. I explained this recently to a visitor at an open studio, who turned out to be an engineer – he promptly replied: 'so you cheat at origami!' However, although large pieces of paper are time-consuming to fold, paper folding carried out on a very small scale, using just a few pleats, can be done quite quickly and is helpful in making decisions about the size and placement of folds before tackling a woven piece. Once again I would recommend Paul Jackson's excellent books on folding.

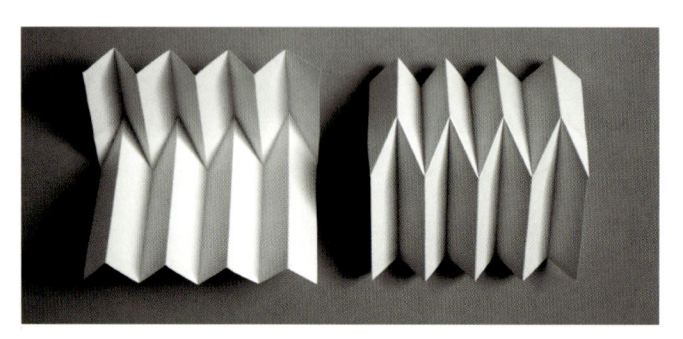

Origami V-folds shown from both sides. Diagonal folds provide a resolution of a conflict created by a reversal of the mountain and valley folds that is combined with a short section where all the vertical folds are mountain folds (left) or all are valley folds, when viewed from the other side (right).

Using just a few pleats makes it quick and easy to form origami V-folds. The diagonal creases that can be formed in this way are not very strongly defined so this will only work well over a few pleats, maybe four or five, depending on the thickness of the paper.

Start by folding accordion pleats and then make all the folds universal folds so they are easy to bend either way.

Fold the whole group of pleats at an angle and press firmly to create diagonal folds.

Open out the pleats and reverse the mountain and valley folds on one half of the paper, using the diagonal folds to allow the paper to fold neatly into place without crumpling. This will result in there being a short section where all the folds are mountain folds on one side (and therefore valley folds on the other). It tends to be easier to make the diagonal folds when working from the valley fold side.

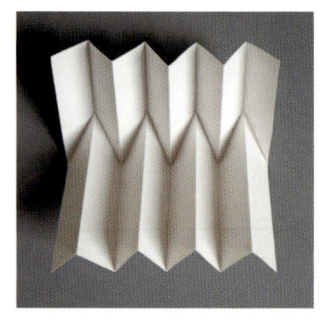

The finished origami V-folds, showing the side with overlapping mountain folds.

Self-folding origami neckpiece. An unfinished piece of fabric is shown in the foreground. Warp: Silk/steel and spun silk. Weft: Crepe silk and paper.

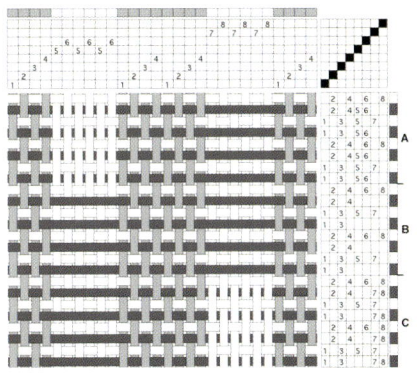

This origami draft has one reversal of the mountain and valley folds and shows the side of the fabric where there is an overlap of valley folds.

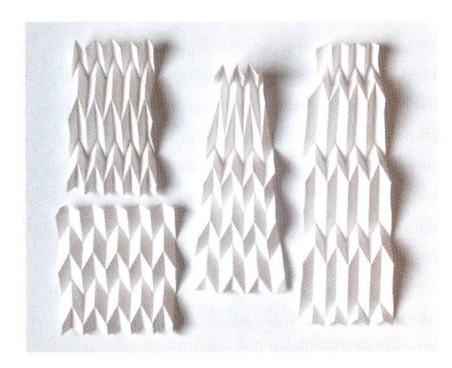

An origami fabric on the loom, showing the cords that will produce reversals of the mountain and valley folds.

These paper folds show different possible placements of reversals for more complex designs. The angles of the diagonals can be varied for more or less of a three-dimensional effect. When weaving, the size of these angles will depend on the *length* of fabric that is woven with all folds as mountains or all folds as valleys.

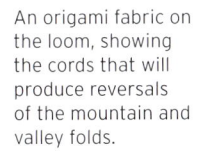

CHAPTER 5: Fold Here

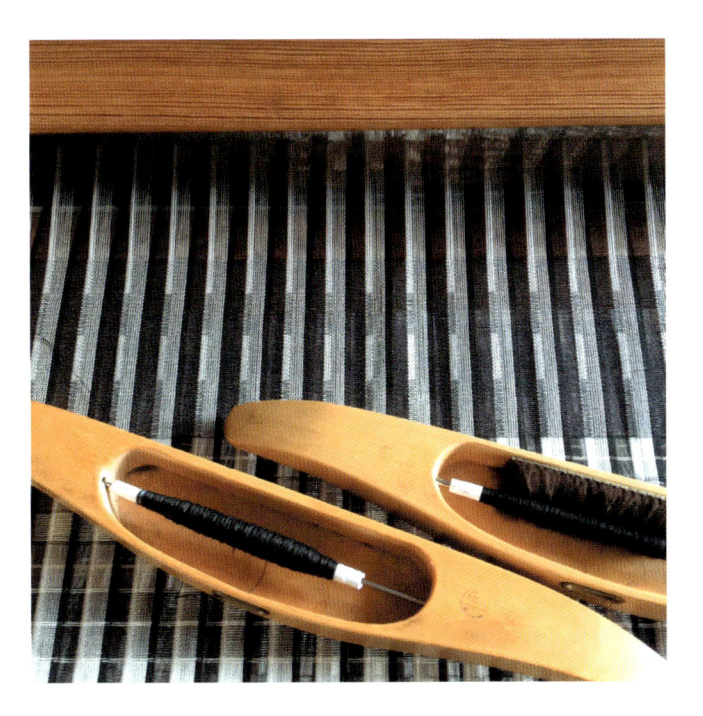

An origami neckpiece with several reversals. Warp: Silk/steel and spun silk. Weft: Crepe silk and paper.

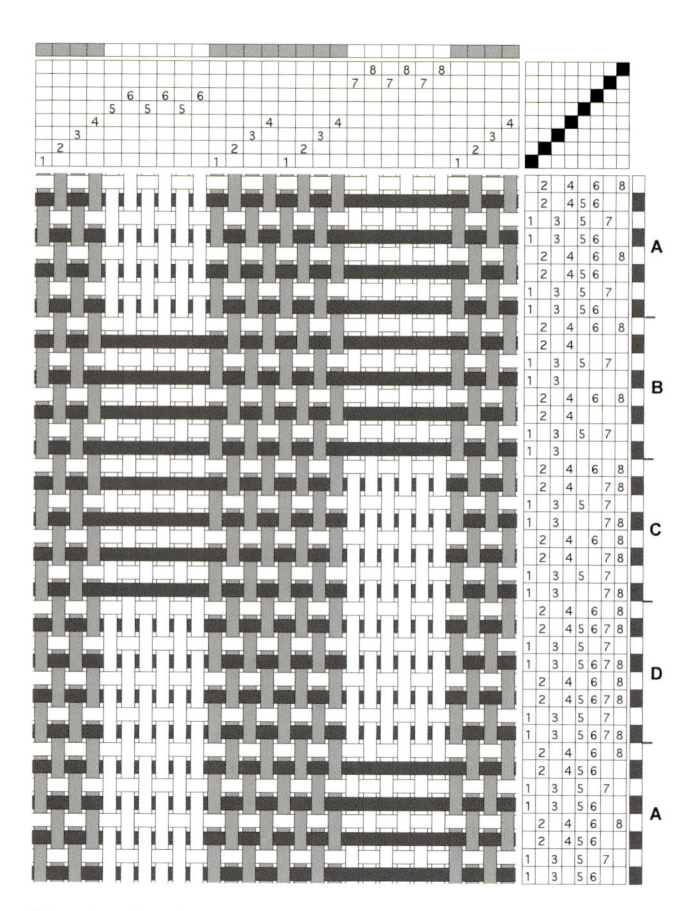

This origami draft has two reversals. Near the top of the draft there is an overlap of valley folds, and this is followed, lower down, by an overlap of mountain folds. Bending back and forth in this way will keep the overall fabric within a single plane. Using the same type of reversal repeatedly or changing the angle will cause the piece to curve, so there is plenty of scope for making differently shaped pieces.

Stretch Properties of Pleated and Origami Jewellery

An important issue with textiles that are intended as jewellery is how they are to be fastened. Conventional jewellery findings often do not work well as they can be heavy and prone to distorting the textile. Working with pleating avoids this problem as pieces can be made to stretch over the head or hand. For neckpieces this means that pleats need to be fairly deep so that the piece will give a reasonable length when expanded to stretch over the head but still pleat up to fit snuggly around the neck. With bracelets only a limited amount of stretch is necessary for them to slip over the hand, so that pleat widths can vary from wide pleats that tend to work well for origami pieces to narrow pleats that are more suitable for multiple-section pieces like the triple spiral bracelets.

ORIGAMI AS INSPIRATION

Origami has proved inspirational to many designers in different media, with diverse applications and on different scales. Over several decades, the origami artist Paul Jackson has been an influential teacher with his 'Sheet to Form' workshops directed at students in disciplines ranging from jewellery, ceramics and product design through to engineering and architecture. His books are an excellent source of information on the basic principles of folding and provide examples of many different applications.

The technique described here produces self-folding woven origami by using the V-fold and working with a limited number of shafts, but many other approaches are possible depending on the equipment available and the choice of origami fold. Reiko Sudo and Hiroko Suwa have designed a woven origami fabric in polyester, 'Polygami', for the Nuno Corporation, while Samira Boon works on a much larger scale, using carefully arranged combinations of different materials to produce dramatic self-folding origami structures for use in architecture. A quite different approach can be seen in the work of Susie Taylor who has developed a technique with differently tensioned sections of warp to form projections from the surface of the cloth, which can then be folded against the fabric. She describes her technique in an article, 'Woven Origami', while her website also includes a video that provides a vivid demonstration of the process. With such diverse approaches to working with woven folds it is clear that there is much still to be explored in this area. Both the 'natural' origami of leaves and insects' wings and the origami tradition itself are full of ideas to be drawn upon and developed – so keep looking and keep folding!

CHAPTER 6

Light Work

> Watching a *jamdani* weaver patiently inserting the additional weft threads is an impressive experience today; it is not difficult to imagine why earlier writers reached such heights of poetry and hyperbole in describing the human fabrication of 'woven air'.
>
> Sonia Ashmore, *Muslin*

When designing fabrics with a high level of translucency there are really two aspects to keep in mind – being light and looking light. A cloth woven from very fine yarn in an open sett will certainly be light in substance and will also look light, perhaps even transparent. But with lightweight fabrics there is also the possibility of playing off open areas of cloth with denser ones, and in this way visually emphasizing the translucency or transparency of the fabric as a whole. The various methods of producing such delicate effects offer different advantages and fabric qualities.

SIMPLE SOLUTIONS

Open Sett

The simplest approach is to use the most stable of the basic weaves – plain weave – combined with a fine yarn and an open sett. This combination can produce good levels of translucency and even transparency, as in the very fine cotton muslins woven in India and Bangladesh that have been described as 'woven air'. Denser areas of inlay in such fabrics, as in the *jamdani* muslins, only serve to emphasize the adjacent transparency of the cloth. The main issue is stability, because as the sett is opened up the transparency of a fabric will be increased but so also will the risk of creating an unstable, sleazy cloth where threads can easily become displaced. The character of the yarn is highly influential and the fine unmercerized cotton singles that have traditionally been used for muslins can give good stability in very open setts. When working with other materials the specific quality of the yarn is important; for example, the stiffness of hard silk often helps to keep it in place more reliably than degummed silk. But even after degumming silks do vary, with soft, glossy cultivated silk yarns producing a more unstable cloth than tussah silk yarns, which tend to have more 'tooth'. Linen yarns, particularly singles, often work well in an open sett because although the fibre is quite smooth, the yarns are slightly slubby and irregular.

Yarn twist also exerts an influence on cloth quality so the fairly hard twist of voile yarns gives good stability in a relatively open fabric. Beyond a certain amount of twist yarns will begin to produce a crepe or crepon effect, especially in very open weaves, but provided that such textures are acceptable for a particular design, these fabrics can still be light and translucent if the yarns are fine enough.

'Dandelions'. Delicately inlayed motifs enhance the sense of 'woven air' in this fabric by Rezia Wahid. Egyptian cotton, silk organzine and spun silk. (Photo: David Westwood) A further example of Rezia Wahid's work can be seen in Chapter 3.

This scarf has alternate ends of white linen and a very fine black hard silk that is also used as weft, creating a light grey fabric with a slight shimmer. The combination of linen and stiff hard silk in an open sett creates a delicate, transparent but reasonably stable fabric. Although the silk weft can easily be slightly displaced locally this is not severe enough to seriously threaten the overall stability. The stiffness of the yarns also means that for a piece that looks so delicate, the fabric has a surprising amount of body. (Designer unknown)

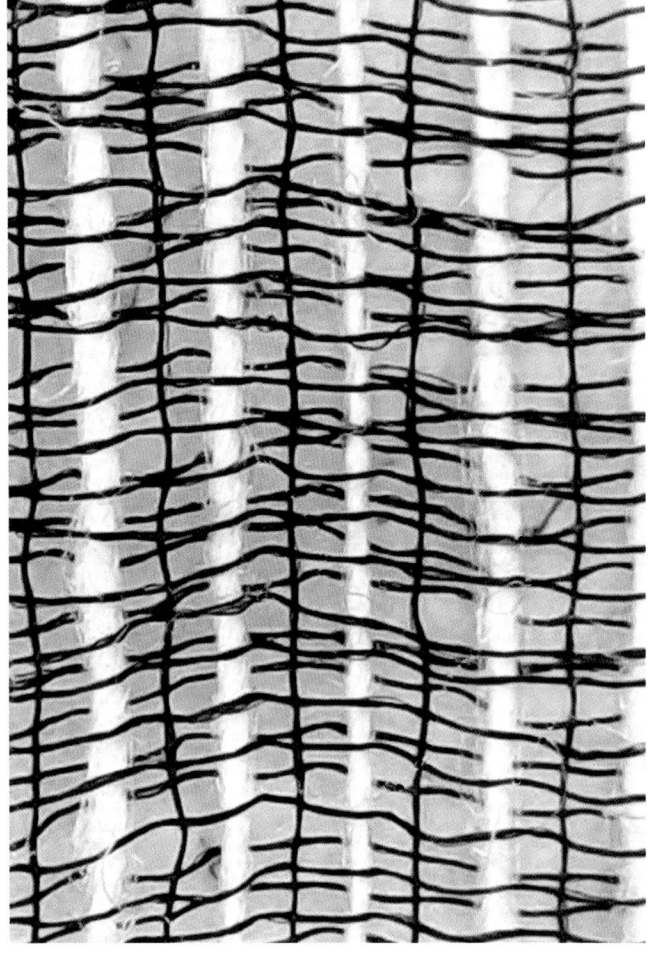

A detail of the scarf in linen and hard silk.

Samples of linen with very open setts. The right half of the warp for both samples is linen 44 lea, while the left half is linen 66 lea, both set at 22 epi.

Right-hand sample: Weft: Linen 44 lea, 22 ppi. Left-hand sample: Weft: 60 lea, 22 ppi. With the 44 lea yarn in both warp and weft, the sett of 22 epi/ppi (42 per cent of maximum sett as calculated using the Ashenhurst formula) is just about stable enough for practical use – threads can be displaced but fall back into position fairly well if the fabric is gently pulled on the bias. However, with the combination of 66 and 60 lea (percentage setts of 34 per cent and 36 per cent respectively), stability is really breaking down – threads are easily displaced and cannot readily be persuaded back into position. Setts of 26–28 epi/ppi would probably be better for these yarns, giving setts of 40–43 per cent for 66 lea and 42–46 per cent for 60 lea.

CHAPTER 6: Light Work

Cramming and Spacing

This is a classic strategy of playing density off against translucency, where fine, openly set areas of fabric are contrasted with denser stripes. Although this is a simple technique it is highly effective in conveying an overall impression of delicacy and a particularly light and airy effect results from leaving definite gaps in the fabric. These gaps also clearly reveal the character of the weft yarn so textured or overtwisted yarns can be particularly effective.

An interesting aspect of this technique is that a crammed and spaced fabric may convey a greater sense of translucency than a fabric that has even spacing, even if both have the same average sett. I noticed this when making such a comparison as part of an experiment to test whether natural pleating might have been used in ancient Egypt. Although both arrangements had the same average sett and developed similar pleating, the crammed and spaced fabric gave a greater *impression* of translucency than the evenly spaced one. This was an interesting result in relation to my investigation, given that the garments shown in many Egyptian paintings appear highly translucent, even transparent and that the method of spacing the warp in ancient Egypt tended to produce a somewhat crammed and spaced effect (*see* the Bibliography for details of my article about this work).

This crammed and spaced fabric by Rita Beales is woven in her own handspun linen. The weft is quite highly twisted causing it to crinkle attractively in the spaced areas. (Crafts Study Centre, University for the Creative Arts. T.81.38. Photo: David Westwood)

SHEER STABILITY

Moving beyond plain weave there are several structural options for achieving openness, and some of these also have the potential to give high levels of stability. Gauze offers the most extreme solution since it is possible to make exceptionally stable fabrics that are translucent or even transparent, but traditional lace weaves can also be effective in creating open but stable fabrics and often work well played off against areas of plain weave.

Gauze

In comparison with other techniques that produce lightweight, translucent fabrics, gauze offers perhaps the most flexibility of design. The stability given by the crossed-warp mechanism allows a very wide variety of materials and setts to be used, while still achieving a cohesive fabric. Cloth qualities can range from translucent, or even transparent, fabrics suitable for window treatments to scarves that look delicate but are robust enough to be practical.

This unusual combination of delicacy and robustness comes from the ability of the gauze structure to be both stable and flexible. With most weaves, if a thread catches on something rough so that a loop is pulled out of the fabric, it is quite difficult to get it back into place. In contrast, if a loop of weft is pulled out of a gauze weave it is generally only necessary to pull the fabric firmly across its width to get the loose weft thread back into place. Putting tension on the weft causes the crossed threads of the gauze units to 'open up' so the weft thread can slip into its correct position. As far as the warp is concerned, the tight crossing of the threads means that they are not usually vulnerable to displacement. Instructions for setting up gauze are given in Chapter 3.

However, stability in the obvious sense of avoiding sleaziness is not the only issue when working with these structures. Another perhaps unexpected way in which yarns can become displaced in these open weaves depends partly on their stiffness and partly on their levels of twist. Perfectly balanced yarns will generally stay in place, particularly if they are fairly flexible, but stiffer, unbalanced yarns may move during wet finishing and create gentle waves in the fabric or possibly even a definite pleated effect. Single yarns obviously fall into this category, but there are also many plied yarns that are not perfectly balanced. Yarns that are stiff, on account of the fibre, the extent of fibre alignment or both, can give surprising results.

An example is shown here of a gauze with a weft of singles linen that moves out of position to produce a wavy effect, and this movement also pushes the warp yarns together at intervals creating a crammed and spaced arrangement. Yarns that are more highly twisted may well form definite pleats as described in Chapter 5. These issues need to be kept in mind – such wavy or pleated effects in gauze or lace weaves can be highly attractive but may not be what you are aiming for.

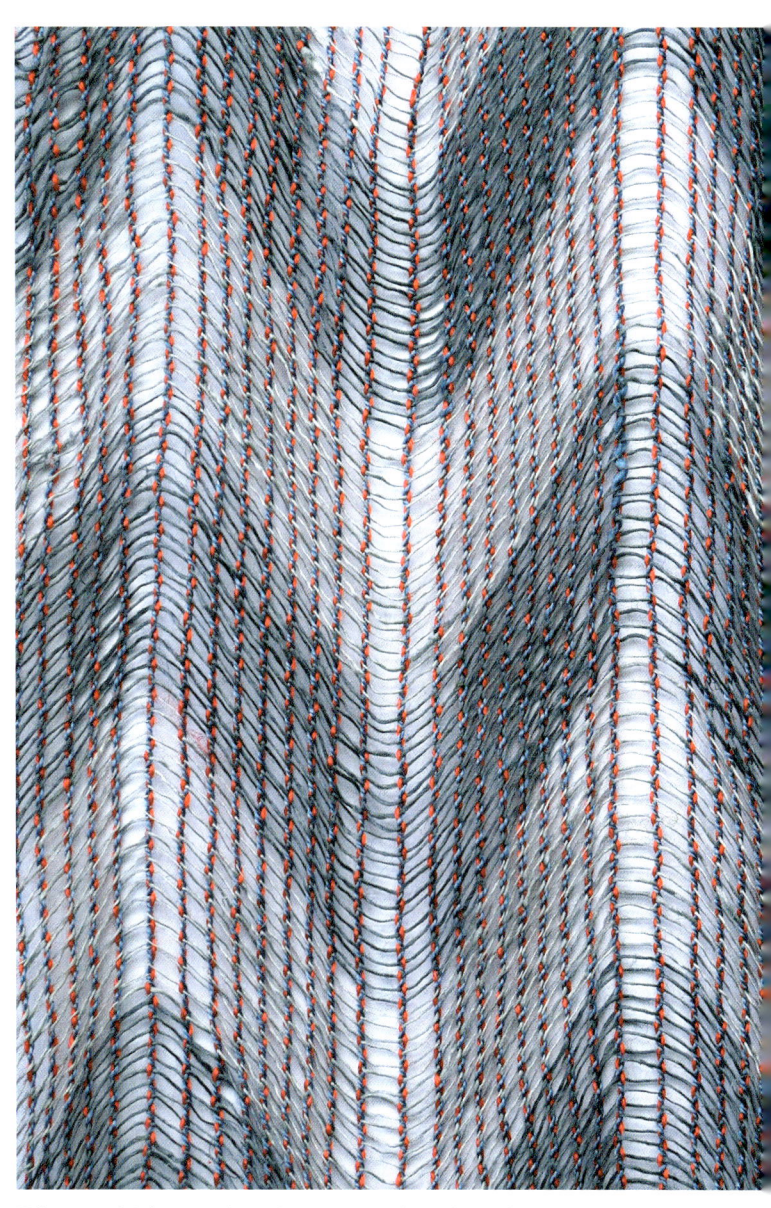

This gauze fabric was set up at an even spacing but spontaneous movements of the linen weft during wet finishing have created a waved effect. This has also pushed the warp threads together at intervals, so that the fabric has organized itself into a crammed and spaced arrangement.

Mock Leno and Swedish Lace

These structures do not offer quite so much stability as gauze since beyond a certain degree of openness or float length they are subject to the same problems of sleaziness as any other weave. However they still offer a good range of weights and translucencies of fabric, particularly for curtains and table linen where long floats are not likely to cause problems. They can also work well for scarves, but here it is necessary to keep an eye on the float length and sett for the sake of practicality.

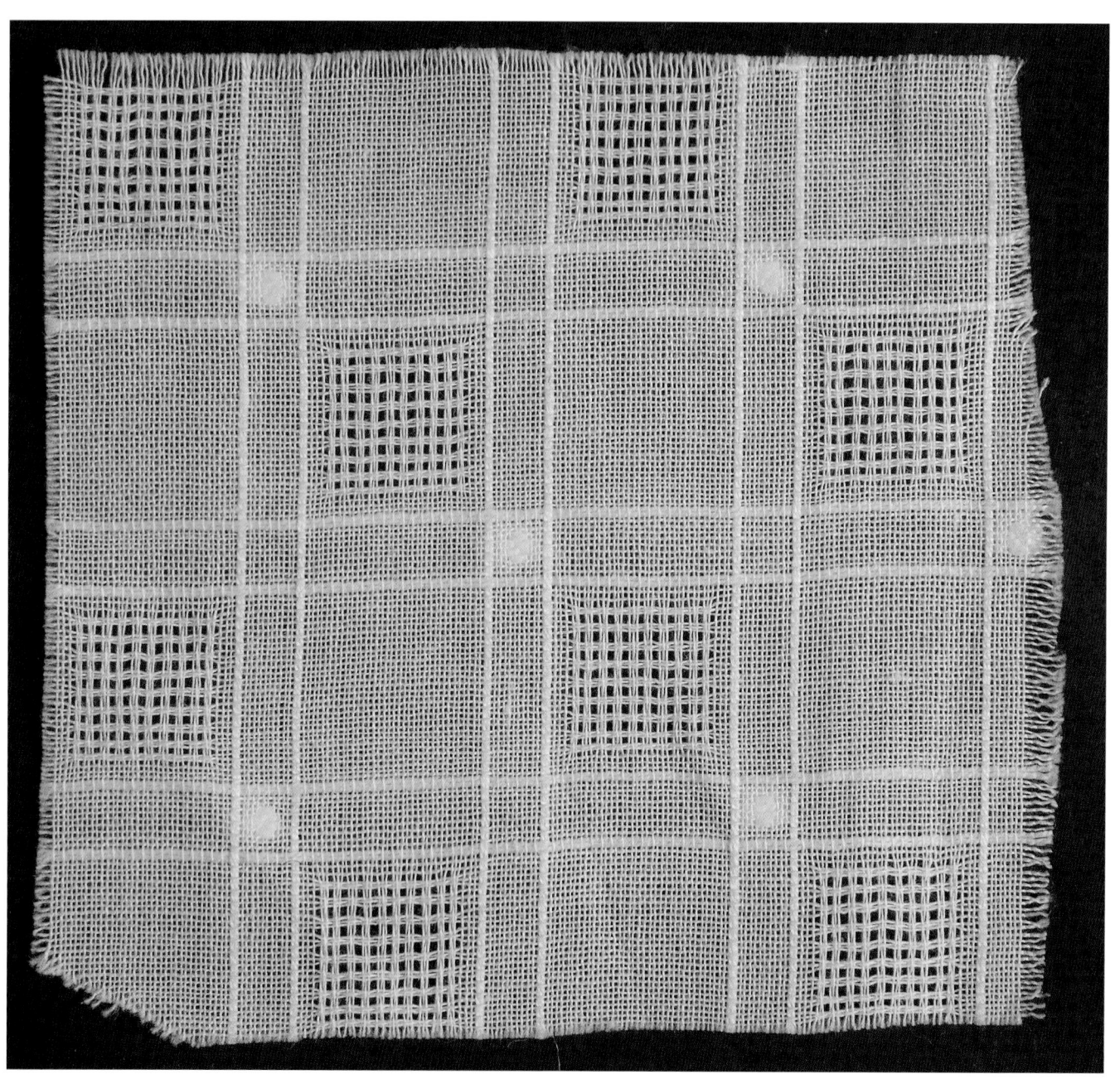

This very fine cotton fabric has blocks of mock leno played off against openly set plain weave, and these areas of varying translucency are emphasized by the contrast with heavier accent threads and dense spots of supplementary weft. The unknown designer has played with almost all the possible techniques for conveying delicacy.

Rita Beales, working from the 1930s to the 1970s, produced exceptionally fine quality table linen in Swedish lace, always handspinning her own linen yarn. This table mat has blocks of Swedish lace played off against plain weave. The contrasting heavier yarn at the border gives the piece robustness while also emphasizing its overall delicacy. The Crafts Study Centre holds a large collection of table linen and fabric lengths by Rita Beales and has published an excellent account of her life and work, written by Patricia Baines. (Crafts Study Centre, University for the Creative Arts. T.81.17. Photo: David Westwood)

OTHER STRUCTURES

Plain weave, gauze and the lace weaves are particularly effective in creating delicate effects but there are other structures that can be used, although it becomes more difficult to maintain the combination of delicacy and stability when longer floats are introduced. A delicate effect will depend a good deal on the fineness and character of the yarn but weaves that include some areas of plain weave in their construction are particularly suitable because of the scope for playing off different densities of fabric against one another. For example Stacey Harvey-Brown has produced some unusual translucent fabrics using adaptations of the honeycomb structure combined with monofilament wefts. Although the plain weave areas in these fabrics are relatively

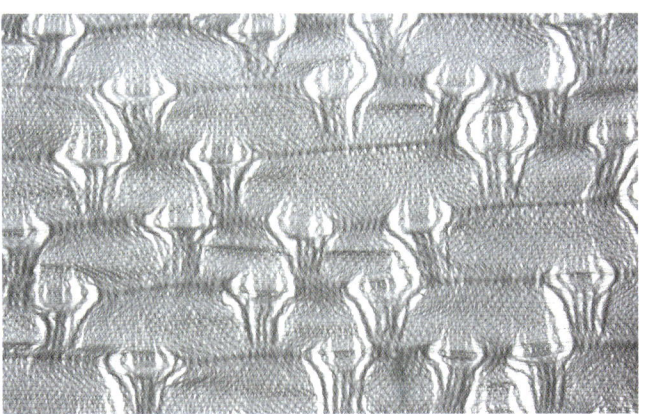

This fabric by Stacey Harvey-Brown is in a variation of honeycomb, with a cotton warp and monofilament weft. (Photo: Stacey Harvey-Brown) *See* Chapter 5 for another example from this series of pieces and refer to Stacey's book *Hybrid Honeycombs* for further details.

CHAPTER 6: Light Work   115

open it is the ability of the yarn and structure to open up gaps in the fabric and the consequent contrast of densities that particularly conveys a sense of transparency. This technique of playing off open and denser areas can be used with many different structures.

LOOKING AT AND LOOKING THROUGH

Variations in density within a cloth can be highly effective in emphasizing the overall translucency of a fabric, but there is another aspect to consider. With a cloth of this type, the experience of viewing the cloth when the light is falling *on* it will be very different from that when looking *through* it. Dense areas that show up as dark and opaque against a translucent or transparent background when they are viewed against the light will appear very different if the fabric is viewed with the light falling on it. This is particularly an issue with fabrics used as curtains because they may be hung in contexts where both situations exist side by side, as when curtains cover window frames or areas of wall as well as the windows themselves. Keeping this in mind makes it possible to design to make the most of both viewing conditions.

Fabrics used for scarves and garments will most often be seen mainly with the light falling *on* them but there still are opportunities for thinking about the aspect of looking through them and how they will be affected by the colour and texture of garments that are visible underneath. A bright colour may give a glowing effect if seen through a dark transparent fabric, while a pale overlay will mute any brightness, an effect that is beautifully shown in many Mughal paintings where people wear brightly coloured garments overlain by white muslin. Often the artist has carefully allowed a little of the bright garment to be seen, perhaps just at the ankles, creating a vivid sense of the transparency of the muslin. A more recent example of playing with

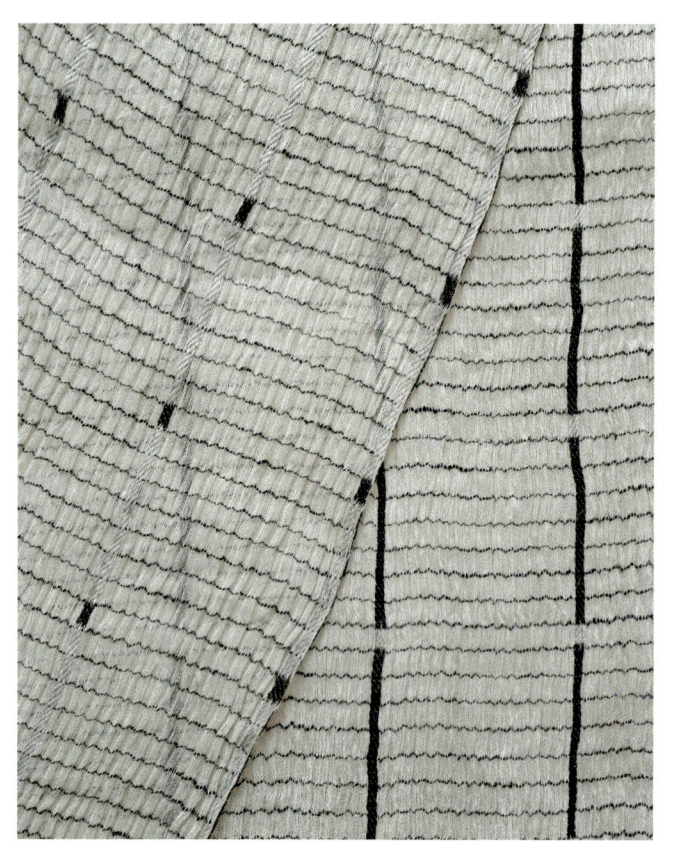

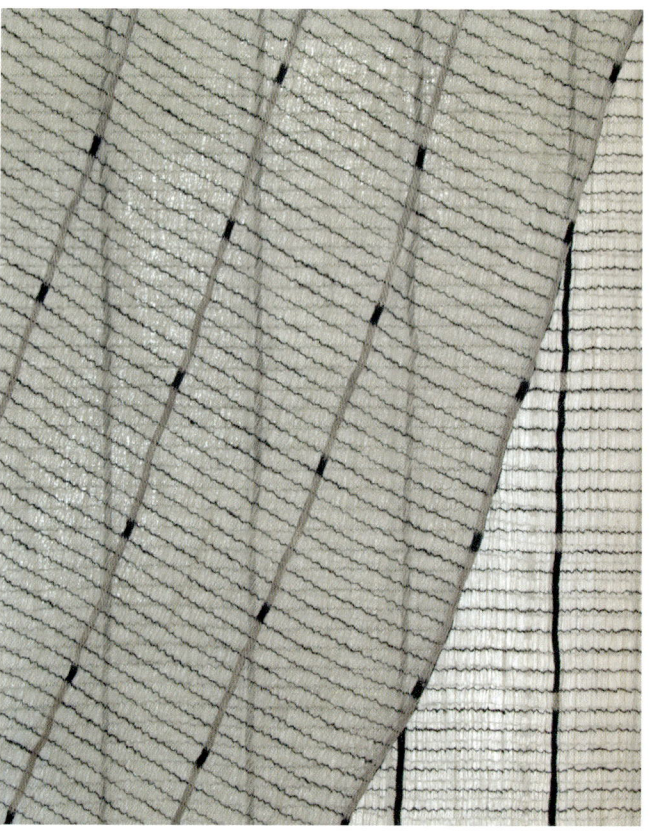

This 'Spot Stripe' fabric combines many of the features that have been discussed so far. Most of the cloth is plain weave with a fine linen warp and crepe silk weft that produces a crepon effect. The cloth is translucent and the presence of occasional picks of a heavier black linen thread and densely packed backed twill stripes do not detract from the lightweight effect, but the impression varies depending on how it is viewed. When light falls on it, as shown on the left, the white side of the backed cloth merges into the background giving a double-sided effect with spots on one face and a broken stripe on the other. Against the light the effect of the piece is different with the dense backed weave stripe being visible throughout.

In this 'Feather Flurries' design by Reiko Sudo, feathers are trapped between two layers of transparent black organza. Chapter 10 includes another view of this fabric.

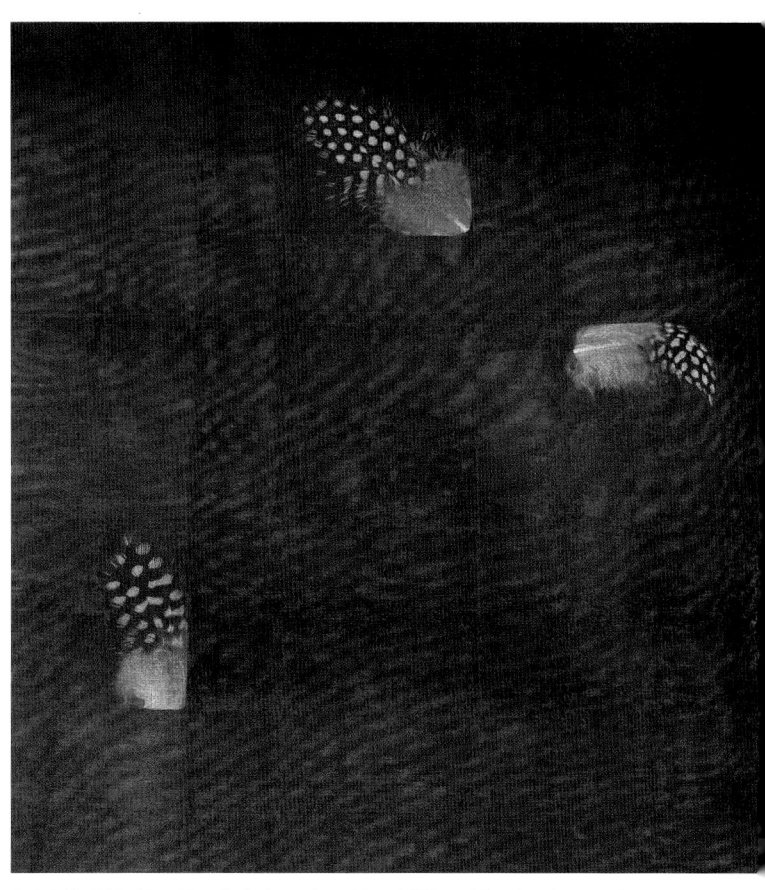

A detail of 'Feather Flurries' shows how the shifting of the two layers of fabric creates beautiful moiré effects.

transparency in this way is an evening dress by Schiaparelli, where a shocking pink Thai silk is muted with an overlay of white semi-transparent organza (V&A, Museum number: T.397-1974). Although such effects of looking through one fabric to another work well when separate pieces of fabric are used together, a further option open to the weaver is to achieve the entire effect within a single piece of cloth by making the translucent cloth one layer of a double cloth.

Another option with double cloth is to create transparent cloths for both layers, because beautiful results can be produced by allowing additional threads to be trapped between the layers or by introducing inclusions. As with variations in fabric density, the presence of such denser elements only serves to emphasize the transparency of the cloth. The construction of two transparent layers also offers the chance for attractive moiré effects to emerge. Although the term is normally associated with the finishing process that creates watered silks, the interference effect that is responsible can occur wherever two openwork grids or patterned surfaces are slightly out of line with one another. Given the flexibility of textiles, the warp and weft threads of the two layers of a double cloth are rarely perfectly aligned so if they are translucent or transparent then moiré effects are likely to emerge (a black and white double cloth that shows this effect is included in Chapter 7).

Many of the remarkable textiles produced by the Nuno Corporation over the last few decades have been recorded in a series of elegant books. One of these is called *Suké Suké*, which in Japanese has several meanings relating to transparency, such as sheer, gossamer, diaphanous or translucent, but it can also mean 'revealing, allowing the other side (inside) to show through.' The book contains beautiful examples of fabrics that have this quality, including a design called 'Feather Flurries' in which double cloth pockets of transparent organza contain feathers.

This silk scarf has a border of striped single cloth but the black warp separates into two layers of transparent fabric, while the white threads become enclosed between them. Looking through one transparent layer these white threads can be faintly seen rippling gently about while on the other side they interlace occasionally with the cloth, creating tiny white dashes. (Designer unknown) Chapter 7 includes another view of this subtle and interesting piece.

The silk single-and-double scarf shown here is a good example of the ways that threads caught or partially caught between two layers can appear differently when viewed from the two sides, so creating fabrics that are both translucent and double sided. Other ways of combining these characteristics would be to use objects as inclusions that are double sided or to make the layers of cloth different colours so that the inclusions 'read' differently from the two sides. Double cloth may not be the first structure that springs to mind when aiming for a translucent effect but it is possible to use relatively open setts because the two layers support one another, making double cloth an interesting option for unusual lightweight designs.

CHAPTER 7

Both Sides Now

> Because the front side of a leaf and the underside are functionally very different – the former captures sunlight to produce photosynthesis and the latter absorbs carbon dioxide and releases oxygen and vapour – they typically have different visual features.
>
> Jose Carranza-Rojas and Erick Mata-Montero

When dealing with fabrics that are different on the two sides what should these be called – double sided, double faced, differently sided? It is obvious that all textiles have two sides, but 'double sided' suggests that the two sides are different and maybe also that both of them are at least usable. 'Double faced' perhaps goes a bit further, implying that both sides are of equal value, or equally attractive. 'Differently sided' is certainly unambiguous but sounds a bit clumsy so here I will adopt 'double sided' as a convenient term.

The previous chapters on ribbing/pleating and on translucency started from the idea of *aiming* for these characteristics, but this chapter is a little different because although it is not unusual to set out with the deliberate intention of designing a double-sided fabric, it may also happen that such a characteristic simply emerges while the focus of the design is on some other issue. This is borne out by the fact that textiles that are different on the two sides appear in all the other chapters in this section.

Although objects with differently coloured or patterned sides often serve as direct inspiration for the design of double-sided fabrics, the different surfaces on the two sides of many natural forms such as leaves and shells have generally emerged as a result of functional requirements. For example, many mollusc shells have a highly ridged outer surface that provides strength and protection while the inner surface in contact with the body of the animal is smooth. Sometimes the inner surface is iridescent – a spectacular effect that also gives extra strength through the fine multilayer structure of nacre (mother of pearl). In textiles it can often happen that designing for particular functions or characteristics such as warmth, flexibility or texture may naturally result in a fabric that is different on the two sides even if that was not the original intention. So with textiles, as with leaves and shells, the function and character of the two sides can go hand in hand.

THE FACE AND THE BACK OF THE CLOTH

The fact that a double-sided effect may be deliberately intended or might also arise incidentally raises issues about the dominance of one face over the other. My view on this is influenced by my experience as a student – after looking at the 'face' of many of my samples, people seemed invariably to turn them over and say 'Oh, I like the back!' After a while I took this on board and accepted that for many fabrics it was necessary from the outset to be designing for both sides of the cloth even if the difference emerged incidentally when my initial idea was focussed on one face. In some cases it may be possible to make both faces equally attractive, so that these cloths are definitely 'two for the price of one' but sometimes one of the faces may seem more obviously attractive or interesting and consequently be regarded as the right side.

This leads on to the question of whether both sides of the fabric will be seen while in use. A garment might be intended to be worn so that only one side shows, though if carefully sewn it might be made reversible to be worn either way round. There is also the option of designing a garment so that a little of the alternative side is on show, as for example by turning up cuffs or folding down a collar. With a scarf both sides are going to be easily visible at once. Furnishings may also be arranged to use both sides though perhaps only one side may be visible from any viewpoint, as with curtains where one side is visible from within the room and another from outside. These issues are important in deciding how the different sides are to relate to one another and the extent to which they need to look attractive viewed together. The most obvious differences naturally result from the use of colour, but subtler effects are also possible by using materials of contrasting quality, such as glossy and matt.

HOW TO BE DOUBLE SIDED

When working from a visual source with contrasting sides and deliberately aiming for a double-sided effect it is easy to jump immediately to the idea of a double cloth, but it is a pity to shut out other possibilities so quickly. I absorbed this idea from my tutor at college, who used to visibly wince when a student announced that they proposed to weave a double cloth, having given no thought to any other possibility. Initially I wondered why she disliked double cloths so much, but gradually realized that her main concern was that the choice was being driven simply by visual ideas without integrating these with design decisions about the substance and quality of the cloth.

Although a true double cloth may seem an obvious solution, there are many ways of producing a single layer of cloth that has two different sides and further possibilities when doubling up only one element, either warp or weft. As a result, two thirds of this chapter is taken up with double-sided fabrics that are not double cloths. The various ways of creating double sides naturally have different effects on the substance and drape of the cloth, and as these qualities are as much a part of the design as the visual effect it makes sense to look at the implications of choosing one technique rather than another.

SINGLE-LAYER CLOTHS

The interplay of structure and material is particularly important with single-layer cloths, since some structures offer a wider range of possible cloth qualities than others. For example, achieving a double-sided effect in plain weave will generally require a firmer fabric than when an uneven twill or a satin is used, while more complex float weaves can create a wide range of different cloth qualities, depending on material, sett and the length of floats. With gauze the range of possibilities for double-sided fabrics is immense, from thick and soft to extremely delicate.

Plain Weave

A double-sided fabric can be made in plain weave by using alternating colours in the warp and an alternation of thick and thin yarns in the weft (or vice versa), and the technique

Samples of double-sided fabrics in plain weave, patterned by reversals of the alternating colours in the warp.

In the background: Warp: Spun silk 60/2 Nm, 40 epi. Weft: Spun silk 60/2 Nm × 2 (thick yarn), spun silk 210/2 Nm (thin yarn), 32 ppi. In the foreground: Warp: Spun silk 60/2 Nm, 44 epi. Weft: Spun silk 60/2 Nm × 2 (thick yarn), spun silk 120/2 Nm, 28 ppi; Spun silk 210/2 Nm, 30 ppi; Silk grenadine 40/44 denier, 32 ppi (thin yarns).

is applicable to a wide range of weights and qualities of fabric (Chapter 3 shows examples ranging from rugs to lightweight fabrics suitable for scarves). If the contrast between the thick and thin wefts is very marked the fabric will have a definite ribbed texture, and quite a firm handle, but it is also possible to get distinctly different sides with wefts that are only modestly different in thickness. This works well to produce more softly draping fabrics suitable for scarves.

When working with such lightweight fabrics there is an advantage in using a rather strong contrast of colours in the warp to be sure of achieving a double-sided effect. It is also useful to have a fairly open sett to get a good drape, and in this case each colour will tend to show through on the reverse side and may give an attractive, slightly iridescent effect. The weft colours will obviously also influence the result and can be chosen to reinforce one or other of the warp colours.

Gauze

Though not particularly thought of as a double-sided weave, gauze will in principle always have this characteristic whenever different colours are used for the ground and whip ends. This is because the warp threads do not *twist round* one another (as is sometimes carelessly stated) but *cross over* one another, so the weft will always push the whip ends to one face and the ground ends to another, though this double-sided character is more obvious in some cases than others. With fine, soft-textured wefts, the colours of whip and ground ends may be almost equally visible and so the difference between the two sides may not be noticeable. But if the warp is soft and flexible while the weft is relatively thick or stiff, the whip and ground ends can easily be pushed apart and there will then be a clearer difference between the two sides.

However, the ways in which different colours appear on the two faces are more subtle and complex than might be expected, as both the thickness and spacing of the weft yarns have an influence. Assuming that whip ends are pulled down, it will be the *ground* ends that pass over the weft on the face of the cloth as it is woven, and these will show up best when a fairly thick weft is used, as this will keep these ends on the surface of the fabric for a greater distance. In contrast, with a fine but openly spaced weft it will be the *whips* that spend most time on the surface and show up best on the face of the cloth.

The relative thickness of the ground and whip ends and differences in tensions can obviously also affect the result, with the special technique of Russian cords, described in Chapter 3, providing an extreme example. The situation is further complicated if the weft yarns are unbalanced, because such yarns often do not lie horizontally across the warp, but tend instead to assume a wavy path, potentially changing the visibility of the different warp colours as they go. Clearly, with an effect that is so subtly influenced by

This double-sided gauze has thick wool wefts so it is the blue ground ends that show up most clearly on the face of the fabric as it is woven (shown to the left), while the whip ends show up clearly on the other face of the fabric (right).

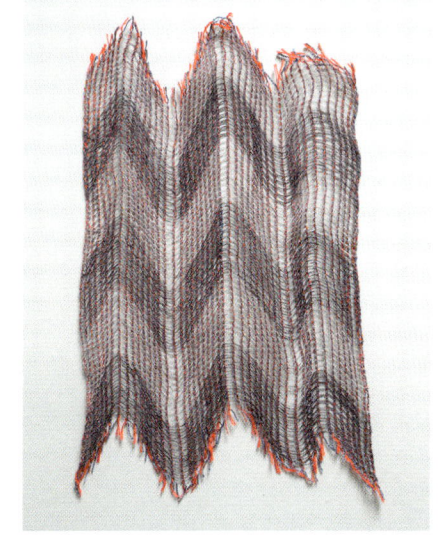

This fabric was woven on the same warp as the piece with the wefts of thick wool but here the weft is fine, openly spaced linen, so now it is the red whip ends that show up most clearly on the face of the cloth as it is woven. Left: The face of the cloth. Right: Reverse side of the cloth.

many factors, only sampling will determine whether any particular combination of yarns will give a distinctly double-sided effect.

Gauze is an especially attractive option for creating a double-sided effect because of the very wide range of fabric qualities that can be produced. In particular it is possible to create much more open and delicate fabrics than are possible with any other technique for creating fabrics that are different on the two sides.

Twills and Satins

Even Twills

At first sight it might seem that the even twills, such as 2/2, are not double-sided fabrics, but because of twist/twill interactions there *is* still a difference between the two sides, with the twill line appearing clearer on one side of the fabric (details are given in Chapter 4), and this may be quite subtle or very obvious depending on yarn and sett. Although it may be almost taken for granted that the visual effect of the twill line is attractive, this does not mean that the side with the most distinct line is universally regarded as the 'right' side. The flexibility and warmth offered by the twill weave may be desired without a wish for a particularly obvious diagonal line. In her study of Tibetan fabrics Gina Corrigan describes a traditional garment, the chuba, which is made of a twill fabric. Being densely set and woven from firmly twisted yarns, this fabric has a very marked steep twill line on one side, but people construct the garment so that the right side is that with the more subdued line. This is also the case with the clothing from Norse Greenland described by Else Østergård.

Satin weave scarf with a warp of ecru silk and a weft of bright red wool, giving a fabric that is glossy on one face with a soft, matt effect on the other. The softly coloured silk warp has a muting effect on the bright colour of the wool weft, which faintly shows through the warp, giving the fabric a hint of iridescence. (Designer unknown) Another view of this piece is given in Chapter 4.

Uneven Twills and Satins

Even if the same colour is used in warp and weft these weaves can look subtly different on the two sides, because warp and weft floats will reflect light differently, as in the case of the patterned effects in damask. But the difference will be very noticeable when warp and weft have different textures or colours; if the colour contrast is very strong there may also be interesting interactions between warp and weft, precisely because this is simply a single-layer cloth in which both elements will usually be visible. Depending on the extent of warp or weft dominance, there will be an intermixture of colours, perhaps even an iridescent effect.

Alternating Float Weaves

Many but not all of these structures are double sided. In the case of Han damask and the related five-span float weave, particularly striking effects result from an alternation of thick and thin wefts, as for example in the Miao wedding blankets described in Chapter 4. Like other structures mentioned so far, these float weaves can work well when patterned with spots of the reverse structure or with plain weave or other structures. The principle of thick and thin alternation can also be used warpways rather than weftways and the weight of the fabric can be greatly varied whilst still using the same principle.

Swedish lace is another alternating float weave with warp floats on one face and weft floats on the other, so this will also be different on the two sides if yarns of different colour or texture are used in warp and weft. The classic form of

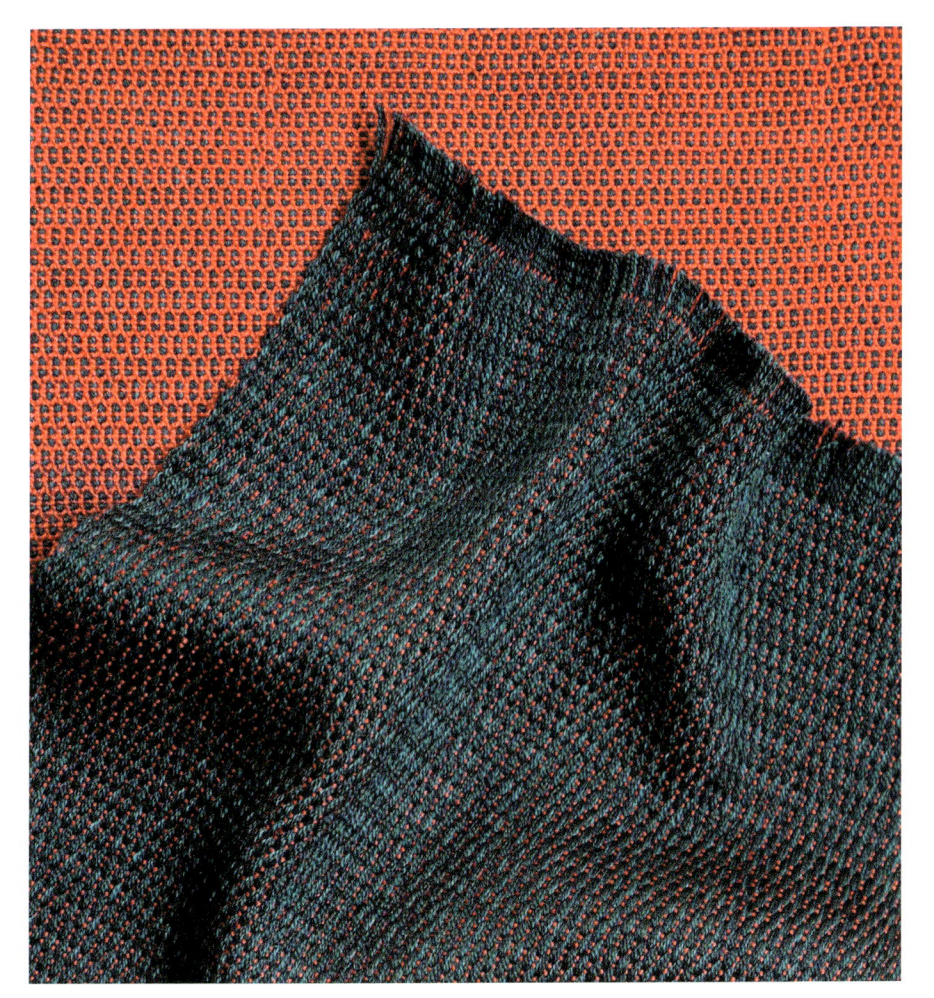

A five-span alternating float weave with thick and thin yarns running warpways, woven in a fairly lightweight quality suitable for scarves or garments. Warp: Spun silk 60/2 Nm × 3 (thick yarn), spun silk 60/2 Nm (thin yarn), 48 epi. Weft: Spun silk 60/2 Nm, 40 ppi. An iridescent effect is produced through the contrast in colour between the dark blue-green of the thick yarn, which dominates the face of the cloth, and the red yarn that is used for the thinner warp and weft.

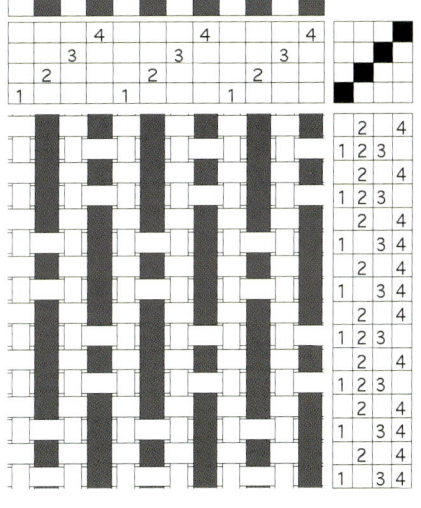

A draft of five-span alternating float weave, indicating how a thicker yarn is used for the float ends with finer yarn for the plain weave ends.

huckaback also has this characteristic (though there are alternative ways of drafting this structure so that there are warp and weft floats on both faces). As in the case of Han damask, using thick and/or different coloured yarns for the float ends or picks will emphasize the contrast between the two faces.

Other Float Weaves

Waffle Weave and Brighton Honeycomb

With waffle weave an attractive double-sided effect can be produced by using contrasting colours on the longest floats on one side of the fabric. This creates a coloured grid on one face and small spots of colour at the bottom of each cell on the other. Ann Sutton has some beautiful examples in her book *The Structure of Weaving*, where she has used brushed mohair and organza ribbon in this way, to dramatic effect.

As well as the diamond-shaped areas of warp and weft floats most frequently seen in waffle weave, the structure can also be constructed with rectangles and this creates two floats that are much longer than the others and can potentially be accented. The tea towel shown here has this type of structure, and in this case both long floats in the warp are in a contrasting colour, but only one of the long weft floats. The coloured threads are used on only one side, creating a fabric with very different effects on the two sides. Washing accentuates this difference and also creates a deeply cellular effect that makes for a very effective, absorbent tea towel.

A waffle weave tea towel with rectangular rather than square cells. The two sides are shown, before and after washing. (Designer unknown)

Drafts of the waffle weave tea towel, showing that the structure has two long floats in both warp and weft. Both the long floats are in a contrasting colour for the warp, while only one is accented in this way in the weft. In principle, both long weft floats could be emphasized for a bolder effect.

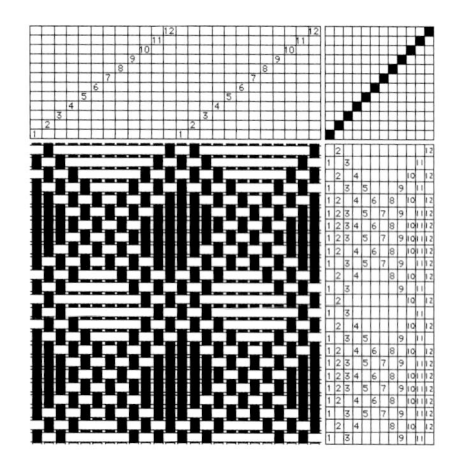

Structural draft of the waffle weave tea towel.

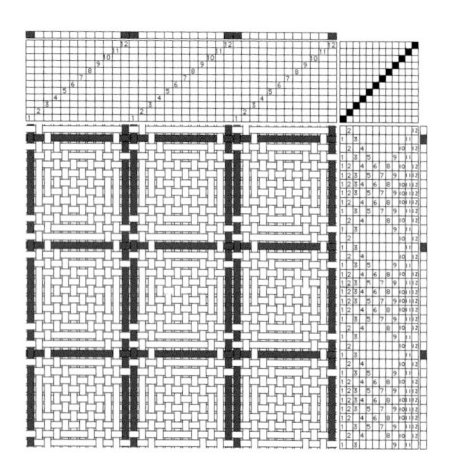

Draft as a thread diagram showing one face.

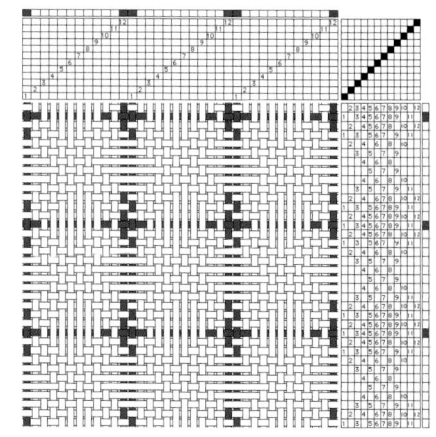

Thread diagram showing the reverse face.

CHAPTER 7: Both Sides Now

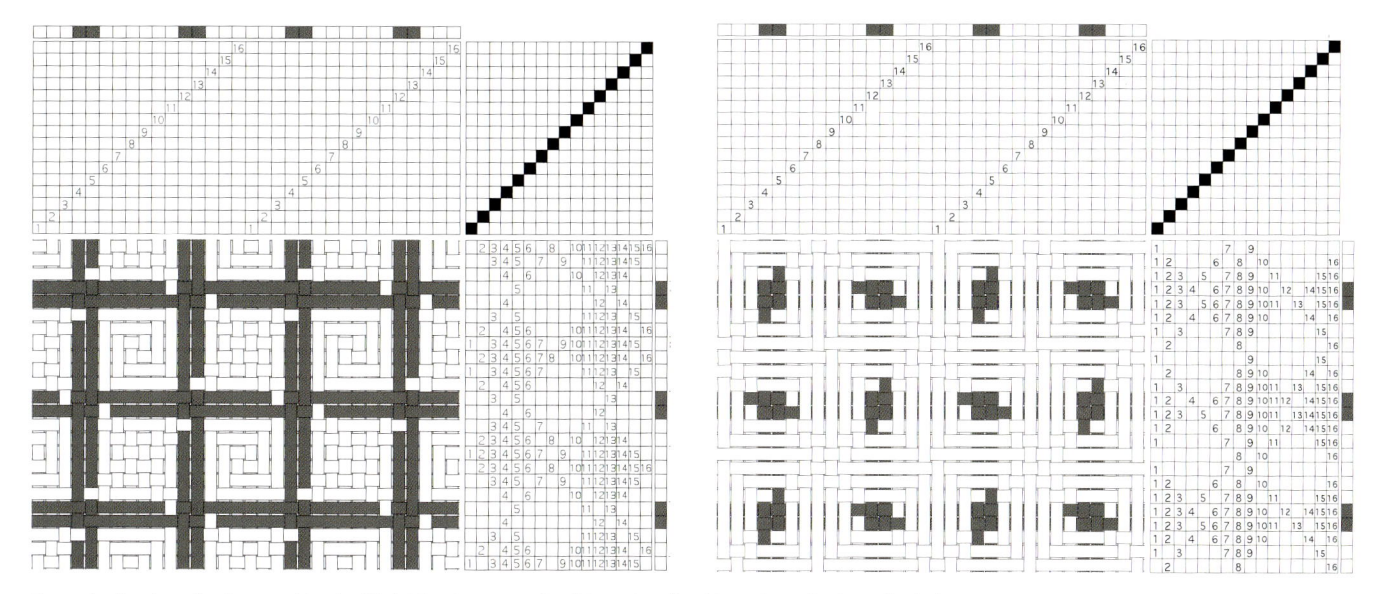

These drafts show the face and back of Brighton honeycomb with contrasting threads on the long floats in both warp and weft.

Brighton honeycomb is inherently a double-sided structure even if carried out in monochrome but as with waffle weave it can be interesting to use different yarns for the longest floating ends and picks. This emphasizes the cellular nature of the structure and also accentuates the difference between the two sides. Because of the staggered arrangement of cells this is another structure where there are two ends and picks in each repeat that are producing long floats that outline the cells, though the effect is very different from waffle weave, where such contrasting threads remain held within the grid-like structure. Brighton honeycomb allows much more movement of the threads, so although both ends and picks can be emphasized in this way, it is possible to outline the cells quite noticeably simply by using contrasting threads on either warp or weft alone (an example is given in Chapter 8).

Honeycomb/Distorted Weft Weave

This structure is very different on the two sides but the long weft floats on the back can make this side rather vulnerable, so it is often used for situations such as furnishings where the back will not be exposed. However, this is an adaptable weave that can be interpreted in many ways so could be constructed for both face and back to be functional.

Deflected Double Weave/False Double Weave

This is a special case of a structure that is set up on the loom as a single layer but that may develop the appearance of a double cloth during the finishing process because of the way that the threads shift position. Different colours weave only with one another and float over or under one another as necessary creating very bold effects although only some of the structures constructed on this principle are different on the two sides. There is scope for creating a very wide range of fabric qualities, including lighter weight fabrics than could easily be achieved with true double cloths, so these structures are especially useful for scarves and garments (examples are given in Chapter 4).

DOUBLING ONE SET OF ELEMENTS

Supplementary Warps or Wefts

Supplementary warps or wefts may often be used only in isolated areas to avoid affecting the overall drape and quality of the cloth but provided these extra threads show differently on the two sides, the overall effect will be that of a double-sided fabric. Extra warps or wefts could interlace with the main cloth only in certain areas, being cut away elsewhere, or wefts may be inserted as inlays. For example, the Moorman technique described in Chapter 4 could be used in this way. In cases where the ground weave is already double sided then a weft inlay will add further complexity, as in the scarf by Noriko Matsumoto.

This soft, warm scarf by Noriko Matsumoto is woven in 1/3 twill using a high-twist woollen merino yarn with a white warp and natural brown weft, so it is in any case a double-sided fabric. But she has also inlaid some of the white yarn to create oval motifs that are clearly visible on the weft-float face of the fabric but show only subtly as ghostly shapes on the warp-float face.

This crepon scarf is in plain weave with blocks of warp-faced compound tabby. Warp: Spun silk 60/2 Nm, 48 epi. Weft: Crepe silk 60/66 denier, S, 48 ppi. Using the same direction of twist for both warp and weft when weaving crepons helps to reduce curling at the corners of the fabric.

It can also work well to use the supplementary warp or weft to pattern the cloth only in narrow stripes, which also avoids impacting on the weight of the cloth. Another option for maintaining a light, softly draping fabric is to use one warp and weft but allow the fabric to become double sided only in certain areas of the cloth. The crepon scarf shown here has alternate ends of black and white with a crepe silk weft, giving a background of plain weave crepon. Small blocks of warp-faced compound tabby push the black ends to one face and the white to the other, while the contraction of the crepe yarn performs a useful function in pushing the warp yarns together in the blocks of warp-faced compound tabby. At this open sett the differently coloured yarns on the two faces would not otherwise conceal one another.

The crepon scarf shows how an overall double-sided effect can be achieved even when large areas of the cloth are the same on both sides, because of the changing relationship of identical and double-sided areas of the fabric. Another example can be seen in a silk and pashmina shawl, which is differently sided in only limited parts of the cloth but does have two sets of weft. It also has a structure that is single cloth in some places and backed cloth in others and the relatively light picking means that the backed cloth areas are very soft, giving the piece an excellent drape.

This softly draping silk and pashmina shawl has a large area of backed cloth that is identical on both sides, forming a chequerboard of light and dark grey squares in weft-backed sateen. The only double-sided areas are some small stripes of satin and the sections at each end of the shawl where the weft-backed sateen forms solid blocks of colour. Although only part of the shawl is actually different on the two sides, when the piece is worn the overall impression is that of a richly coloured double-sided fabric. (Designer unknown. Lent by Vasu Reddy)

A detail of the silk and pashmina shawl.

Warp-Backed or Weft-Backed Cloths

If either the warp or the weft is doubled throughout this will naturally impact on the substance of the cloth, which will become firmer in the direction of the doubled element (other things being equal). This can be an advantage in situations where it is useful to have a good deal of body to the fabric, as Deirdre Wood found when working on her wall hangings. She comments:

> The contrasting colours of double sided fabric are usually only glimpsed fleetingly but I thought if lengths of narrow strip woven fabric were firm enough they could be twisted before the edges were joined by sewing, revealing both sides of the cloth at once. This led to the idea of turning the fabric completely back on itself, to create spiralling triangles for example, using the entire length of the fabric uncut. Again, contrasting colours and materials could be viewed simultaneously, the potential of which seemed very exciting.

'Triangular Blue and Grey Construction' by Deirdre Wood. This piece is constructed from a single strip of backed twill cloth. (Photo: David Westwood)

DOUBLE CLOTHS

When designing with true double cloths the impact on fabric quality of bringing in an additional layer is a major concern. If each layer of cloth is kept at a sett that would have been appropriate for a single cloth, the fabric may become quite firm and heavy. This robust quality may certainly be ideal for some purposes, but when designing fabrics for garments or scarves it is easy to end up making the cloth too firm by not taking account of the way that the layers will support one another. It is a potential weakness of double cloth that it can be an easy visual solution that may inadvertently create problems of cloth quality. This can be avoided because in many cases it should be possible to open out the sett, sometimes to an extent that would be unstable in a single cloth. Also, given that the two layers do not have to be at the same density, finer yarns or a more open sett could be used for one layer, with the other firmer cloth providing support. Interesting effects of transparency can be produced in this way, allowing one cloth to be viewed through another, a point that has already been discussed in Chapter 6. Decisions about sett will also depend on how, if at all, the two layers are to interchange or be stitched together.

Detail showing the point where the strip is turned to reveal the other side of the fabric. (Photo: David Westwood)

Impact of Stitching or Interchanging of Layers

Stitching together or interchanging layers has the advantage of making cloths more cohesive but can also make the fabric firmer or stiffer, depending on the frequency of the exchange or stitching, so this may be another reason to experiment with what may seem rather open setts. These techniques offer obvious possibilities for pattern, but contrasts of fabric quality between the two layers can also be interesting, offering an immense range of possibilities for textured effects through differential shrinkage. This can be produced through differences in material, yarn twist, fulling capacity, or combinations of any of these.

A classic interchanging double cloth can give an identically textured effect on both sides, but if the cloths are stitched together, or combine in places to form a single layer of cloth, then a double-sided effect can be produced with a flat surface on one side and texture on the other. At its simplest, double weave used in this way for stripes can produce ribbed effects rather similar in appearance to the warp-float/weft-float pleats already described in Chapter 5, though with a different, less elastic quality. However, this type of construction has many possibilities and cloth qualities can range from fabrics firm enough for upholstery to more lightly stitched fabrics suitable for clothing. If the cloths are joined at scattered intervals then very bold and irregular textures can be produced.

This double cloth by Nuno has a plain weave face cloth that is bound into the twill back layer by scattered stitching points. The back layer of cloth has shrunk to give a randomly crinkled effect to the surface cloth. Here it is clear that one side of the fabric is the right side but the back layer is necessary to create the effect.

This linen and crepe silk dress fabric has an unusual style of stitching in which the crepe weft of the lower silk cloth passes over a linen warp of the top cloth, but this is done repeatedly over the *same* thread for about a centimetre. This gives a very interesting effect of small vertical lines running down the fabric and ties the cloths together so that the shrinkage of the crepe silk weft throws the top layer of cloth into relief. (Designer unknown)

The face of the cloth shows the textured surface consisting of silk warp and linen weft.

The back of the fabric has a silk warp and crepe silk weft.

This scarf with a silk warp and wool weft is composed of two layers, one black, one white, that largely remain separate but join together down the centre. In this case both sides of the single cloth form identical horizontal black and white stripes but these read differently in the context of the black and white sides of the fabric. The shifting of the separate layers against one another creates attractive moiré effects. (Designer unknown)

COMBINING DOUBLE AND SINGLE CLOTHS

Designs that combine double and single layers of cloth can often be more interesting than those that are double cloth throughout. Such combinations offer many possibilities both in terms of fabric quality and visual impact, particularly if contrasting colours are used, allowing for colour-and-weave effects in the single cloth areas to be played off against solid blocks of colour in the double areas.

Combining single and double layers naturally impacts upon the fabric quality because the single areas of cloth will feel firmer than the double areas. This will be most noticeable if the single layer is plain weave but less closely interlaced structures such as twills will also feel firmer than the double areas. This will be particularly obvious when high-twist yarns are used for textured effects because the greater density of yarn in the single areas may limit the movement and shrinkage of such yarns as compared with the double areas. This can work well to produce contrasts of texture between the two cloth qualities and can also be used for fabric shaping, which will be discussed in Chapter 8.

A cloth can also be different on the two sides while splitting into more than two layers, a strategy that has further repercussions on the fabric quality, as can be seen in the scarf shown opposite, where some warp threads become 'sandwiched' between layers of cloth and interplay differently with each side of the cloth.

COLOUR RELATIONSHIPS IN DOUBLE-SIDED FABRICS

Finally, it is worth emphasizing a general point that has already been mentioned in connection with specific pieces. In fabrics where only part of the fabric is different on the two sides, maybe even only a small part, there will be a changing relationship between the double- and identically sided parts of the cloth, especially if strong colour contrasts are involved. Areas of cloth that are identical on both sides will still 'read' differently in the contexts of the different colours against which they are seen.

The impact of one colour on another is an important principle of design in all fields, and is beautifully explored by Josef Albers in his classic *Interaction of Color*. This book includes remarkable investigations of the interplay of colours and the impact of context; these were studies that formed part of his teaching programme at Black Mountain College, after he and the weaver Anni Albers had moved to the USA to escape Nazi Germany. These dramatic demonstrations, together with the complete text of the book, are now available as an app allowing you to make your own experiments (see Online Resources).

'Ripplemarks' scarf in double cloth and 1/3 twill. This has a linen warp and uses a contrast of linen and high-twist wool in the weft to create a piece that is textured on one side and flat on the other. Warp: Linen 66 lea, 56 epi. Weft: Crepe wool 52/2 Nm and linen 66 lea, 56 ppi (28 ppi each cloth).

The border of this scarf is a firm single layer of striped cloth that is the same on both sides, but the warp then separates to form two layers of much softer transparent cloth that use only the black yarn, while the white threads are caught between the two cloths. This double section is different on the two sides, because on one face the loose threads of white yarn are faintly visible rippling randomly beneath the black cloth, while on the other face they emerge periodically, creating tiny white dashes against the black background. So an attractive range of effects is achieved within this one piece, creating a subtle, softly draping scarf, which sadly I cannot attribute properly, saying only: designer unknown. *See* Chapter 6 for another view of this interesting and unusual piece.

CHAPTER 8

Off the Grid

> The form, then of any portion of matter, whether it be living or dead, and the changes of form which are apparent in its movements and in its growth, may in all cases alike be described as due to the action of force. In short, the form of an object is a 'diagram of forces'.
>
> D'Arcy Thompson, *On Growth and Form*

As weavers we seem to have an ambivalent attitude towards the grid-like structure of woven textiles. On the one hand an attraction to the interlacement of warp and weft must be one of the reasons for taking up weaving, as opposed to a technique that offers more freedom such as textile printing. But although we clearly love the neat stripes and checks that naturally emerge from the woven structure, most weavers seem also to be fascinated with the idea of breaking out of this grid.

Some techniques create a purely visual effect, as warp and weft threads remain straight while changes in the proportions of adjacent blocks or of the sett of the yarns create an attractive illusion of curvature. Various strategies such as crammed and spaced twills, overshot weaves and network drafting fall into this category. The alternative approach, to be discussed here, is to use structures that really do cause warp and weft threads to move from their normal straight alignment. Several classic methods of distorting the grid have already been mentioned in earlier chapters but there are also other weaves that can usefully be combined in various ways to create such effects. Such structures may be used to create curves within a piece of cloth that still retains an overall rectangular shape but many can also be effective in shaping entire pieces of cloth and so can be used to produce 'loom-to-body' clothing that requires little or no cutting.

THE DISTORTED GRID

One of the most striking off-grid effects is produced by the ondulé technique, where a fan reed is used to progressively shift the position of warp threads to create dramatic curves. Needing special equipment, this is unfortunately beyond the scope of this book, but the effect is beautiful and Norma Smayda's excellent account of this technique is highly recommended. A related development is the RailReed technique, devised by Kadi Pajupuu, which consists of a reed with sliding sections that can be closed up and opened out. This makes it possible to create variations in density across the warp, similar to the effects produced with an ondulé reed and this ingenious technique is well described in Tina Ignell's article 'Inventions' about Kadi Pajupuu and her work.

The focus here is on techniques where threads are not *moved* out of the grid but rather *move themselves* due to the influence of the material, yarn twist, weave structure, sett or any combination of these. Although some movement may occur as soon as the fabric is cut from the loom, generally wet finishing will be needed to achieve the final result. Some effects are small in scale, creating only minor deflections, while others cause striking distortions or changes of shape. With some techniques the quality of fabric may be quite firm, but other methods, particularly those that rely on yarn shrinkage, may give a springy or even elastic quality to the cloth.

This detail of a gauze scarf with a moderately twisted weft shows how it creates a large-scale crepon texture but with a definite zigzag element to the pleating.

At its simplest the crisp precision of the woven construction can be very gently disturbed by using contrasts of yarn twist or material that cause ripples to develop in the fabric. For example the random effect of crepon pleating can break up the formality of any sharp-edged stripes or pattern blocks to create a softer, more organic effect. Any pattern is still there but modified in an irregular way, rather like the weather patterns that James Gleick describes in his book *Chaos*: 'the repetitions were never quite exact. There was pattern, with disturbances. An orderly disorder.'

Spiralling Yarns

During wet finishing, unbalanced yarns form spirals within the cloth and this can cause curves or zigzags to emerge when relatively open cloths are woven. This works particularly well in gauze and the results can vary considerably depending on the amount of twist. A lightly twisted weft may shift position, creating gentle waves that can be emphasized by using stripes of contrasting colour. With more highly twisted yarns the results may depend on how the fabric is handled during wet finishing – a gentle wash will cause curves or zigzags to emerge, while pulling firmly lengthways may generate definite pleats, though still with a zigzag component.

Gauze samples with a warp of spun silk 60/2 Nm for the ground thread and spun silk 120/2 Nm for the whip threads, 6 gauze units/inch. The weft yarns are linen 60 lea and 50 lea and although these are 'normal-twist' yarns, their single construction means they are sufficiently unbalanced to create a waved effect after washing.

Loomstate gauze sample.

Gauze sample after washing.

CHAPTER 8: Off the Grid

Contrasts of Materials

Stripes of materials with very different properties can disturb the fabric in rather similar ways to the effects of twist. The contraction of a yarn that shrinks readily, such as silk or wool, will create gentle ripples in any adjacent stripes of a stiffer yarn like linen.

Chequerboards of Differential Tension or Take-up

Introducing tension variations into the warp offers another way to create curves. The techniques for varying warp tension employed by Peter Collingwood, Ann Sutton and Andreas Möller have already been described in Chapter 3. By creating variations in the density of the cloth these methods naturally also cause weft threads to curve – an effect that could be emphasized by inserting a contrasting weft wherever there is a switch in tension. Fabrics produced in this way tend to have a fairly firm quality.

In contrast, blocks of structures that take up or contract differently will allow curves to emerge while creating a more springy and flexible fabric. For example, when working with high-twist yarns, a chequerboard of Z × Z and Z × S interactions in plain weave will produce curves because the different textures produced by these combinations take up differently. The effect can be enhanced if the Z × Z blocks are in plain weave and the Z × S blocks in twill, as this increases the difference in take-up between the blocks. Moving to more complex structures, chequerboard arrangements of weaves that pull in different directions offer many possibilities for creating curves in fabrics with a flexible or elastic character.

This plain weave scarf with a wool and linen warp and cotton weft has random textures created both through contrasts of material and through yarn twist. The warpways shrinkage of the wool throws adjacent linen stripes into ripples, while the high-twist cotton weft gives a crepon effect.

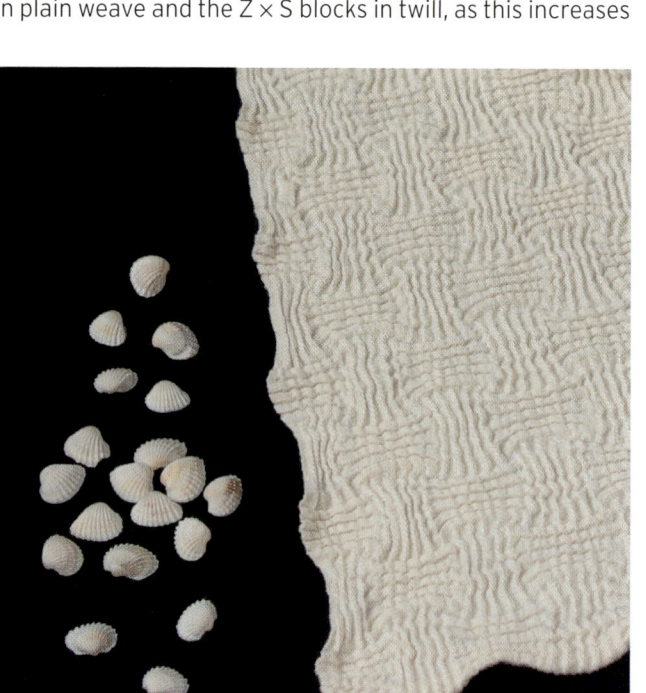

In this 'Two-way Furrow' scarf by Wendy Morris the different directions of furrows pull against one another to create striking curves in the fabric. The effect is created with blocks of warp-float and weft-float twill stripes that run warpways and weftways in a chequerboard arrangement. (Photo: Wendy Morris)

A detail of 'Two-way Furrow' scarf. (Photo: Wendy Morris)

Deflected Thread Structures

This is a diverse group of weaves but they all rely on the same principle. Sharon Alderman sums this up concisely in her book *Mastering Weave Structures*: 'when nothing lies between a pair of warp ends or weft picks, they will move together. It really is as simple as that. We shall see over and over again how this simple fact underlies all structures with deflected warps and wefts.'

Alternating float weaves do this on a small scale, something that is seen very well in the Miao wedding blankets described in Chapter 4, where thick float wefts cause distortions of warp and weft on the back of the fabric. In structures with longer floats the distortions become more dramatic, creating large-scale undulating or zigzagging lines that run across one face of the fabric. This effect works particularly well if these floating threads contrast with the ground weave due to their colour or thickness, as seen here in the fabrics by Paulette Adam. Variations in structure can create widely different effects and Sharon Alderman gives some beautiful examples of the range of possibilities with such linear zigzag or spider weaves.

Another way to use floats is to make a chequerboard composed of plain weave and a structure with fewer intersections. Many variations on this idea are possible, such as plain weave combined with half hopsack in the structure popularly known as Ms and Os. Even in monochrome the curving effect is obvious but as with so many of these effects, a contrasting thread to emphasize the curve is especially successful.

Honeycomb provides another example of this class of structure by contrasting blocks of plain weave with areas where warp and weft do not interlace at all. Attractive circles and ovals can emerge and these can be varied in ways that move them far beyond the classic appearance of honeycomb. Fabrics formed on these principles are often quite firm in character, but this will vary depending on the yarns that have been used.

Linear zigzag weaves, designed by Paulette Adam, in which high-twist yarns assist the distortion of the weft yarn. (Photo: Karl Ravn)

Bold curves emerge in this honeycomb fabric by Stacey Harvey-Brown. (Photo: Stacey Harvey-Brown)

CHAPTER 8: Off the Grid

Brighton Honeycomb

This structure includes long floats that move freely during wet finishing, developing an effect of rounded cells on one side of the fabric. Threads that contrast in colour, fibre or both can be used to emphasize the curved path that is taken by the longest floating ends and picks. Although both warp and weft can be emphasized in this way, the movement of threads is so strong that even contrasting threads in only one direction will create quite a bold outlining effect. The relaxation of yarns involved in this structure tends to give a springy character to the fabric, particularly if high-twist yarns are used.

Deflected Double Weave

The name of this group of weaves derives from the deflections that can often be seen during wet finishing as groups of threads shift position. Particularly dramatic effects can be produced through differential shrinkage by using yarns with contrasting characteristics, as can be seen in the work of Denise Kovnat (shown in Chapter 4). This highly adaptable principle of construction can create a wide range of different fabric qualities, depending on the relative proportions of floating and weaving areas of cloth and the yarns involved.

This draft and series of samples show how the contrasting threads on the longest picks in Brighton honeycomb can shift position and outline the cells once the fabric is cut from the loom and wet finished.

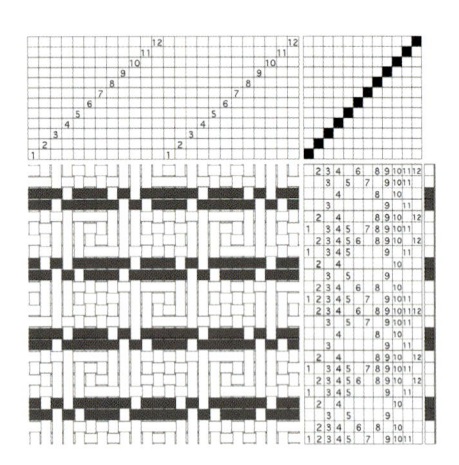

Draft of twelve-shaft Brighton honeycomb, showing accent threads in the weft.

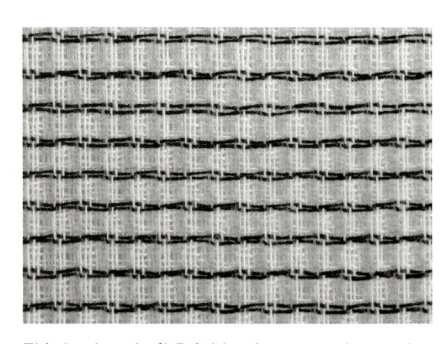

This twelve-shaft Brighton honeycomb sample was photographed while still on the loom and shows how the contrasting weft threads lie almost straight within the structure. Warp: High-twist woollen merino 14.5 Nm, S, 32 epi. Weft: As warp, together with spun silk 30/2 Nm in black for the picks that form the longest floats, 32 ppi.

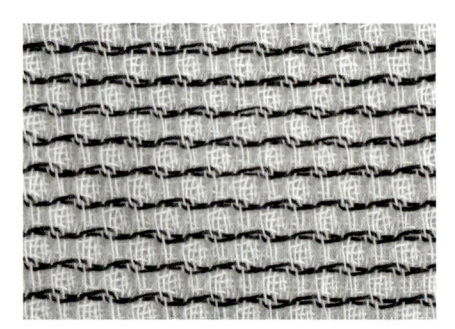

Released from tension and cut from the loom, the contrasting threads begin to ripple slightly.

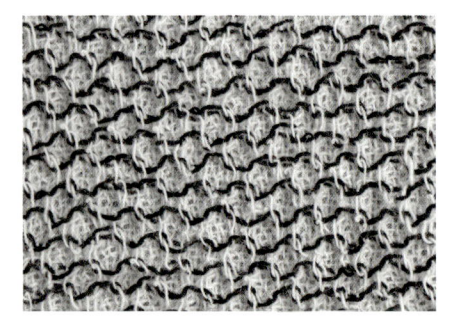

The sample after wet finishing, showing how the contrasting weft threads have curved to outline the cells.

SHAPING WHOLE PIECES OF FABRIC

The techniques discussed so far cause the deflection of threads within pieces of cloth that nevertheless retain a rectangular shape. But given that individual yarns can move out of the grid, why does a piece of woven cloth itself need to remain a rectangle? Techniques that shape the fabric itself offer many possibilities both for wall pieces and for functional textiles. The principle of constructing shaped pieces of fabric is well known in knitting but its application in woven textiles has been relatively neglected. Currently such ideas are receiving a good deal of interest because of an increasing concern to avoid waste.

Garment Shaping for Minimal Waste

Traditionally, many garments were very economically cut through a careful layout of rectangular and nested triangular pieces, as can be seen in the books by Max Tilke and Dorothy Burnham, but fashionable garments have frequently been cut in ways that create considerable waste. Current concerns about the sustainability of fashion are stimulating interest in less wasteful methods and although economic cutting layouts will always be important another interesting option is to use techniques that allow a garment to be constructed or shaped as weaving progresses.

The earliest 'loom-to-body' clothing relied simply on the draping of rectangular pieces of cloth, but techniques for producing shaped garments on the loom also go back some way – the Romans wove semi-circular togas on the warp-weighted loom. More complex examples are the seamless shirts that date from the seventeenth to nineteenth centuries, where weavers gave virtuoso demonstrations of skill by using multiple layers of cloth to produce elaborate shirts that came completely finished from the loom (Norgate and Bennett give a detailed account of some beautiful Scottish examples).

Current experiments in shaping woven clothing on the loom use methods that lend themselves particularly well to handweaving but also have some scope for adaptation to industrial production. During the nineteenth century some fabrics were woven *à la disposition* to create patterned areas of cloth designed to fall appropriately on parts of a garment, forming decorative borders at the edges of skirts or sleeves. Using different yarn qualities or structures to shape the fabric is essentially applying the same principle to the substance of the cloth rather than simply its decoration.

The Japanese designer Akihiko Izukura has been pursuing such ideas for many years with his 'Zero' textiles, but the current sense of urgency to find sustainable ways of living is now attracting many other designers to experiment with such techniques. Although there are many ways to pursue this idea of loom-to-body garments, the examples given here will concentrate on techniques where shaped pieces of fabric emerge from woven rectangles through the interplay of yarns and weave structures.

A DIAGRAM OF FORCES – A WAY TO THINK ABOUT SHAPE

In discussing different forms in nature D'Arcy Thompson puts forward an idea that he calls 'the theory of transformations' in which he uses a system of coordinates that can be manipulated in various ways to show how one form may be related to another through varied rates of growth. The way that he uses coordinates to expand or contract the different parts of an organism seems to echo the 'slash and spread' and 'slash and close' methods of pattern drafting that garment designers use to produce differently shaped pattern pieces from a basic block.

This idea of manipulating coordinates can also be a useful way to visualize possible ways of shaping garments from woven rectangles through contrasts of material, yarn twist and weave structure. In this case the analogy is closest to the 'slash and close' method of sliding pattern sections over one another, because such shaping on the loom relies on the ability of some yarns, structures or combinations of the two to shrink more than other parts of the cloth. Varying the shrinkage in only one direction, either warp or weft, will give simple flared, waisted or bulging shapes, while varying the shrinkage in both warp and weft allows for greater complexity of form.

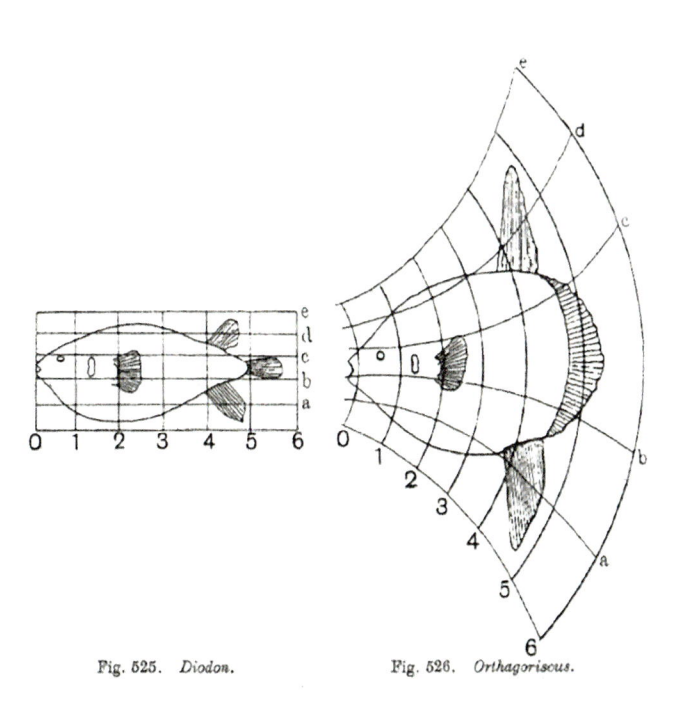

This diagram by D'Arcy Thompson shows how his coordinate system suggests a relationship between two fish that appear at first sight to have very different forms.

Fabric Shaping with Amount and Direction of Yarn Twist

Many methods of shaping fabric can be done entirely in plain weave, with the simplest technique being the contrast of high-twist yarns with those of normal twist. If yarns of several different twist levels are available, this will allow for gradual shaping, but an alternative strategy is to interleave high- and low-twist yarns to provide stripes of intermediate shrinkage.

Other ways of using twist for shaping rely on different directions of twist. A normal-twist warp crossed by a high-twist yarn of only one direction will develop a crepon effect, while alternating Z and S yarns will break up the pleating to produce an overall crinkled texture, the classic crepe effect. Because crepon pleating takes up more fabric than crepe, switching from one to the other will result in a widening of the fabric.

The classic crepe texture relies on separate shuttles of S and Z that are used to create narrow stripes, usually 2S, 2Z, but it is also possible to weave a 'quick crepe' by winding S and Z yarns together on the same bobbin. To keep the weight of the fabric consistent throughout the piece the crepon section can be formed by winding two threads of the *same* direction on to one bobbin. The example shown here was actually produced accidentally by a student – Lotte Dalgaard and Paulette Adam include it in their book

The top half of the sample has been woven with a doubled thread of the same twist direction while the lower part has been woven with S and Z wound together on the bobbin. (Photo: Karl Ravn)

A sample of fabric in the loom state.

The scarf after wet finishing.

In this 'Curve' scarf, differently coloured stripes of S and Z yarns, grading from wide to narrow, produce a shaped effect during wet finishing. Warp: Crepe wool 30 Nm, S and Z. Weft: Spun silk 60/2 Nm. 28 epi/ppi.

This wool and linen jacket uses graded stripes of S and Z yarns to shape both the body and sleeves of the garment. Warp: Crepe wool 30 Nm. Weft: Linen and crepe wool. The warp is running across the body and around the sleeves. The stripes are faintly visible because the S and Z yarns reflect light differently.

to demonstrate the change of texture that can happen by mistake if dyed yarns of different twist become mixed up (undyed yarns often have identification tints to avoid this problem). However, it provides a good example of how an effect that would be annoying if unintended can be put to good use deliberately!

S and Z yarns can also be used in a different way to produce a more gradual form of shaping. The two twists are used in separate shuttles and the width of the S and Z stripes is varied in a graduated way, using decreasing numbers of threads between reversals. This progressively increases the extent to which the opposing twists 'fight' one another, so the fabric develops a gentle, consistent flare. The equivalent technique can be applied with the high-twist yarn in the warp and a normal yarn in the weft.

Another option is to use high-twist yarns in both warp and weft. When S and Z yarns cross one another a wavy texture is produced that takes up more fabric than when yarns of the same twist are used. As described above, a chequerboard of these different yarn interactions will introduce curves into the fabric. The same principle can be used to shape entire pieces of cloth, though this works best with relatively small pieces.

This collar is shaped using S × S and S × Z interactions. Warp and weft: Crepe wool 30 Nm. In this piece the same-twist stripe is in plain weave and the opposite-twist stripe in 2/2 twill. The more open weave of the twill assists the formation of the wavy texture and so enhances fabric shaping.

Fabric Shaping with Contrasts of Material

These techniques rely on contrasts of materials that shrink differently during wet finishing. Because the range of properties in textile materials is so great, there are possibilities both for extreme and subtle contrasts of shrinkage and consequently for gentle or dramatic changes of shape. For

'Cinnebar', a wall piece by Deirdre Wood, made from sections shaped through differential shrinkage of linen and silk. These curved strips have been assembled so as to play not only with the shapes of the pieces themselves but also the negative spaces that form between them.

This knitted sample by Alison Ellen shows how combinations of different stitches can shape a 'rectangular' piece of fabric, as each section has been worked with the *same* number of stitches and the *same* number of rows. The variations produced in length and width can be used to shape garments, a technique that is described in detail in Alison's books. Although most woven textiles do not have the flexibility of knitting, similar shaping principles relying on changes of structure can still be very effective. (Photo: Colin Mills)

example, the contrast between wool and linen is quite strong, while that between silk and linen is less extreme. Different kinds of silk also vary in their properties, with tussah being more elastic and inclined to shrink than cultivated silk, so even a pure silk fabric could be given a subtle shaping. Different wool fibres also have a range of properties so differential fulling could be a further way to shape fabric.

Deirdre Wood makes dramatic wall pieces using contrasting materials to shape the fabric. Gradations across the warp from silk to linen allow her to create narrow strips that become curved when cut from the loom and wet finished. She explains that these curves rely on the different shrinkage properties of the two types of yarn and describes the process of actually weaving the fabric as 'a bit tricky, like trying to steer a bus with loose steering!'

Fabric Shaping with Structure

Some weaves tend to relax considerably during wet finishing and consequently take up yarn to a greater extent than more firmly woven structures, so juxtaposing weaves with such different properties can cause rectangular pieces of cloth to change shape. Weavers can usefully take inspiration from the use of such structural shaping in knitted garments, as beautifully shown in the work of Alison Ellen. Unlike the more familiar techniques of increasing and decreasing, the use of stitches with different characteristics can be a highly effective method that does not so much *impose* a shape as *allow it to emerge* from the interplay of material and structure.

In comparison with knitwear designers, weavers have until recently made relatively little use of such structural principles of shaping, but things are beginning to change as part of the drive for greater economy in the use of materials. Many 'relaxing' weaves have already been discussed and include classic structures with long floats, such as waffle, Brighton honeycomb and the double deflected weaves. A sudden transition from such a weave to a firmer structure will tend to result in a frilled effect, which can work well on smaller items, producing shaped collars or attractive borders for scarves. But by setting up the loom to weave a number of blocks a gradual transition can be achieved that is more suitable for shaping entire garments.

Structures such as waffle and the various alternating float weaves are particularly economical on shafts and also allow plain weave to be woven on the same threading. This can allow a fabric to be woven with a gradation of structures – all blocks in the 'relaxing' weave, an intermediate mixed stage and a section that is all plain weave. Another possibility is a gradation from a weave with very long floats, through intermediate float lengths and so down to plain weave. Other structures that work exceptionally well for fabric shaping are combinations of double and single cloth and ribbed/pleated structures.

Fabric Shaping with Double and Single Cloths

Combinations of double and single cloths have great potential for fabric shaping, but do not inevitably create this effect. If a fabric is very openly set then a transition from double to single cloth will probably not change the width of the fabric, but with a closer sett the greater density of the single cloth may cause it to spread. The most effective approach is to use high-twist or other shrinking yarns because their scope for contraction will be greatly altered by the transition from double to single layer cloth. This can produce really strong changes of shape especially if both S and Z twist yarns are brought into play – some examples are given below under the section on 'Combining Techniques'. Fulling is another technique that could work well in taking advantage of the different densities of the single and double cloths, especially if combined with different qualities of wool or a mixture of wool and a fibre resistant to fulling.

Ribbing/Pleating with Warp-Float and Weft-Float Weaves

Uneven twills, satins and alternating float weaves can be used in narrow stripes to create an effect of soft pleating (as described in Chapter 5) and these structures offer several different strategies for shaping fabric. One simple method is to vary the thickness of the yarn that runs across the pleats, as this can be a determining factor in whether or not pleating will occur. So with warpways stripes of 1/3 and 3/1 twill, pleats will form easily if the weft is much finer than the warp, while progressively increasing the thickness of the weft along the length of the fabric will weaken the pleating, causing the piece to flatten and widen.

Another technique is to use reversals of the warp- and weft-float stripes. With alternate stripes of different colours this will bring the 'back' colour to the face and vice versa. Weaving long stretches of pleating between reversals will create bands of colour across the warp without changing the width of the fabric, but progressively reducing the distance between reversals will both flatten the pleating and widen the fabric.

A third option is to combine different widths of rib or pleat. Wide ribs take up more fabric than narrow ones so switching from wide to narrow pleats will cause the fabric to widen. A transition from a ribbed structure to a flat structure such as plain weave or twill will obviously also create a curved shape.

Samples showing pleated fabrics shaped by increased weft thickness (left) and reversals of structure (right) using warp- and weft-float stripes of Han damask. Rust stripes: Spun silk 60/2 Nm × 3 (float ends) and spun silk 60/2 Nm (plain weave ends). Brown stripes: Spun silk 60/2 Nm. Warp sett: 20 epcm for both samples. Weft for left-hand sample: Spun silk 210/2 Nm, 24 ppcm; spun silk 120/2 Nm, 20 ppcm; spun silk 60/2 Nm, 18 ppcm. Weft for right-hand sample: Spun silk 210/2 Nm, 24 ppcm.

This sample is based on the classic *Rippenköper* structure of 1/2 and 2/1 weftways twill stripes. The left-hand side of the sample has ribs composed of six picks, while those on the right are of three. After wet finishing the six-pick stripes take up more fabric than the three-pick stripes, causing the fabric to develop a curved shape. Warp: Linen crepe 24 Nm. Weft: Yarns of varying thickness, including linen, hemp and allo.

This sample has *Rippenköper* stripes on the left and 1/2 twill weave on the right, creating a curved shape.

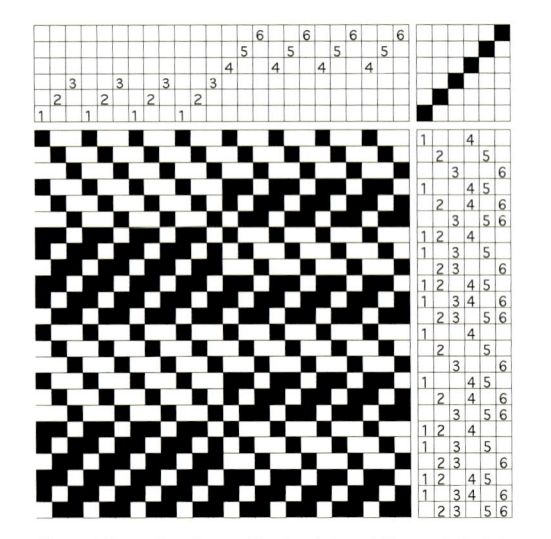

Rippenköper structure with six-pick and three-pick stripes.

COMBINING TECHNIQUES

Several possible methods of shaping have been described separately for the sake of clarity but these can obviously also be used in many different combinations. For example, when using the contrast between high-twist and normal twist, this could be emphasized by also changing from a soft fibre to a stiff one. So a contrast between crepe wool and normal wool will shape the fabric, but the greater contrast between crepe wool and linen will enhance the effect, as shown in a scarf by Lotte Dalgaard.

144 CHAPTER 8: Off the Grid

This curved scarf by Lotte Dalgaard contrasts a high-twist wool yarn with a stiff linen normal-twist yarn and also includes a narrow stripe of metal yarn at the selvedge that further enhances the shape.

CHAPTER 8: Off the Grid

This skirt is shaped by varying the amounts of double cloth and 1/3 twill in different parts of the cloth. The loomstate fabric is shown on the left. Different colours and directions of yarn twist are used for the two layers of double cloth. This means that the garment is double-sided, while the way that the different directions of twist 'fight' in the single layers of cloth results in these parts of the fabric being wider and flatter than if the same direction had been used for each. Warp: Linen 24 Nm and 14 Nm, 48 epi. Weft: Crepe wool 27.5 Nm, S and 30 Nm, Z, 48 ppi.

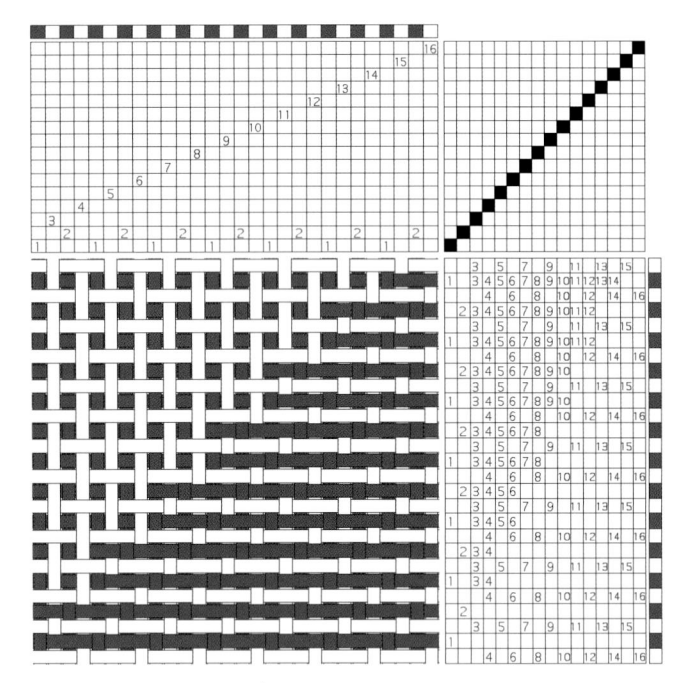

Draft of double cloth and 1/3 twill with double two-tie threading.

Another useful combination of techniques is to use both S and Z yarns when working with high-twist yarns and double- and-single cloths. While the yarns of different twist direction are weaving the separate layers of the double cloth, the yarn twists will not affect one another, but once they combine to form a single cloth the opposing twists will 'fight' and produce a flatter, wider fabric than if the same twist was used for both layers.

When combining double and single cloths and aiming for a gradual change in shape, the double two-tie threading is particularly useful. Double plain weave and four-shaft uneven twills have two ends and picks in common, so using a double two-tie threading extends the number of blocks that can be produced. Instead of having only two blocks on eight shafts there will be three, while this extends to five on twelve shafts and seven on sixteen shafts. Double plain weave can also be combined with warp-faced compound tabby in a similar way.

If the various shaping techniques that have been described are used in both warp and weft then even more varied effects will result, ranging from interesting borders to greater complexity of the overall shape of the piece. There is plenty of scope for combining different shaping strategies to enhance the effect, and the more techniques that are brought into play, the more extreme the changes of shape that are possible.

The skirt is shown here together with a top garment where both body and sleeves have been shaped through warp stripes of S and Z yarns, grading from wide to narrow, and crossed by a linen weft. The warp for the top is running across the body and around the sleeves, and the changing direction of yarn twist causes a difference in light reflection that is faintly visible.

A sample of fabric shaped through a combination of double cloth and spots of uneven twill, using a double two-tie threading, showing the fabric before and after finishing. Warp: Spun silk 60/2 Nm, 56 epi. Weft: Crepe wool 27.5 Nm, S and 30 Nm, Z, 56 ppi.

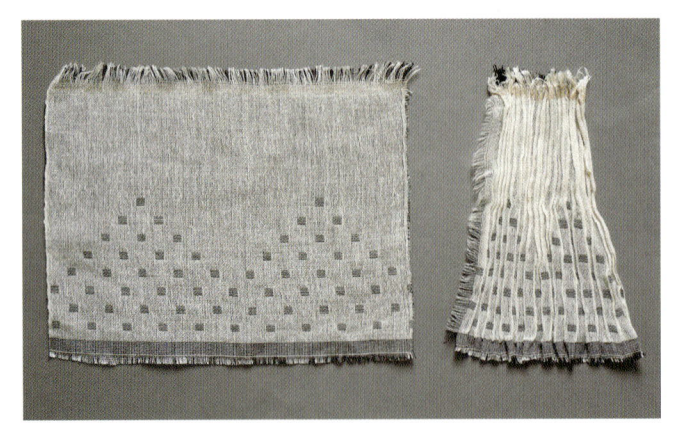

Light face of the fabric.

Dark face of the fabric.

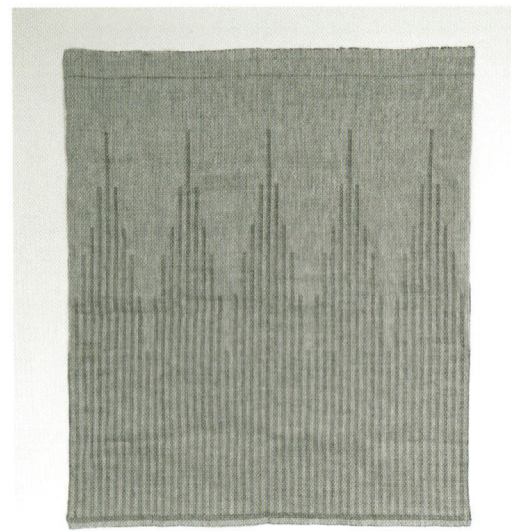

This skirt is shaped with a combination of uneven twill and double cloth. The loomstate fabric is shown on the left. One of the seven blocks provided by the double two-tie threading is used for double cloth throughout to give a striped effect on the lower part of the skirt while the other six blocks allow a graded transition from double cloth to twill to give a gentle flare to the garment. *See* the Introduction for a detail of this fabric. Warp: Linen 26.5 Nm and 14 Nm, 48 epi. Weft: Crepe wool 27.5 Nm, S and 30 Nm, Z, 48 ppi.

DOWN TO ZERO

While the techniques described here are effective in shaping simple items such as gently flared skirts, other garments raise more problems in achieving a good fit. Even with simple, loose tops there can be difficulties in shaping necklines and fitting the garment to the slope of the shoulder, while clothing that aims for a closer fit can be especially challenging. Consequently, loom-to-body shaping techniques can usefully be viewed in the context of other methods of minimizing waste in garment design. In *Zero Waste Fashion Design*, Timo Rissanen and Holly McQuillan give a useful survey, referencing historical examples as well as current practice, encompassing economic cutting layouts, rectangles used on the bias, the inventive use of selvedges and radical new methods of cutting that utilize slashes or holes in the fabric. Such techniques can provide a useful complement to fabric shaping on the loom.

Draping methods that use the fabric on the bias are especially effective in avoiding the blocky, square-cut effect that could be regarded as a weakness in some garments that come straight from the loom. Madeleine Vionnet, famous for her extensive use of the bias cut, often used simple rectangles of cloth but positioned these on the body so as to fall on the bias. So although the bias cut is often thought of as wasteful many of her designs were surprisingly economical in

148   CHAPTER 8: Off the Grid

This fabric by Lotte Dalgaard uses a contrast of high-twist and normal yarn in the warp to give a curved shape, but an alternation of narrow stripes of high-twist yarn with wider stripes of linen in the weft also creates a beautifully scalloped border. The piece is shown with the warp running horizontally.

their use of fabric. Betty Kirke's survey of Vionnet's work is an inspirational account of the techniques of this great designer.

A wide variety of interests and practice can be seen in the work of designers currently experimenting with minimal waste techniques, ranging from collaborations between handweavers and garment designers right through to mainstream fashion design for industrial production. A good example of a collaborative relationship is that between weaver Lotte Dalgaard and clothing designer Elisabeth Hagen, who works by draping uncut lengths of fabric and frequently makes use of the selvedge as part of the design. *Thread Magic* by Lotte Dalgaard and Paulette Adam includes several examples of her work, showing the value of close co-operation between weaver and garment designer. Practitioners who choose to integrate the processes of weaving and garment design by constructing loom-to-body clothes include Emily Olsen and Anna Piper, while there are a number of mainstream fashion designers with a long-standing interest in minimizing waste, notably Issey Miyake and Yeohlee Teng. The techniques used by these designers and the many others now joining the field of minimal waste design can serve as a useful source of inspiration for handweavers who are interested in shaping their own clothes.

150

PART 4

Designing Through Making

[The designer] shapes the situation, in accordance with his initial appreciation of it, the situation 'talks back', and he responds to the situation's back-talk. In a good process of design this conversation with the situation is reflective.

Donald Schön, *The Reflective Practitioner*

The final part of this book deals with the practical process of designing through making, both when sampling and when scaling up to produce full-size pieces. When designing, it is important to keep a balance between purposeful planning and a flexible attitude that can take advantage of any interesting, unplanned results that arise from the interplay of structure and material. Some of this back-talk may be both unexpected and unwanted, but it is wise to be cautious about rejecting such results as failures, since an undesired effect in one context may be successful in another – all results provide information. The need to respond to feedback may seem most important at the sampling stage but some qualities of the fabric may only become obvious once a full-scale piece has been produced. A willingness to reflect on results at every stage is helpful in achieving a fully resolved design and can also allow designing to become a truly evolutionary process in which one idea leads on to a whole series of others.

A warp set up for warp-float/weft-float pleating, with a finished sample to the right-hand side. Several structures were tried out on this warp: soft pleating was tested in two different ways, with Han damask for both warp- and weft-float stripes and then with Han damask combined with plain weave. The finished samples and drafts for these are given in Chapter 5. This warp was also used for some samples that show different methods of fabric shaping, which can be seen in Chapter 8.

CHAPTER 9

From Sample to Full-Scale Fabric

At the beginning you work with the materials – you don't know them very well and you try to make them do what you think you want them to do. As time goes on you understand the way to make them do what *they* want to do, but your way.

Sheila Hicks

IMITATING NATURE'S LAVISH PROTOTYPE TESTING

Earlier in this book I quoted Michael French's comment that in nature, complexity in itself does not seem expensive, since natural selection has the time to 'try' endless variations. Julian Vincent picks up this evolutionary point in his article 'Survival of the Cheapest' by pointing out that while materials are expensive, for living organisms shape is cheap. For weavers, good quality materials are certainly expensive, and so this provides an incentive to follow nature's example and design for optimum use of the material, but weaving is a slow craft both while sampling and when producing full-size pieces, so for us shape is also expensive in terms of the time required.

However, there is no way round this, so weavers need to be willing to imitate the lavish scale of nature's prototype testing and keep on sampling, sometimes trying many small and subtle variations in order to achieve a good design. This is the process of designing through making, a reflective practice that demands responsiveness to the materials and a willingness to react to feedback. Sheila Hicks deftly captures the essence of this approach by emphasizing the need to work *with* the properties of the material, while still keeping hold of your original ideas.

TECHNIQUES IN WEAVING

Since both materials and design are expensive it makes sense to work as efficiently as possible, so practical aspects of weaving technique are important if everything is to run smoothly. Unfortunately, discussions about methods can prove contentious – it sometimes appears that everybody believes that the very best way to do anything is the way that *they* were first taught! This is a pity, since with the great variety of methods available helpful techniques can usefully be exchanged.

For example, I was taught to beam the warp through a raddle while watching carefully for problems, but a tangle would still occasionally cause breakages. Once I started to use difficult, high-twist yarns this became a serious issue but Lotte Dalgaard taught me to insert a stick between the raddle groups and gently move it forwards to clear the raddle cross – any tangles can easily be felt before they reach the raddle. Why bother *looking* for tangles when *feeling* them is so much more reliable? I have passed this technique on to students in my classes, along with warnings against various other 'normal' methods that I have found by experience to work badly with fine, high-twist yarns. Sharing techniques in this way is always worthwhile because rather than there being some 'holy grail' of ideal technique, different methods are likely to prove effective depending on the situation.

Rather than laying down rigid rules that should always be obeyed it seems better to think simply in terms of methods and results. The job of the designer-maker is to be observant and willing to adjust their technique, working out what method in any particular situation can give the best result, if necessary experimenting with unconventional methods, even inventing them. I attended a fascinating lecture by Peter Collingwood in which he described the challenges of working with an innovative stainless steel yarn designed by Junichi Arai (described in Chapter 2). Some of his key difficulties were later summed up in an interview with Linda Theophilus, in connection with his solo exhibition at the Minories Art Gallery, Colchester:

> I hadn't tried [macrogauzes] in anything other than linen until Junichi Arai gave me a sample of stainless steel yarn (Alphatex). I have made a 3D macrogauze for the Kiryu Performing Arts Centre. It has nine identical panels of 32 inches wide. It weighed 100 kilos. Completely different from my linen ones that only have the weight of the rods really. Also, when I turned the weaving on, the nature of the thread moved it all sideways, so I had to add rollers to the loom. The weight of the yarn together with the weights I use in the process proved very difficult when I moved the batten up and down – I had to make a head rest so that I could lean forward to lift the combined weight physically.
>
> Exhibition catalogue *Peter Collingwood – Master Weaver*, p.26

As a result of these adaptations Collingwood succeeded in thoroughly mastering the material and went on to use it to produce a huge, dramatic wall piece for the Kiryu Performing Arts Centre in Japan.

DESIGNING THROUGH SAMPLING

Sampling Productively

Sampling is the basis for designing through making and clearly it is helpful to start out with some ideas about what you want to achieve. What are the samples for? What are you trying to find out? Having clear ideas makes it easier to plan sampling warps, which if carefully thought out may be designed to answer a number of questions. On the other hand, it does not pay to be excessively rigid because it is precisely the opportunity to experience the properties of the material and respond to them reflectively that is the

Tying bundles of warp with slip knots and lacing them to the front stick is a good way to avoid wasting yarn when sampling and needing to cut off frequently.

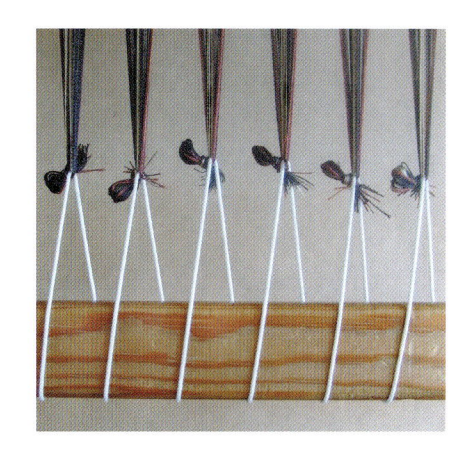

strength of this approach. It is good to start out with some ideas in mind but also to accept that the purpose of the samples may well evolve during the process of designing through making.

It is important to cut off pieces frequently and apply any finishing techniques to get rapid feedback about how things are going. Weavers are sometimes reluctant to do this because of wasting both yarn and time through repeatedly tying on, so it is worth taking advantage of the speed and efficiency of the lacing method. This involves tying the warp into small bunches with slip knots and then lacing these to the front stick. Cutting off frequently is easier to accept with a method that wastes very little yarn, saving materials as well as time so it is worth using this technique when sampling, even if you prefer the traditional technique of tying on when working on full-size pieces.

The importance of prompt feedback was impressed on me by one of my tutors at college who described working for a textile company where she was not in a position, as we were in college, to weave and finish her own samples and quickly see the success or failure of an idea. Instructions were sent off for samples to be woven elsewhere and when she finally saw them, there were occasions when she said to herself 'If I'd known *that* would happen I would never have suggested it!' As a student I thoroughly absorbed this idea that prompt feedback was the essence of designing through making and it has been the basis of my work ever since.

Getting regular feedback means that adjustments can quickly be made if things do not seem to be working well. For example, the sett might seem too open but it will be impossible to be certain about this until a sample has been finished. Also there is always the possibility of completely unexpected results. Large changes in the fabric can obviously be expected in some cases, such as with woollen fabrics that are to be fulled or with structures that allow plenty of yarn movement, but there are other, subtler and

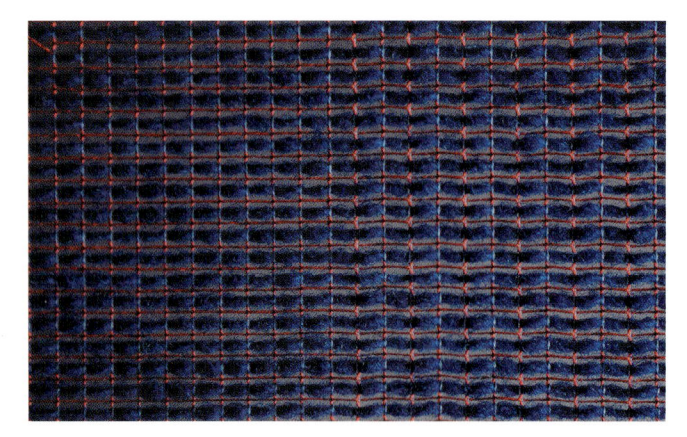

The gauze sample shown here was set up with half the gauze units as regular and half as mirrored units (as described in Chapter 3) and was woven with alternate picks of thick wool and fine silk. While still on the loom there was a subtle difference between regular gauze units (left) and mirror units (right), but this became much more obvious after wet finishing.

The wool and silk sample after wet finishing, showing the difference in effect of regular and mirrored units. It would be difficult to anticipate such a striking result from the subtle difference that could be seen in the fabric while still on the loom.

The open structure of gauze allows plenty of scope for yarn movement during finishing. Here the gauze has a warp of spun silk 60/2 Nm for the ground thread and spun silk 120/2 Nm for the whip threads, 5 gauze units/inch. The weft is ramie/silk 60/2 Nm at the top and mohair 36/2 Nm at the bottom. Although these yarns are plied they have sufficient residual twist to create a waved effect after washing. Left: Loomstate sample. Right: Sample after washing.

less easily anticipated ways in which finishing may alter the character of fabrics. Gauze samples have been chosen here to make the point because they are particularly likely to produce unpredictable results.

Further examples of such transformations can be seen elsewhere in this book. However, it is not only aspects of cloth quality, but also the appearance of colours that may be altered by finishing as the cloth relaxes and becomes more closely integrated. This is particularly the case with strong colour contrasts in warp and weft, such as those that create shot effects, as the balance of colours can be difficult to judge while the fabric is still on the loom. I have certainly been caught out in this way!

Getting prompt feedback also allows for making local changes within the sample such as tying in some threads of different colour, weight or yarn quality. It is particularly easy to do this towards the end of the warp when the back stick is free from the beam – tying a new thread to the old and pulling on its 'partner' allows a quick change over of two ends at once. However, try to avoid tying together yarns of different twist direction because unless they are perfectly balanced they will untwist one another and break. Changing just a few threads can be a quick way to test whether an idea is worth pursuing with a completely new warp. Making such ongoing changes may cause some samples to look rather messy, but this is no bad thing in the early stages of designing, while you are playing with various ideas and the samples are just for your own information. A friend of mine who visited a rather well-known art college to look round the workshop reported back that the students there didn't seem very adventurous – she thought all the samples looked too tidy!

Sampling can sometimes seem an uphill struggle, especially when there is a definite idea in mind, a particular cloth quality or effect that is hard to achieve. When any of us after much experiment finally finds a satisfactory solution it can sometimes seem obvious and we may be left wondering why we didn't think of it in the first place! It is important not to get discouraged by this because the apparently direct route to the solution is an illusion, a path that can only be seen after the event. The wobbly route that has initially been followed must be accepted as part of reflective practice, an essential element of designing, and indeed of thinking in general. Ann Sutton, who has experimented so widely with many different aspects of weaving, quotes the poet Antonio Machado: 'Traveller, there is no path, you make the path by walking'.

Keeping and Using Records

An important aspect of sampling is keeping proper records. These do not necessarily have to be elaborate; samples to be shown to customers must obviously be neatly presented, but for pieces that are simply the results of your experiments more informal records can be adequate as long as they are clear. A notebook by the loom to write down everything as you do it and a prompt labelling of samples, before you forget which is which, is a minimum requirement. Something rough that you do straight away will be more use than a more formal system of write-up that you do not get round to. Sharon Alderman captures the essential point of records: 'I think of my own records as a way of sending information to my 'future self'. I feel kindly towards Sharon-in-the-future and don't want her to work any harder than she must to complete a particular job.'

Records for both samples and finished pieces are valuable, not only in enabling you to replicate a fabric at a later date but also as a guide to new work. Looking at earlier work, particularly after a lapse of time, can trigger fresh ideas, perhaps because new materials have become available or new techniques learnt that make it possible to pick up an idea and run with it again. Much of what is gained from earlier work will be the tacit knowledge that comes from experience, but there are also more formal ways of using the recorded information, particularly when wanting to make a similar cloth but with thicker or finer yarns.

It is obvious that if the thickness of the yarn is changed then the sett must also change, so it may seem as if only the structure remains the same, but there is something else that can remain invariant, at least to some extent. The *relationship* between the yarn thickness and the sett can be transposed, that is to say the same *proportion* of the maximum sett (or same *percentage sett*) can be a guide to producing a new fabric. The Ashenhurst and cloth setting formulae can be used to determine the proportion of maximum sett that was used in the original sample. This can then be applied to the maximum sett that has been worked out for the new yarn (see the box for an example). The same principle can obviously be used if you prefer to estimate setts on the basis of wraps/cm or inch.

I have said 'to some extent' as it is important not to be too rigid in applying such calculations because yarns obviously vary in other ways than merely their thickness. Many characteristics may influence how they behave – stiffness, smoothness, potential for shrinkage or fulling and so on – but information transposed from earlier samples is likely to prove better than a guess when setting up a new warp. Once

USING THE PERCENTAGE/PROPORTION OF MAXIMUM SETT AS A GUIDE FOR NEW DESIGNS

A balanced plain weave fabric in linen 44 lea is set at 32 epi, 32 ppi, which is 60 per cent of the maximum sett as calculated by the Ashenhurst formula, giving a softly draping fabric suitable for scarves or lightweight garments. This information could be used to make a cloth with similar draping qualities, but in finer or heavier yarn. It is simpler to use the figure as a proportion (0.60) for the calculation rather than as a percentage.

A fabric in linen 25 lea:
Linen 25 lea: 80 diameters/inch. Maximum plain weave sett: 40 epi, ppi

$40 \times 0.60 = 24$

A sett of 24 epi, ppi will give a similar fabric in the new yarn.

A fabric in linen 66 lea:
Linen 66 lea: 130 diameters/inch. Maximum plain weave sett: 65 epi, ppi

$65 \times 0.60 = 39$

Taking account of available reed sizes a sett of 40 epi, ppi will be suitable.

a sample has been woven, this can be cut off, finished and assessed to see whether the sett needs adjusting. Another caveat is that there will obviously be limits to the range over which such information can be used without considerably changing the character of the fabric. For example, beyond a certain level of increased yarn thickness a scaled-up scarf fabric will probably begin to seem rather heavy for a scarf.

Another relationship that can usefully be treated as an invariant is that between yarns of different thickness, particularly where these are quite extreme. For example, if there is a thick warp but a much finer weft, or if yarns of contrasting thickness are alternated in either warp or weft, then an attempt can be made to maintain the *ratio of yarn diameters* between the thick and thin yarns, even if the new design is to be carried out with heavier or finer yarns. This can be important for some effects that depend on a rather precise relationship between the yarns. For example, the self-pleating uneven twill pleats described in Chapter 5 can be produced entirely with normal-twist yarns, but if a lightweight, softly draping fabric is required then the size relationship of the warp and weft yarns needs to be maintained within certain limits. A detailed example of scaling up this type of fabric is given in my book *Weaving Textiles That Shape Themselves*.

When transposing such information it may not be possible to find a yarn combination that perfectly matches the original relationship, but in any case it is undesirable to be too rigid in applying transposed information. This is where experience must play its part in deciding whether increasing or decreasing the contrast in yarn sizes is likely to prove more successful. Also samples can easily be set up to test more than one possibility. If the yarn contrast is between warp and weft, once a warp yarn is chosen then several yarns that are close to the desired thickness for the weft can be tried out. If an alternation of yarn thicknesses is used only in the warp, different yarn combinations could be tried across the warp or the design could be turned so that the thick/thin alternation is tested in the weft instead.

Yarns can obviously be chosen to maintain such a relationship on the basis of their counts, provided that all the yarns involved have the same count system. However, it is also convenient to match up yarns on the basis of their diameters so it is useful to draw up a table of all your yarns and work out the diameters/cm or inch for each of them. These figures are needed anyway for calculating setts and they provide a quick and easy way of comparing yarn thicknesses that is independent of the various count systems.

THE RELATION OF SAMPLES TO FULL-SIZE PIECES

Practical Issues of Cloth Quality

When scaling up from small samples to full-size pieces a useful general principle is to try to avoid doing things while sampling that might be physically impossible in the finished piece. For example, the usual advice to lay the weft at an angle or in an arc can cause problems if the ultimate width of the intended finished piece is not taken into account. This is a simple matter of geometry. I have heard of weavers being advised to lay the weft in at an angle of 45 degrees, but though this could be managed on a width of 10-15 cm, it will not be possible on a much wider piece where an angle of 15-20 degrees is likely to be the maximum that can be achieved on a normal loom. Such a reduction in angle when moving from sample to finished piece obviously reduces the amount of weft available for take-up, changing the quality of the cloth.

Another problem can arise if aiming for quite close picking, because it is easy to beat the weft down closely on a small piece but achieving an equivalent impact across a wide warp needs a great deal of force – you have to ask yourself if you are really that strong! The combined effect of varying both the weft angle and the strength of beat can make it difficult to achieve the same picking on a full-size piece as on a small sample, so it is wise to keep these issues in mind while sampling and to lay the weft at a modest angle and be realistic about the strength of beat in relation to the intended width of the final fabric.

Laying the weft at an angle is generally the most reliable technique, at least when working with relatively balanced cloths. An arc has the disadvantage of a section at its centre where the angle is reduced, providing less yarn for take-up. This can change the quality of the cloth in the centre of the piece, particularly when using high-twist weft for crepe or crepon, as there may be a loss of texture in the centre of the warp. Also, as the beater hits the peak of the arc first the weft may become pushed out at the selvedges. Of course, in the case of an extremely weft-faced cloth, laying the weft at an angle may provide insufficient weft and it may be necessary to use a deep arc. It is best then to push this down at intervals to distribute it evenly before beating (as for rug weaving).

Achieving consistent picking is one of the most difficult tasks, both when sampling and in finished pieces, and not only when aiming for a closely picked fabric. It can involve

A linen tester (piece glass) provides a quick and easy way to check that you are keeping to your intended weft sett.

learning to 'place' the weft rather than just 'beat' it, a skill that is especially necessary when aiming for an extremely light picking, and weavers new to working on openly set fabrics sometimes seem surprised that you can actually *choose* the weft sett rather than just swinging the beater and accepting what happens. In terms of consistency a simple visual check may work well enough on the section of fabric that can be seen, but as it disappears over the front beam, there is the danger of allowing the sett to drift. It is useful to check on the picking occasionally with a linen tester or by inserting a marker (counting thread or simply a pin) and counting as you insert the intended number of picks for a given length.

Impact of Scaling Up

Even if the cloth quality of a sample is perfectly replicated in a larger piece there is still a question of whether it will be suitable for purpose on this larger scale. I have had interesting discussions with Denise Kovnat, who captures some key points when she comments: 'sometimes what pleases me as a sample has to be reworked for a scarf or other item. The drape can be problematic or even the design when it's expanded to the larger format.' She gives the example of a small sample where the fabric seemed suitable for a scarf, but as she increased the scale of her samples she began to feel that the fabric would be rather heavy in a piece that was large enough for a scarf. Further experiments were necessary, trying different weights of yarn, to achieve the lightweight quality she wanted. The reverse experience can also occur – a small piece of fabric may feel quite firm and appropriate for upholstery but when a larger piece of the same cloth is woven it may become clear that it has sufficient drape that it could also work well for heavy curtains.

Visual Design Issues

When it comes to the visual aspects of scaling up the design it is necessary to think through what this really means. Are you going to make a bigger piece of *exactly* the same cloth? Or will any stripes or other patterns be scaled up, so that the effect of viewing your small sample close up will be replicated in the experience of viewing a larger piece from further away? For example, a sample with a relatively small-scale pattern might work well as a scarf if simply woven as a larger piece of fabric, but if intended for a curtain that would be mostly viewed at some distance then the impact of the pattern might be reduced. In that case it might be better to try to scale up the pattern itself.

However, scaling up any blocks of colour or texture has implications for the weave structure – can that be scaled up too, perhaps by using heavier yarns, or will that alter the handle and draping qualities of the cloth too much? If the yarns stay the same while any stripes or blocks are scaled up, then the overall visual effect will still be altered. Photographing or scanning your sample and pasting sections together to visualize a larger piece of cloth can be helpful in judging the effect of different relationships of scale between the various elements of the design.

Drawing and collage are other useful techniques for visualizing a full-size piece but it is wise to avoid introducing effects that cannot be replicated in a real fabric. For example, collage is helpful because paper can be dyed to the intended colours, but to be really useful these need to be accurate. Also it is often advisable to cut stripes or squares of paper cleanly rather than tearing them – the softness of a torn edge can make an attractive collage but are you going to be able to replicate that charming irregular edge in your final fabric? Textured yarns or heavy milling may create an irregular or fuzzy edge to a stripe but smoother yarns will give a crisp edge.

In practice many textiles, ranging from wall pieces to clothing, will be viewed at a variety of distances, and so it is worth aiming to make them succeed under a range of viewing conditions. This can often be achieved by combining a clear overall design with smaller-scale details that only become obvious as one comes closer, as in the pieces shown here.

'Ikat Triangle', a wall piece by Deirdre Wood, makes a dramatic impact seen from a distance, but also reveals beautiful details as one comes closer. (Photo: Joe Low)

Viewed close up, it becomes possible to see the subtle diagonal line of the backed twill, the black and white details of the selvedges and the soft transitions of colour between the ikat stripes. (Photo: Joe Low)

Other examples of combining design elements on different scales are shown throughout this book. For example, Reiko Sudo's 'Feather Flurries' (illustrated in Chapters 6 and 10), gives an overall impression of feathers drifting in space but when seen close up subtle moiré effects and the fine details of the guinea fowl feathers come into view.

Moving from sample to full-size fabric poses particular difficulties, but problems of visualization arise at all stages of design and it is useful to try a variety of techniques, as no single method will be completely effective. In the early stages many weavers use yarn wrappings, which are very helpful in showing the texture and colour of the yarn and the proportions of any stripes, but although this works well for strongly warp- or weft-faced textiles, it is not easy to simulate the visual effect of the close intermixing of warp and weft that occurs with more balanced weaves. In contrast, computer drafting is helpful for getting a sense of this warp and weft balance but the visual effect of the colours on the screen cannot completely replicate all the surface qualities of textile fibres. Employing a combination of several techniques can really help in visualizing the final fabric. Above all, it is important to keep the function of the cloth in mind, as emphasized by Marianne Straub:

> It is essential to visualize the cloth as it will be used: for example, hanging at a window, covering a chair or made up into a garment. By 'seeing' the cloth in context it is easier to determine its quality and pattern scale; and in this way the cloth's design is related directly to its function.
>
> Marianne Straub, *Hand Weaving and Cloth Design*

It is clear that a successful process of scaling up from samples requires several different issues to be kept in mind and brought into balance with one another – the visual impact, the desired cloth quality and also the purpose of the fabric. Only by working with materials, learning directly of their possibilities and limitations, seeing how they behave at different setts, with different structures and on varied scales can we achieve a resolution of these various requirements and succeed in making the materials do what they want but our way.

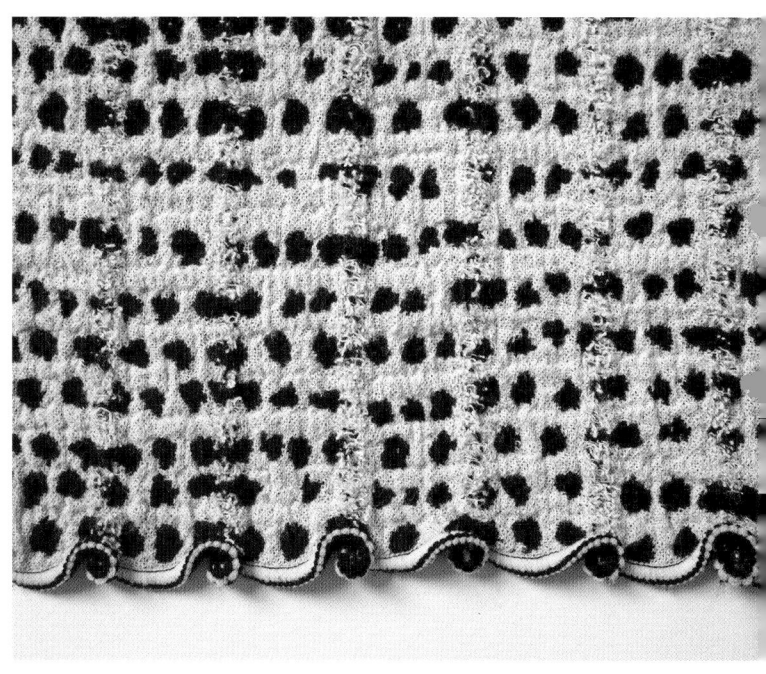

This detail shows how high-twist yarns are used to give an overall textured surface, but gaps in the warp also allow lines of crinkling weft yarns to emerge, creating further texture. The strong contraction of these unconstrained yarns also creates an attractive edge by pushing the tightly stitched border into a series of waves.

In this scarf by Junichi Arai, the bold black and white pattern of irregular spots can be clearly seen from a distance but it is only close up that the character of the fabric can be fully appreciated.

CHAPTER 10

Reflective Practice and the Butterfly Effect

> Tiny differences in input could quickly become overwhelming differences in output – a phenomenon given the name 'sensitive dependence on initial conditions.' In weather for example, this translates into what is only half-jokingly known as the Butterfly Effect – the notion that a butterfly stirring the air today in Peking can transform storm systems next month in New York.
>
> James Gleick, *Chaos*

> Chance favours only the prepared mind.
>
> Louis Pasteur

It is clear that there can be various starting points for a design – forms and processes in nature, the resources of materials and weave structure, designs in other media, or the desire for a particular fabric quality. But sources of inspiration can be more subtle and complex than is often assumed, as there may be multiple influences on a single design. Once an idea has taken root other related examples may spring to mind – frequently there seems to be no getting away from them. On one occasion, having become interested in the idea of cracked surfaces through which another surface might be glimpsed, I found that suddenly they seemed to be everywhere – cracked earth, cracked ice, seeds that were cracking open and so on. It is as though the awareness of the initial idea opens your eyes to the existence of other related examples.

Wendy Morris has explained that the idea of her 'Two-way Furrows' design (shown in Chapter 8) arose initially after seeing a stitched/patchwork textile but that later, as the design developed, some cockles in her shell collection influenced her choices about shape, texture and the decision not to use colour in this particular piece. Although a specific object may spark the original idea, the way that other influences and connections feed into the design process can only enrich the final result.

The practicalities of designing through making also have their impact through the need to react to the behaviour of materials and structures and make adjustments accordingly, allowing the design to gradually evolve. This approach of responding to feedback is in strong contrast with the idea of design as a preformed plan that will be precisely carried out without alteration. Plans are useful resources but successful design also requires a responsiveness to the interplay of material and structure that may throw up unexpected problems or possibilities that could not have been predicted – designing through making is an emerging process. Henry Petroski and Donald Schön are two writers who in different ways argue for this responsive approach to design.

FORM FOLLOWS FAILURE

A favourite axiom in modern design is that 'form follows function' but in his book *The Evolution of Useful Things*, Henry Petroski suggests that it is the imperfection of existing objects that really pushes the design process forward. People notice that a design fails to function as well as it might and through repeated attempts at improvement it gradually evolves, a process he characterizes as 'form follows failure'. His entertaining book gives the history of many classic everyday objects such as the paper clip and the zip fastener, but his fundamental point is that this process is going on in *all* branches of design. This is a useful counter to the rather negative reaction that usually greets a failure of any kind, instead accepting that to fail or at the very least to feel some sense of dissatisfaction is a natural part of the design process. Petroski emphasizes that when designing any object there are many, sometimes conflicting, requirements, so it is hard to produce something that satisfies all of them in every way. Even if a design should seem to have reached perfection life is always moving on and sooner or later, with changing needs or fashions, there may be a new push to improve it. Having trained as a biologist I can well appreciate the point that evolution is never finished.

REFLECTIVE PRACTICE

Donald Schön is another writer who emphasizes the way that designs inevitably evolve, because the complexity of dealing with many variables means that designing becomes a kind of 'conversation' with the material or situation.

> Because of this complexity, the designer's moves tend, happily or unhappily, to produce consequences other than those intended. When this happens, the designer may take account of the unintended changes he has made in the situation by forming new appreciations and understandings and by making new moves. He shapes the situation, in accordance with his initial appreciation of it, the situation 'talks back,' and he responds to the situation's back-talk. In a good process of design this conversation with the situation is reflective.
> Donald Schön, *The Reflective Practitioner*

Designing through making exemplifies this approach, and the conversations to be had with textile materials and weave structures can be intriguing as well as challenging.

EVOLVING DESIGNS

Often it is only when a solution to one problem has been achieved and there is time to reflect on the result that it becomes clear what needs to be tackled next and this may happen repeatedly, creating a series of related designs as each idea leads on to the next. My pleated scarves and jewellery pieces developed in this gentle evolutionary way. The first time I wove accordion pleats it was the structure of the dragonfly wing that helped to resolve the problem of creating pleating that looked delicate but that would hold its shape (as described in Chapter 1). But the full-sized scarf behaved in ways that I had not anticipated from my small preliminary samples and this suggested the idea of using a pleated fabric for neckpieces.

Dragonfly pleat scarf. The fabric naturally falls into tight pleats along its length but fans out broadly at the ends. This contrast of effects suggested the idea of a neckpiece that might fan out in a similar way, rather in the style of a ruff.

I was not sure how to persuade a linen fabric to maintain the radiating shape of a neckpiece so this idea remained on hold until a visit to Denmark introduced me to the Danish Yarn Purchasing Association, an organization that buys unusual yarns in bulk and distributes them to the members in smaller quantities. This gave me access to a silk/steel yarn with intermediate properties between textile and wire, and its stiffness and capacity for moulding have proved ideal for pleated neckpieces.

The first pieces were in the form of simple radiating pleats, woven as a single layer and joined at the selvedges, but I soon began using the 'memory' of the silk/steel yarn to introduce additional folds. It then seemed natural to emphasize the three-dimensional effect with contrasting colours on alternate sides of the pleats, and a further variation was to alternate the colours on the edges of the pleats to make the pieces double sided.

This all worked well enough until I began experimenting with the Möbius strip, when it became clear that folding a *pleated* structure into this form raised a potential problem. The strip is given only a *half* turn before the ends are joined and this disrupts the pleating, so one pleat face must be dropped to keep the pleating consistent. I realized this would bring two identically coloured pleat faces together, so opted

Möbius neckpiece. When a pleated fabric is used for this structure it needs to have an *odd* number of pleat faces for the pleating to remain regular. Silk, steel and linen.

The double-layer Möbius neckpieces solved the problem of alternating colours on the sides of the pleats, but this new situation also 'talked back' and fairly quickly suggested the next idea. The length required for a neckpiece is about twice that needed for a bracelet, so it is possible to make pieces that can be worn either way.

to use a single colour for the sides of the pleats, though retaining a contrast of colours for the edges.

However, the 'back-talk' of this situation reminded me about the odd properties of the Möbius strip. A favourite game is to ask people what they think would happen if they cut through the strip all the way along its centre. Almost everyone guesses that this would produce two separate strips, but the counterintuitive result is actually one long strip with *two complete* turns. Clearly this odd behaviour can work in reverse – a long piece with two complete turns can be folded up into a double Möbius strip. A pleated strip that is to be given *complete* turns, rather than a half turn, can obviously have a regular arrangement of pleats, which allows the option of a consistent alternation of colours on the sides of the pleats.

Two neckpiece/bracelets. A neckpiece with two turns is shown surrounding an identical piece that has been folded into a double-layer Möbius bracelet. Silk, steel and paper.

When folding the strip into a bracelet the twist needs to be evenly distributed by laying the piece in a figure of eight with the colour that is to form the *outside* of the bracelet lying on top – arranged here to place the pale side of the piece on the outside. The two loops of the darker side can then be folded together to form the double Möbius strip. It is not essential for the pleats to mesh with one another but it makes the bracelet firmer, so there are coloured dots on two of the pleats that can be matched up to make this easy.

Double Möbius neckpiece, folded from a double-length strip with an *even* number of pleat faces. Silk, steel and linen.

Intrigued by the potential of such twisting structures I looked for other curiosities. There is a wealth of useful information about the Möbius strip in Clifford Pickover's entertaining book on the subject and he also includes another attractive shape that seems to work well for jewellery, the trefoil knot. Once again this is a structure that needs a little care in assembly when it is made from a pleated fabric, because the strip needs to be given three complete turns before being interlaced in the *same* S or Z direction of twist that has initially been given to the strip.

Trefoil knot neckpieces, which can be worn in different ways to reveal either of the two different coloured sides and more or less of the knot structure. Silk, steel and linen.

With so many pleats and folds my work had begun to acquire a rather origami-like appearance, and at roughly the same time I became aware of fascinating examples of 'natural origami' (described in Chapter 1) – the next line of enquiry was obvious and is still ongoing.

Origami neckpieces. Silk, steel and paper. They can be worn either with the mountain fold side or the valley fold side uppermost, giving a different impression.

Erica de Ruiter describes a similar gentle evolution of ideas, starting with an attempt to solve a problem. She writes that, 'My favourite challenge is to reduce an interesting draft to fewer than four shafts', and the draft in this case was that of warpways pleats created with 1/3 and 3/1 twills, requiring eight shafts (a structure that is described in Chapter 5). It was a simple matter for her to reduce this to a six-shaft draft by using 1/2 and 2/1 twills but to get to less than four shafts was more of a challenge. She began to think about the possibilities of combining thick and thin yarns in both warp and weft, with a changing arrangement of thick and thin warps in narrow stripes and this proved to be a good solution. She experimented with this first as a three-shaft draft but after further research finally achieved the seemingly impossible, a structural pleat on only two shafts (refer to her article 'Magic Pleats – from eight shafts to two').

THE BUTTERFLY EFFECT

Reflecting on existing work and tackling any problems that arise can suggest new ideas and so allow a series of designs to evolve one from another. But sometimes very unexpected things may happen, often resulting from some apparently insignificant change that has been introduced either deliberately or by accident. The complex interplay between material and structure means that small changes may have unexpected and even dramatic effects – woven textiles display 'sensitive dependence on initial conditions', popularly known as the Butterfly Effect. Some attractive textures, particularly those depending on yarn twist or juxtapositions of strongly contrasting materials, may be poised on a knife-edge and even a slight change may cause them to turn into something completely different that may or may not be desirable!

Although it is natural to feel disappointed when a design turns out differently from expectations such unforeseen results can sometimes be a gift, suggesting new lines of enquiry, so it is important not to be so focussed on what you are *intending* to do that you miss such opportunities thrown up by chance. An excellent example of seeing the potential of something that happened by mistake is the 'shadow boxes' technique developed by Andreas Möller (illustrated in Chapter 3). He is a highly inventive weaver who certainly seems to tackle everything with a prepared mind.

My most memorable mistake occurred when I was relatively new to weaving and was aiming to produce smooth silk scarves in stripes of 1/3 and 3/1 twill. Having completed one scarf with a plied silk yarn in both warp and weft I introduced a 'small' change by using my handspun singles tussah silk as weft. When washed, this scarf spontaneously developed an effect of coarse pleating. Sadly, my mind was not as well prepared as it should have been – I was just annoyed – but in retrospect this was an ungrateful reaction to such an excellent free gift. Gradually I began to see the possibilities and have been exploring them ever since. This incident also taught me that it would be better to encounter an unexpected result at the sampling stage rather than in a finished piece!

It is clear that you can get quite a surprise even when trying to do something conventional, but unexpected results are even more likely when different structures are combined with an aim of producing new effects, or traditional weaves bypassed altogether in favour of working from first principles. The weave plan, the section of the draft showing the interlacing, is described by many handweavers as the 'drawdown', making it sound derivative from the threading and liftplan, but although that is physically the case when weaving the fabric, the process of drafting does not have to go in that direction. By directly planning the weave structure itself, you have complete freedom to try whatever you like, though it is necessary to check back regularly to see if you are exceeding the capacity of your loom. Working in this way offers particular opportunities for creating something really original and personal.

ORIGINALITY

Clearly it is not easy to invent something completely new – a familiar axiom is that there is 'nothing new but that which is forgotten'. If you start from scratch and just think about the effect that you want to create, you may well find you are re-inventing the wheel. Theo Moorman was modestly hesitant to claim originality for the weave structure that bears her name, suggesting that other weavers somewhere, perhaps in ancient Peru, must surely at some time have come up with the same idea:

Certainly I 'invented' the weave, that is, worked it out by long and patient experiments until I arrived at the present cloth structure, but I know only too well how easy it is to discover for oneself something in common use. When I was little more than a student I 'invented' leno weaving.

Theo Moorman, *Weaving as an Art Form*

However, an alternative saying is that 'everything has already been thought of – the only problem is thinking of it again', which does at least capture a sense of rethinking as challenging rather than pointless. Even if you find that your idea or chance discovery is already known it will still have a fresh quality derived from the process of working it out for yourself. After accidentally discovering self-pleating twill stripes I eventually learnt that highly accomplished fabrics exploiting this principle were already being woven in Roman Egypt as far back as the second century AD. Although it turned out that all I had done was to discover the effect again, finding it out for myself has left me with an ongoing fascination with this type of fabric.

PLAYING WITH AND AGAINST THE RULES

In designing, a balance needs to be struck between the open attitude that is natural when tackling a subject as a novice and the skill and control that are built up through experience. Although ignorance is usually regarded as a bad thing it can have its uses – people may have a sense of adventure in the early stages of learning a new skill, before they have been thoroughly instructed on how to do it properly! They can be more likely to try interesting experiments while they remain unaware that these are not supposed to work, and more likely to discover things by accident while doing things they are not supposed to do. In a sense my whole career as a weaver of textured textiles has been based on the beginner's mistake of overtwisting handspun yarn.

Of course once you have stumbled on something interesting it is important to build up sufficient knowledge to be able to exploit it effectively. The skill and understanding that come with experience are necessary to do really good work but it is worth keeping something of the openness that you had at the beginning. Even when you are very experienced some of the most interesting things happen when working at the very edge of your knowledge, struggling with a new idea or material. The Danish psychologist Lene Tanggaard, who has made a special study of the creative process, precisely captures how it can be an ongoing cycle: pushing at the limits

'Spectrum Patches', one of Ann Sutton's series of pieces from the exhibition *No Cheating*. The different ways of playing with colour also create subtle variations in texture in the different pieces. A detailed view of another piece from this exhibition is shown in Chapter 4. (Photo: James Newell)

of existing knowledge and then using newly acquired knowledge as a fresh starting point for further experiment. She challenges the conventional axiom so often quoted about creativity that one needs to 'think outside the box'. Instead she argues that creativity is about working 'along the edge of the box' – producing new ideas by constantly expanding the boundaries of existing knowledge (for more information refer to the book on creativity by Stadil and Tanggaard).

The great advantage of having experience in any field is that it offers a *range of choices* about how closely to engage with any conventional rules. Ann Sutton has often worked by playing creatively within the conventions of weaving, and explicitly drew attention to this approach in the exhibition *No Cheating*, for which she made a series of pieces that used careful permutations of weave structure, aiming to break new ground while remaining within certain 'rules of the game' that she had chosen:

six progressive ideas from each warp;
no change of colour or weft yarn without real reason;
to break fresh ground (living dangerously here);
everything to be shaft controlled;
no cheating.

Exhibition catalogue, *No Cheating: Serial Woven Studies*

However, it can also be interesting to deliberately break some of the rules. Flying in the face of conventional wisdom about materials, structures or finishing techniques amounts to positively inviting the unexpected to occur and can create beautiful results. According to Ann Sutton 'the rule-breaker of all time' was the Japanese designer Junichi Arai:

Very long floats are generally considered a bad idea, but in this scarf by Junichi Arai they create a design of bold blocks by very simple means. Most weavers must have seen what happens when a gap is left in a plain weave fabric that has alternating colours in the warp, but Arai not only noticed but also thought how he could use the effect. He has achieved the blocks by allowing the weft to go only part way across the cloth at certain intervals, another break with convention.

A quadruple-layer scarf by Junichi Arai. A double layer of fabric creates a reversible design of spots on a plain ground in a piece that is also a tube. A section of the fabric has been stretched to show the openness of the sett. In theory, even with multiple layers supporting one another, using such an open sett should make a highly unstable fabric, but here it is used with a very high-twist weft to create a wonderfully stretchy fabric with a bouclé surface.

Not for him the aim of most weavers: a perfectly flat smooth cloth. Some of his cloths buckle wildly and intentionally into 8 cm pockets. The felting quality of wool is not avoided but used to the greatest effect: many cloths are, in most handweavers' thinking, deliberately 'ruined'. On a trip to some North of England mills with his cloths, conventionally-trained designers expressed horror at some of the technical liberties which had been taken: 'He breaks every rule that I've ever been taught' muttered one designer crossly, at the same time asking me where she could buy some of the results for her own use.

Ann Sutton, 'The Textiles of Junichi Arai, Hon RDI', *Journal of Weavers, Spinners and Dyers*

In 1984, Arai co-founded the Nuno Corporation, together with another highly inventive designer, Reiko Sudo. Nuno ('fabric' in Japanese) rapidly became known for unusual designs, some of which played creatively within the rules while others freely challenged them. Since Arai left the corporation it has remained under the directorship of Reiko Sudo and continues to be greatly admired for its innovative approach to design. Reiko Sudo explains how simple aspects of everyday life or comments in conversation can be the starting point for a design: 'Often it's just a casual thought or something in everyday life. I might see something that catches my attention, something a little bit unusual that starts me thinking – how about using this in textiles?' For example 'Feather Flurries', one of her most famous designs,

'Feather Flurries'. In this design by Reiko Sudo, guinea fowl feathers are trapped between layers of black silk organza. This fabric exemplifies Nuno's adventurous approach to textiles, since its manufacture requires an unusual alliance of modern technology and handwork. The organza double cloth is woven on powerlooms but these are stopped periodically so that the feathers can be inserted by hand. Further views of this piece are given in Chapter 6.

had its starting point in a conversation with a friend who suggested the idea of using holograms of moving pictures on textiles. 'Well, the researchers I met just laughed at this. But it started me thinking about motion, about fabric that had motion in it. Which led to thoughts about flight and feathers.' (This interesting interview with Reiko Sudo is included in a book edited by Lesley Millar.)

These inventive fabrics result from making strategic decisions to break certain conventions about how things are normally done. But this does not mean it is wise to try to work without *any* constraint, breaking all the rules at once, as this simply tends to result in a rather incoherent design. Accepting some limitations can be really worthwhile, because struggling against them can be much more interesting than total freedom – as Lene Tanggaard suggests, you want to be at the *edge* of the box, *pushing at the limits*, rather than right out of it. Imposing certain limitations that you choose yourself, as Ann Sutton did for her *No Cheating* exhibition, is a good way to focus the mind. The combination of choosing rules but at the same time challenging their limits can be a productive way of generating new ideas. And however wild the idea, the material itself is always there as the final arbiter:

> ...the inherent discipline of matter acts as a regulative force: not everything 'goes'. To circumvent the No of the material with the Yes of an inventive solution, that is the way new things come about – in a contest with the material.
> Anni Albers, *On Designing*

EXPERIMENT AND REFLECTION

Inevitably in a book of this length it has been necessary to concentrate on certain aspects that have caught my attention and interest, so it is a personal choice. There are many weave structures that could produce widely different cloths through variations in scale and density, and also through contrasts of yarns – thick and thin, stiff and flexible, stable and shrinking – to push them beyond their 'classic' forms. And many desirable fabric qualities could be considered from the viewpoint of possible ways of achieving them. For example, in contrast to a light, delicate effect the alternative problem of achieving a warm, bulky fabric could be investigated. In this case simply using heavy yarns would obviously achieve this effect, but more interesting strategies could follow nature's model of economical design by pursuing all the different possible ways of trapping air within the fabric, with fine yarns in backed, double or multilayer cloths, structures like waffle weave that naturally tend to bulk up, or possibly combinations of any or all of these.

This book has been shaped around two possible starting points for design, firstly the resources of material and weave structure and secondly, desired fabric qualities based on sources of inspiration or the practical requirements of a brief. But these apparently different approaches cannot really remain separate. Materials and weave structures may suggest observational studies that are worth following up, while any source of inspiration can be interpreted in many ways with different materials and structures. Whichever approach may be taken as a starting point, the process of practical design requires us to be reflective practitioners who are willing to move back and forth between ideas and resources as a design evolves.

Bibliography

The bibliography contains books and articles that I have referred to in the text, together with others that include useful information.

Albers, Anni, *On Weaving (Expanded Edition)* (Princeton University Press, 2017)

Albers, Josef, *Interaction of Color [50th Anniversary Edition]* (Yale University Press, 2013)

Alderman, Sharon, *Mastering Weave Structures* (Interweave Press, 2004)

Aldersey-Williams, Hugh, *Zoomorphic* (Laurence King, 2003)

Ashmore, Sonia, *Muslin* (V&A Publishing, 2012)

Autio, Laurie, (ed.) *Eight Shafts: Beyond the Beginning: Personal Approaches to Design* (Complex Weavers: in press)

Baines, Patricia, *Linen Handspinning and Weaving* (Batsford, 1989)

Baines, Patricia, *A Linen Legacy: Rita Beales 1889-1987* (Crafts Study Centre, 1989)

Ball, Philip, *Shapes: Nature's Patterns: a tapestry in three parts* (Oxford University Press, 2009)

Ball, Philip, *Flow: Nature's Patterns: a tapestry in three parts* (Oxford University Press, 2009)

Ball, Philip, *Branches: Nature's Patterns: a tapestry in three parts* (Oxford University Press, 2009)

Ball, Philip, *Patterns in Nature: Why the Natural World Looks the Way it Does* (University of Chicago Press, 2017)

Barber, E. J. W., *Prehistoric Textiles* (Princeton University Press, 1991)

Barker, Alfred F., and Midgley, Eber, *Analysis of Woven Fabrics* (Scott, Greenwood and Son, 1922)

Barrett, Clotilde, and Smith, Eunice, *Double Two-tie Unit Weaves* (Weaver's Journal Publications, 1983)

Becker, John, *Pattern and Loom* (Rhodus, 1987)

Black, Sandy, *Eco-Chic: The Fashion Paradox* (Black Dog Publishing, 2008)

Braddock Clarke, Sarah E. and O'Mahony, Marie, *Techno Textiles 2* (Thames and Hudson, 2005)

Burnham, Dorothy, K., *Cut my Cote* (The Royal Ontario Museum, 1973)

Carlstedt, Catharina and Kongbäck, Ylva, *Rep: A Guide to Swedish Warp-Faced Rep* (LTs Forlag, 1987)

Ciszuk, Martin, 'Rippenköper or repp twill', *Vävmagasinet: Scandinavian Weaving Magazine* (No. 2, 2010, p. 41)

Cochrane, Grace, *Liz Williamson: Textiles* (Craftsman House, 2008)

Collingwood, Peter, 'Two Weft Distortion Effects in Plain Weave', *The Journal for Weavers, Spinners and Dyers (Peter Collingwood Special Edition)*, (Summer 2009, pp. 16-18)

Collingwood, Peter, *Textile and Weaving Structures* (Batsford, 1987)

Cooke, W. D., Mohamed El-Gamal and Brennan, Angela, 'The Hand Spinning of Ultra-fine Yarns, Part 2, The Spinning of Flax', *CIETA* (Bulletin 69, 1991, pp. 17-23)

Corrigan, Gina, *Tibetan Dress: In Amdo and Kham* (Hali Publications, 2017)

Dalgaard, Lotte, *Magical Materials to Weave* (Trafalgar, 2012)

Dalgaard, Lotte and Adam, Paulette, *Thread Magic* (Forlaget Mellemværk, 2020)

de Ruiter, Erica, 'Magic Pleats – From Eight Shafts to Two', *Fabrics That Go Bump,* Madelyn van der Hoogt (ed.), (XRX Books, 2002, pp. 66-67)

de Ruiter, Erica, *Weaving on 3 Shafts* (Erica de Ruiter, 2017)

Dunsmore, Susi, *Weaving in Nepal* (British Museum Publications, 1983)

Dunsmore, Susi, *Nepalese Textiles* (British Museum Press, 1993)

Dunsmore, Susi, *The Nettle in Nepal* (John Dunsmore Nepalese Textile Trust, 2006)

Edom, Gillian, *From Sting to Spin* (Urtica Books, 2019)

Ellen, Alison, *Hand Knitting: New Directions* (The Crowood Press, 2002)

Ellen, Alison, *Knitting: Colour, structure and design* (The Crowood Press, 2011)

Ellen, Alison, *Knitting: Stitch-led design* (The Crowood Press, 2015)

Emery, Irene, *The Primary Structures of Fabrics* (The Textile Museum, 1980)

Eriksson, Mariana, 'Moorman – a technique with huge scope', *Vävmagasinet: Scandinavian Weaving Magazine* (no. 1, 2017, pp. 42-45)

Forbes, Peter, *The Gecko's Foot* (Fourth Estate, 2005)

Ford, Birte, *Yarn from Wild Nettles: A Practical Guide* (Nettlecraft, 2014)

French, Michael, *Invention and Evolution* (Cambridge University Press, 1994)

Gleick, James, *Chaos* (Cardinal, 1988)

Gordon, J. E., *Structures* (Penguin Books, 1978)

Grömer, Karina, Kern, Anton, Reschreiter, Hans and Rösel-Mautendorfer, Helga, *Textiles from Hallstatt* (Archaeolingua, 2013)

Grömer, Karina and Rast-Eicher, Antoinette, 'To pleat or not to pleat – an early history of creating three-dimensional linear textile structures', *Ann. Naturhist. Mus. Wien. Serie A* (No. 121, 2019, pp. 83-112) (A pdf of this paper is also available online)

Hald, Margrethe, *Ancient Danish Textiles from Bogs and Burials* (The National Museum of Denmark, 1980)

Harvey-Brown, Stacey, *Honeycomb Hybrids* (The Loom Room Publications, 2017)

Harvey-Brown, Stacey, *Beneath the Surface* (The Loom Room Publications, 2020)

Hertel, Heinrich, *Structure, Form, Movement* (Reinhold Publishing Corporation, 1966)

Ignell, Tina, 'Inventions', *Vävmagasinet: Scandinavian Weaving Magazine* (No. 3, 2015, pp. 25-27)

Irwin, Bobbie, *Weaving Iridescence* (Stackpole Books, 2017)

Izukura, Akihiko, *Textile of Akihiko Izukura* (International Association of Natural Textiles, 2001)

Jackson, Paul, *Folding Techniques for Designers: From Sheet to Form* (Laurence King Publishing, 2011)

Jackson, Paul, *Complete Pleats* (Laurence King Publishing, 2015)

Kapsali, Veronika, *Biomimetics for Designers* (Thames and Hudson, 2016)

Kemp, Barry, J. and Vogelsang-Eastwood, Gillian, *The Ancient Textile Industry at Amarna* (Egypt Exploration Society, 2001)

Kirke, Betty, *Madeleine Vionnet* (Chronicle Books, 1998)

Kovnat, Denise, *Weaving Outside the Box: Techniques and Projects for Creating Dimensional Fabrics* (Forthcoming)

Leitner, Christina, *Paper Textiles* (A&C Black, 2005)

Loescher, M., 'The Weaving of Lengthwise Pleats', *The Melland* (Vol.1 No.3, June 1929, pp. 349-351) (*See* also Online Resources for a pdf of this paper)

Masterson, Vicki, 'Texture with Deflected Double Weave', *Fabrics That Go Bump*, Madelyn van der Hoogt (ed.), (XRS Books, 2002, pp. 103-105)

Meinhardt, Hans, *The Algorithmic Beauty of Sea Shells* (Springer, 1998)

Major, John, (ed.) *YEOHLEE: WORK* (The Images Publishing Group PTY Ltd, 2003)

Margetts, Martina, Theophilus, Linda and Wood, Katherine (eEds.), *Peter Collingwood – Master Weaver* (firstsite, reprinted 1999)

Millar, Lesley, (ed.) *21 21: the textile vision of Reiko Sudo and Nuno* (University College for the Creative Arts, 2005)

Möller, Andreas, 'Andreas' "Shadow Boxes"', *Vävmagasinet: Scandinavian Weaving Magazine* (No. 3, 2008, p. 49)

Möller, Andreas, 'Andreas' "Saimaa"' *Vävmagasinet: Scandinavian Weaving Magazine* (No. 1, 2017, pp. 62-63)

Moorman, Theo, *Weaving as an Art Form* (Schiffer, 1975)

Nisbet, Harry, *Grammar of Textile Design* (Scott, Greenwood & Son, 1906)

Nuno Corporation, *Boro Boro* (Nuno Corporation, 1997)

Nuno Corporation, *Suké Suké* (Nuno Corporation, 1997)

Nuno Corporation, *Fuwa Fuwa* (Nuno Corporation, 1998)

Oelsner, G. H., *A Handbook of Weaves* (Dover Publications, 1952, unaltered republication of original edition of 1915)

Olding, Simon, *Rezia Wahid: Woven Air* (Crafts Study Centre, 2007)

Østergård, Else, *Woven into the Earth* (Aarhus University Press, 2004)

Petroski, Henry, *The Evolution of Useful Things* (Pavilion Books, 1993)

Pickover, Clifford, A., *The Möbius Strip* (Thunder's Mouth Press, 2006)

Piper, Anna and Townsend, Katherine, 'Crafting the Composite Garment: The role of handweaving in digital creation', *Journal of Textile Design Research and Practice* (3:1-2, 2015, pp. 3-26)

Richards, Ann, *Weaving Textiles That Shape Themselves* (The Crowood Press, 2012)

Richards, Ann, 'Did ancient Egyptian textiles pleat themselves?' In C. Graves-Brown & Goodridge, W. (eds.) *Egyptology in the Present: Experiential and Experimental Methods in Archaeology* (The Classical Press of Wales, 2015, pp. 139-150)

Rissanen, Timo and McQuillan, Holly, *Zero Waste Fashion Design* (Bloomsbury Visual Arts, 2018)

Robinson, A. T. C. and Marks, R., *Woven Cloth Construction* (The Textile Institute, 1973)

Schoeser, Mary, *Marianne Straub* (The Design Council, 1984)

Schön, Donald, A., *The Reflective Practitioner* (Avebury, 1991)

Smayda, Norma and White, Gretchen, *Ondulé Textiles* (Schiffer Publishing, 2017)

Smith, Ruth (ed.), *Minority Textile Techniques: Costumes from South West China* (Gina Corrigan & Occidor Ltd, 2007)

Stadil, Christian, and Tanggaard, Lene, *In the Shower with Picasso: Sparking your Creativity and Imagination* (LID Publishing Ltd, 2014)

Straub, Marianne, *Hand Weaving and Cloth Design* (The Viking Press, 1977)

Stubenitsky, Marian, *Double with a Twist* (Uitgeverij Stubenitsky, 2019)

Sutton, Ann, *The Structure of Weaving* (Hutchinson, 1982)

Sutton, Ann and Sheehan, Diane, *Ideas in Weaving* (Batsford, 1989)

Sutton, Ann, 'The Textiles of Junichi Arai, Hon RDI', *Journal of Weavers, Spinners and Dyers*, (March 1992, pp. 14-15)

Sutton, Ann, Newell, James and Gillet, John, *No Cheating* (The Winchester Gallery at Winchester School of Art, 1995)

Taylor, Marjorie, A., *Technology of Textile Properties* (Forbes Publications, 1990)

Taylor, Susie, 'Woven Origami', *Complex Weavers Journal* (October 2014, No.106, pp. 20-22)

Thompson, D'Arcy Wentworth, *On Growth and Form* (Cambridge University Press, 1942)

Tilke, Max, *Costume Patterns and Designs* (Rizzoli International Publications, 1990)

van der Hoogt, Madelyn, 'Deflected Double Weave', *Weaver's* (Summer 1999, Issue 44, pp. 54-9)

Watson, William, *Textile Design and Colour* (6th Edition) (Longmans, 1954)

Watson, William, *Advanced Textile Design* (2nd Edition) (Longmans, 1925)

Willetts, William, *Chinese Art: Volume 1* (Penguin Books, 1958)

Williamson, Liz, 'Fulled Seersucker Scarves', *Fabrics that go Bump*, Madelyn van der Hoogt (ed.), (XRS Books, 2002, pp. 103-105)

Wootton, Robin, *How do insects fold and unfold their wings?* (The Amateur Entomologists' Society, 2012)

Online Resources

Josef Albers
Interaction of Color App for ipad
interactionofcolor.com
Available on the App Store

Samira Boon
Studio Samira Boon
Self-folding origami textiles for architecture
www.samiraboon.com

John Boyd Textiles
Horsehair upholstery
www.johnboydtextiles.co.uk

Martin Conlan
Traditional world textiles for collectors, films and interiors
Instagram: slowloristextiles

Crafts Study Centre
www.csc.uca.ac.uk

Alison Ellen
www.alisonellenhandknits.co.uk

Stacey Harvey-Brown
www.theloomroom.co.uk

Denise Kovnat
www.denisekovnat.com
Blog: Random Acts of Colour

Loescher article on woven pleats
Loescher, M. The Weaving of Lengthwise Pleats.
www.handweaving.net. Under Docs search for keyword 'pleats'

Noriko Matsumoto
www7b.biglobe.ne.jp>~norikomatsumoto

Miura-ori
www.sciencefriday.com/educational-resources/tessellation-and-miura-folds

Andreas Möller
en.weberei-hamburg.com

Wendy Morris
Instagram: wendymorrisweaving

Nuno
www.nuno.com

Emily Olsen
Weaver and Designer
emily-olsen.com

Tim Parry-Williams
Instagram: timparry_williams

Anna Piper
Textile Design|Design Research
annapiperdesign.com

Ann Richards
annrweave@gmail.com
Instagram: annrichardsweave

Rippenköper
Priest-Dorman, Carolyn. 2/1 Twills: Rippenköper, Complex Weavers Medieval Textile Study Group, Issue 25, Sept 2000. Available online. A google search for 'Priest-Dorman, Carolyn' and 'Rippenköper' will pick up a pdf of this article.

Ann Sutton
www.annsutton.org

Susie Taylor
Woven origami
www.susietaylorart.com
www.theweavingworkshop.com

VADS: online resource for visual arts
www.vads.ac.uk

Julian Vincent
'Survival of the Cheapest'
A pdf of this article can be found on www.sciencedirect.com

Rezia Wahid
www.woven-air.com

Deirdre Wood
www.deirdrewood.com

Suppliers

The Danish Yarn Purchasing Association (GIF)
To buy yarns from the Association you have to be a member. Yarns can only be bought from the webshop.
info@yarn.dk

A wide variety of unusual yarns, including a good selection of crepe yarns.

Eurestex
Park View Mills
Raymond Street
Bradford
BD5 8DT
Tel: +44 (0)1274 721231
Mobile: +44 (0)7802 790424
email: richard@eurestex.co.uk
www.eurestex.co.uk

A good source of silk yarns in various weights, including dyed spun silk 60/2 and 120/2 Nm.

George Weil & Sons Ltd
Old Portsmouth Road
Peasmarsh
Guildford
Surrey
GU3 1LZ
Tel: +44 (0)1483 565800
sales@georgeweil.com
www.georgeweil.com

Worsted high-twist botany wool yarn 2/36 Nm, 18 tpi and 30 tpi, and balanced yarn of the same count. High-twist silk yarn, 4 × 40/44 denier, S and Z.
A variety of standard yarns, including dyed spun (shantung) yarn 60/2 Nm.
Looms and equipment, including end-delivery hand shuttles and autodenters.

Habu Textiles
www.habutextiles.com
A wide variety of unusual yarns, including metal/textile blends and wool and silk crepe yarns from Japan.

The Handweavers Studio and Gallery
140 Seven Sisters Road
London N7 7N
Tel: 0+44 (0)20 7272 1891
admin@handweavers.co.uk
www.handweavers.co.uk

A very extensive selection of yarns, both standard and specialist, including metal/textile blends, synthetic shrink yarns and high-twist yarns, including Japanese crepe wool yarns and high-twist woollen merino 14.5 Nm.
Looms and equipment, including end-delivery hand shuttles.

Lunatic Fringe
www.lunaticfringeyarns.com

A selection of yarns, including high-twist and shrink yarns, wires and metal yarns.

Magiske Garner
www.magiskegarner.dk
email: info@magiskegarner.dk

Danish webshop with a wide range of yarns including crepe, elastic and shrinking yarns.

Don Porrit Looms
The Studio
Leathley Road
Menston
Ilkley
W. Yorks, LS29 6DPT
Tel: 01943 878329
email: donporritt@yahoo.co.uk

Extremely helpful supplier of looms and equipment (including autodenters).

Index

accent threads 47-48, 51, 114, 123-125, 138
Adam, Paulette 137
Albers, Anni 8, 21, 34-35, 53, 60, 168, 169
Albers, Josef 132, 172
Alderman, Sharon 60, 137, 155, 169
allo 28, 73
Alphatex 34, 153
alternating float weaves 68-75, 97-99, 122-23
angle of twist 25, 37
Arai, Junichi 34, 84-85, 159, 165-166
architecture 14-15
Ashenhurst formula 23-24, 40, 155

backed cloth 16, 82, 127-129
Baines, Patricia 27, 115, 170
balanced yarn 25
Ball, Philip 19, 169
Barber, Elizabeth 38, 61, 62, 169
Beales, Rita 75, 112, 115
beating 156-157
Becker, John 68, 169
Bedford cord 100
bias cut 31, 148
biomimetic textiles 15-16
Boon, Samira 108, 172
Borum Eshøj belt 38
bouclé effect 166
bracelets 105, 108, 162
Brighton honeycomb 77-78, 125, 138
Bronze Age textiles 37-38, 61, 62
building on experience 155
Burnham, Dorothy 139, 169
Butterfly Effect 160, 163-164

China, ancient 32, 39, 61
Chinese minority textiles 68-71, 74, 88
cloth setting 40, 155-156
Collingwood, Peter 7, 153, 169, 170

colour-and-weave effects 42, 81, 86
compound weaves 82-85
Conlan, Martin 69-70, 172
conversion factors for yarn counts 24
cord weaves 100-108
Corrigan, Gina 69, 122, 170
cover factor 41
Crafts Study Centre 115
cramming and spacing 44-48, 112-113
creativity 163-168
crepe
 fabric 39, 140
 yarn 25, 27, 30, 32, 39, 140-141, 145-149
creping reaction 25
crepon 39, 92-94, 127, 140

Dalgaard, Lotte 33, 77, 80, 145, 149, 170
damask 67
deflected double weave 81, 138
deflected thread structures 137
degumming of silk 32, 68
deployable structures 12-13, 92
de Ruiter, Erica 50-51, 62, 94, 163, 170
diameter of yarns 23-24, 89, 155-156
differential shrinkage 52, 81, 139-149
distorted weft weaves 79-80, 137
double-and-single cloths 131-133, 143, 146-148
double cloth 83-85, 129-131
double two-tie unit weaves 86, 146-148, 169
dragonfly wing 14, 101, 161
Dunsmore, Susi 28, 73, 170

economy in nature 10-11, 16-17, 152
Egypt, ancient 26, 37, 92, 112
Ellen, Alison 142, 170

Emery, Irene 36, 54, 61, 68, 82
energy in yarn 25
Eriksson, Mariana 56, 83, 170
evolving designs 161-163

fabric curling, 78, 102, 127
fabric shaping 138-149
feathers 16, 18-19, 117, 166-168
felting/fulling 20-21, 30, 38, 143
Fibonacci series 19
fibres
 alignment 23
 animal 30-32
 banana 28-29
 bast 26-28
 cotton 29-30
 elastomeric 33
 flax 26-27
 hemp 27
 horsehair 31
 man-made 33
 nettle 28
 pineapple 28-29
 ramie 27
 regenerated 33
 silk 32
 stiffness 22-23
 strength 22-25
 swelling 15, 25
 toughness 22-23
 tussah silk 32
 vegetable 26-30
 wool 30
Fisher, Sharon 65
float weaves 60-81
folding of insect wings 12, 15
folding of leaves 13
Forbes, Peter 13, 16, 170
Forchhammer, Berthe 45
form follows failure 160-161
French, Michael 12, 91, 170

garments 8, 9, 139-149
gauze 54-59, 90-91, 93-94, 113, 121-122, 135, 154
Gleick, James 135, 160, 170
Gordon, J.E. 12, 22, 170

Hagen, Elisabeth 80, 149
Hald, Margrethe 62, 170
Hallstatt textiles 37, 61, 62
Han damask 68-69, 97-99
Harvey-Brown, Stacey 16-17, 79-80, 115-116, 137, 170
Hertel, Heinrich 14, 170
Hicks, Sheila 152
high-twist yarns 25, 39-40, 137, 140-141, 143-149
honeycomb 79-80, 114, 137
huckaback 73

identification tint (S or Z) 140
inlay 48-49, 110, 126
insect wings 12, 14-15, 101, 161
iridescence 16, 53-54, 66, 73, 119-123
Iron Age textiles 37-38, 62-63
Izukura, Akihiko 139, 170

Jackson, Paul 104, 106, 108, 170

Kapsali, Veronika 15, 170
Klee, Paul 53
knitting 142
Kovnat, Denise 81, 157, 170, 172

lace weaves 73-5
lacing on 153
leaf fold 13
leaves 10-11, 13-14, 17-18, 119
Leitner, Christina 29, 170
leno 54
linear zigzag weaves 137
linen tester 87, 89, 157
Little, Gilian 20-21
Loescher, M. 100, 172
'loom-to-body' clothing 138-149
lustre 30, 32, 53, 64-66

Mairet, Ethel 32, 44,
Masterson, Vicki 81, 170
Matsumoto, Noriko 126, 172
mercerization 29-30
Miao textiles 68-71

Miura-ori 13, 172
Miyake, Issey 149
Möbius strip 104-105, 161-163
mock leno 74, 114
moiré effect 117, 131
Möller, Andreas 52, 100, 163, 170
Moorman technique 82-83, 164, 171
Moorman, Theo 82-83, 164, 171
Morphotex 15-16
Morris, Wendy 103-104, 135, 160
Mughal paintings 116
multilayer cloth 85
muslin 109

neckpieces 29, 35, 105, 162-163
Nisbet, Harry 91, 171
Nørgaard, Anna 62-63
Nuno Corporation 85, 117, 166-168, 171, 172

Olsen, Emily 149, 173
ondulé weaving 134
openness of weave 109-111
opposite-twist yarn interactions 37-40
origami 12-13, 106-108
originality 164
origin of twill weaves 61-63
Otto, Frei 15-16

paper folding 104, 106-107
Parry-Williams, Tim 43-44, 173
pattern cutting 139, 148
Paxton, Joseph 11, 14
percentage sett 40, 155
Petroski, Henry 160-161, 171
Piper, Anna 149, 171, 173
pleating
　accordion 101-103
　box 104
　crepon 39, 92-94, 140-141
　in insect wings 12, 14-15, 101
　knife 104
　sharp-edged 101-108

　warp-float/weft-float 94-100, 150-151
plying 25

records as a guide to future work 155-156
record keeping 155
reflective practice 151, 161
rep 49-51
retting 26-27
ribbed effect 46, 49-51, 62, 94-100
Rippenköper 62-63, 94-96, 144, 173
rugs 50
Russian cords 58-59

same-twist interactions 37-40
sampling 150-157
satin/sateen 64-68, 122
S and Z twist 25-26, 37-40, 102, 140-141, 146-148
scaling up of designs 156-158
Schiaparelli, Elsa 117
Schön, Donald 151, 161, 171
seed pods 17-18
seersucker 51-52, 57
self-pleating fabrics 8, 29, 35, 90-108, 161-163
selvedges 80, 148-149
sericin (silk gum) 32, 68
sett 40-41, 155
shadow boxes 52-53
shadow stripes and checks 38, 61-63
shaping fabrics 138-149
shells 17, 119, 160
shot effect 53, 66, 73, 120-121
spinning 23, 26, 37
spiralling of yarn 90-91, 93, 135
splicing of yarns 26
spot weaves 73-75
St Aubyn Hubbard, Geraldine 46
stiffness 22-23
Straub, Marianne 34, 44, 46, 158, 171
strength 22-23
stress lines 106

structural colours 18-19
struts 14-15, 101
Stubenitsky, Marian 81, 171
Sudo, Reiko 108, 117, 166-167
supplementary warps and wefts 125-129
Sutton, Ann 84-85, 123, 165-166, 171, 173
Swedish lace 74-75, 94, 115
swelling of fibres 15, 25

table mats 28, 75, 83, 115
Tanggaard, Lene 164-165
Taylor, Susie 108, 171, 173
tea towels 74, 76, 124
Teng, Yeohlee 149, 170
tension variations 51-53
textile analysis 87-88
thick and thin 44, 46, 49-51, 53
Thompson, D'Arcy Wentworth 19, 134, 139, 171
threading drafts as a resource 86
Tilke, Max 139, 171
toughness 22-23
tracking 38-40
translucency 17-19, 109-118
trefoil knot 163
twill 61-65, 122
twill line 122, 158
twist
　amount 23, 37
　angle 25, 37
　direction (S and Z) 25-26, 37-40, 102, 136, 140-141, 146-148
　impact on fabric properties 37-40, 78, 109
　impact on yarn properties 25-26
　twist direction interactions 37-40
　twist-twill interactions 61-62, 64

Uden, Amelia 59
unbalanced yarn 25
undulating texture 40

van der Hoogt, Madelyn 81, 171
V-fold 13, 106
Vincent, Julian 16, 92, 173
Vionnet, Madeleine 148-149
visualizing designs 157-158

waffle weave 76-7, 123-124
Wahid, Rezia 49, 110, 171, 173
Waldron, Margrit 45
warp and weft relationships 41-44
warp-faced compound tabby 102
warp-weighted loom 62, 139
water lily 10-11, 14
Watson, William 60, 171
Willetts, William 32, 61, 68, 171
Williams, Angus 28, 50
Williamson, Liz 52
Wood, Deirdre 129, 142, 157, 173
Wootton, Robin 12, 171
'woven air' 109-110
woven origami 106-108, 172-173
wrapping 23

yarn
　balanced 25
　counts 23-24
　diameter 23-24, 89, 155-156
　elastomeric 33
　high-twist 25, 39-40, 137
　metal 34
　paper 29
　plied 25
　silk/steel 161-163
　single 25
　spiralling 93, 135
　strength 25
　swelling 25
　twist 25-26
　unbalanced 25
　woollen and worsted 30, 93
Yarn Purchasing Association (GIF) 161, 174

Zero Waste Fashion Design 148-149, 171

RELATED TITLES FROM CROWOOD

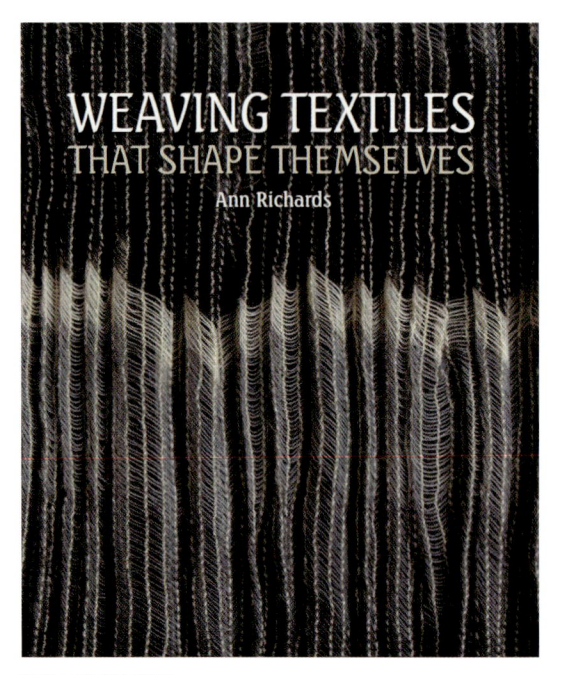

WEAVING TEXTILES THAT SHAPE THEMSELVES
Ann Richards

978 1 84797 319 1

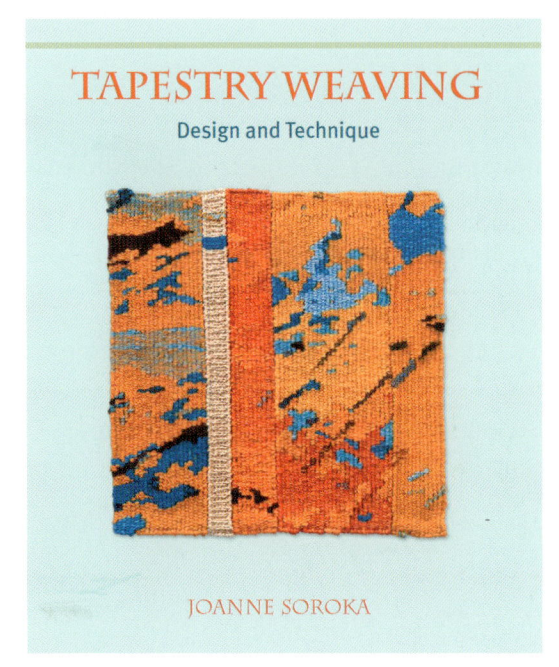

TAPESTRY WEAVING
Design and Technique
JOANNE SOROKA

978 1 84797 280 4

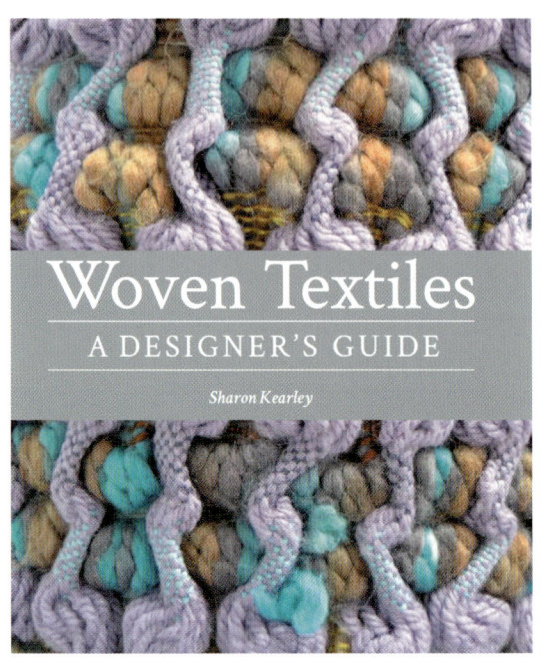

Woven Textiles
A DESIGNER'S GUIDE
Sharon Kearley

978 1 84797 814 1